INSIDE HAWAII'S CAPITOL

Lessons in Legislative Democracy

Jim Shon

Former Representative,
Hawaii State House of Representatives,
1984-1996

AUTHOR'S NOTE

The book was originally completed in 2002, before much oftoday's social media - Facebook, twitter, etc. - were features of political life. It is also a snapshot of Who Was Who in terms of power, position and relevance. One big difference is that the number of Republicans has continued to decline to the point where there are none left in the Hawaii State Senate in 2016.

Inside Hawaii's Capitol
Lessons in Legislative Democracy
Copyright © 2020 Jim Shon

Paperback: 978-1-7338331-6-5
eBook: 978-1-7338331-7-2

HAWAII
INSIGHT
BOOKS

HONOLULU, HI 96822
United States

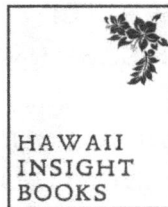

CONTENTS

More books available
at
https://hawaiiinsightbooks.com

HAWAII INSIGHT BOOKS

HOME   AUTHORS   BOOKS   ABOUT   BLOG   CONTACT US   CIVIC EDUCATION

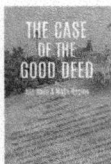

BROADENING YOUR PERSPECTIVE

The Case of the Good Deed
$3.99 – $9.99

The Case of the Rainforest Reunion
$3.99 – $9.99

Poison in Paradise
$3.99 – $9.99

Popular categories
New Releases
Soon
Mystery
Politics

Useful links
About
Books
Blog
Civic Education
Contact

Hawaii Insight Books
Broadening Your Perspective

We are Weavers.
Through our hands
Bright notions ravel,
Velvet Mountains,
Rainbows calling,
Oceans yearning.
We toil and dance to the images
We're learning.
Hues entwining destinies,
Each thread
Held by dependencies,
The opposites pursue their courses,
Appreciate each other's' sources
In Kapakahi harmony.
We are Weavers.
A blue-eyed girl, a golden man.
A pristine valley,
A human alley,
Are woven strong and kind.
It's our differences that bind.
If ever it's denied
We will unravel.
We are Weavers.
We seek to join the strands of time,
The present, past and future
Into a patterned line,
A quilt of forceful images,
A strong and gentle tapestry,
Our vision will expand,
To nurture,
Warm,
Protect,
And beautify
The land.
We are Weavers.

–Jim Shon
1980

DEDICATION

This book is dedicated to the intelligent and hard-working members of my staff. No one accomplishes anything alone in this world, and certainly not in the Legislature. Year after year, we legislators took all the credit when our staff did all the work. They taught me a great deal and kept me on the right path. We owe the legislative staff in all offices our appreciation for making democracy work.

1985: Claire Arakaki, Katherine Ingoglia, Yiok Kawamoto, Steven Montgomery, Leonard Wilson.

1986: Katherine Ingoglia, Steven Montgomery, James Waddington Jr., Leonard Wilson

1987: William Dendle, Robert Grossmann, Claudia Lucas, Steven Montgomery

1988: Claire Arakaki, Bernice Ebinger, Robert Grossmann, Pamela Lichty, Steven Montgomery

1989: Robert Grossmann, Alissa Guyer, Pamela Lichty, Lisa Shibata

1990: Ginny Baresch, Jane Gallagher, Diane McFaull, Amy Mizuno, Debbie Onomura

1991: Diane McFaull, Amy Mizuno, Brian Mohoric, Michael Sullivan

1992: Diane McFaull, Hali Robinett, Jonathan Scheuer, Michael Sullivan

1993: Diane McFaull, Jonathan Scheuer, Michael Sullivan

1994: Debbi Glanstein, Diane McFaull, Laurelyn Veatch

1995: Rand Berkke, Jeff Burgett, Donald Koelper, Suzanne Marinelli, Diane McFaull

1996: Donald Koelper, Diane McFaull, Shanti Mizuno, William Sagar

ACKNOWLEDGEMENT

A special *mahalo* to the late Professor David Yount, without whose encouragement and hours of detailed manuscript editing this book would not be possible.

PREFACE

My last two-year term as a member of Hawaii's State House of Representatives (1995 -1996) can be characterized only as frustrating. The Legislature seemed unable to cope with really complex issues, particularly those that required solutions that cut across bureaucratic lines or demand innovation. We were unable to develop a coherent longterm vision of where the state should go, or even to reach a consensus on little more than artificially juggling the numbers to balance the budget. My constituents did not, in spite of my best efforts to inform them, have much of a feel for what I did for the many important issues addressed by the Legislature, or for evaluating the institution. I was struck by the number of reasonably well-informed people who were unable either to understand how the Legislature worked or to interpret the behavior or decisions of elected officials during the four-month session. Finally, the gap between the daily work of government and the character and content of the intermittent election campaigns was growing wider each year. The democratic system in Hawaii appeared to be losing its ability to respond to its citizens, and the citizens appeared to be losing their ability (and motivation) to appropriately influence the legislative process.

There are several specific objectives of this book:

- To encourage interested citizens to put themselves into the shoes of a Hawaii state legislator and to acquire a small personal taste of the experience – the rhythms of a day in the life, the four-month legislative sessions, a year in the life, etc.

- To increase the public's appreciation for the strengths and weaknesses of today's legislative form of democracy in general, and Hawaii's recent experience in particular.

- To foster a more thoughtful analysis of the state of our democracy, to step back from the media hype and sound-bite rhetoric to reflect on what makes the system operate well and what leads to frustration and to ask why complex problems often seem beyond the modern legislature's grasp.

- To suggest a few modest ways to improve both the operations of government and its relationship with the people it serves.

The purpose of the book is to develop as complete a picture as possible of life within a modern legislature. Each chapter is sprinkled with personal reflections in an attempt to underscore the important points. Most were initially drafted in the spring of 1997, in anticipation of a possible Constitutional Convention, or Con Con, in the near future, and a rousing public debate over how to make democracy work. In 1998, the voters rejected the Con Con, but public disillusionment still cries out for a renewal of democracy in Hawaii.

To stimulate discussion, particularly for educational purposes, many chapters are followed by a number of lessons representing personal conclusions about our democratic process. Readers are invited to ponder these, to agree or disagree, but at least to think about our system. This is not a "dirty laundry" book, nor the lofty memoirs of a powerful politician. It will not please those who take delight in trashing government or elected officials. It is not the sort of book that sells for an outrageous amount in university bookstores. It is more of a citizen's handbook, for those who would appreciate a few insights, biased as they may be, into legislative life.

INTRODUCTION

They are waiting on the shingle – will you come and join the dance? Will you, won't you, will you, won't you, will you join the dance?

– Lewis Carroll

The relationship between the citizens of a community and their government may be likened to a waltzing partnership, each dancer attuned to the other's closeness, breathing, and movements. When it works, the two move as one, and neither is really sure who is leading and who is following. But sometimes the partners are just not in tune with each other. Movements become power struggles, and toes are stepped on. Perhaps the music has changed, and they haven't learned the new steps. Perhaps they don't want to learn. The dancers may feel they are no longer a good match. It's time to take a breather and cool off. With a little understanding, they will dance as one again. Lately, this social contract, this dance between citizens and government, has grown strained. The partners have turned their backs on each other, folded their arms with indignation, and begun to walk away. Perhaps it is time for each to do a little soul searching and examine the importance of their relationship. Before they can be reconciled, however, someone must make the first move. It is my premise that the logical partner to swallow some pride and initiate the reconciliation is the government.

ANOTHER BLACK EYE

In the fall of 1997, among the sensational news reports about the Bishop Estate, Hawaii's largest private landowner, was the revelation that the House Judiciary chair continued to receive $4000 a month from the Estate for legal consulting work. When challenged to step aside on legislative matters dealing with the Estate due to his obvious conflict of interest, his quoted response was that he would do whatever the Speaker of the House decided was in the interest of the House of Representatives. As the public was to learn, another House member also worked for a Bishop Estate subsidiary, and Speaker of the House Joe Souki made money by selling land to the Estate for a new school. During 1998 and 1999, there was a continuous stream of depressing news surrounding the Bishop Estate and its trustees, resulting in criminal indictments – a sad story for the worthy dream of educating Native Hawaiian children. However laudable the purpose, it did not justify the questionable practices. This is one of the most difficult lessons to learn by those in power. The former Speaker of the House, Henry Peters, had been ousted from his position in 1987 due to a conflict of interest issue. How an elected body addresses conflicts of interest is at the very heart of whether the institution is willing or able to adapt to changing public attitudes, expectations, and needs – whether elected officials will learn a new dance. That such conflicts have become public controversies intensifies citizen alienation and cynicism. It must have occurred to more than one frustrated reader that the House Judiciary chair, as quoted in the newspaper, did not state that he would do what he felt was in the best interests of the community. It was the interests of the House and the judgment of his leader, the Speaker of the House, that he chose to emphasize. After all, if the House "belongs" to the public, then protecting "it" is the same as protecting "them." Many people begged to differ. The sense of ownership was no longer, if it ever was, a strong feature of our political culture. Some legislators interpret loyalty to the Speaker and to the institution as taking precedence over a sense of public propriety. There is a difference between community sensibilities and the culture of the House, and this difference is at the core of citizen disenchantment.

Near the end f the 1998 legislative session, these House members were criticized for casting the deciding "no" votes on a bill that would have limited the compensation for Estate trustees. The public outcry was so intense that all three were forced to reverse themselves in a matter of days. (The Judiciary chair lost his race for a Senate seat in the fall of 1998. Speaker Joe Souki was reelected, but he lost his bid to continue as leader of the House.)

PART-TIMERS AND CONFLICTS

It is inevitable that in a part-time elected group, benign conflicts will be common. In today's economy, it is highly likely that many elected officials will have immediate family members who work for the government, either directly or as contractors. If every legislator whose family income was somehow related to the state budget declined to vote on the budget document, you could not find a quorum or a majority to pass it. As long as the economic survival of families in Hawaii requires two or more wage earners, these "benign" conflicts will continue.

There is another more corrupting and destructive conflict that arises when legislative behavior directly affects the official's income, or his or her employer's income. Many legislators in Hawaii have secured outside employment with industries that have direct interests in legislation. One rightly suspects that not all of these arrangements are based on the skills and expertise of the representative or senator. They are employed to improve legislative clout, pure and simple. Or, if they are truly skilled, they may be expected to look out for the special interests of their employer.

Examples of direct conflict occurred when highly controversial insurance issues, such as no-fault auto insurance, came under the jurisdiction of a Senate committee chair who actually worked for that industry. Another senator, an honest and sincere fellow, for a time chaired the Consumer Protection Committee, which regulates the telephone company where he had been employed for many years due to his technical skills. It matters little if the individual legislator makes a good-faith effort to separate his or her roles. The fact remains that the social contract between the community and their elected representatives has been compromised. The only way to resolve this dilemma is to enact rules that require legislators to step aside when bills arise that obviously put their personal incomes at conceptual odds with public policy. In my twelve years of service, I cannot recall a single case when the Speaker of the House ruled that a legislator had a conflict of interest, even when a legislator/

Bishop Estate trustee led the fight against a bill perceived as directly affecting the Estate.

It really doesn't matter whether a representative did perform $4000 worth of service for a powerful employer, or whether a senator could refrain from making biased decisions regarding his employer. In choosing to vote on bills directly affecting their employers, they said loud and clear that they viewed the relationship between the electorate and the Legislature as being of secondary importance.

Part-time legislatures have never been comfortable with making distinctions between benign and direct conflicts. It has always been easier to adopt a blanket policy that denies the existence of real conflicts, or insists that they can be handled on a case-by-case basis. It is time to revisit this policy.

There is more to this drama than stubborn or arrogant officials. The public still supports the notion that a full-time legislature, where the compensation might justify prohibition of outside income (and thus direct conflicts), is not worth the cost. This attitude fits quite nicely with powerful lobbyists whose bread and butter is the education of the ill-informed, inexperienced, part-time representative or senator. Since there is only sketchy reporting of the legislative session and the hours of hard and sincere work done at the state Capitol, the public naturally assumes that the whole lot of them are overpaid and overrated.

Community activists are at a disadvantage in the part-time legislative world, where hundreds of issues reach a climax in April. Because Hawaii's legislative session is only four months long, those who can mobilize their resources and information quickly have the edge. Community organizations, relying on busy volunteers who often work during the day, cannot arrange for necessary decisionmaking meetings as easily as union and corporate decision makers. A legislative timetable more conducive to participation and deliberation would level the playing field.

If citizens were asked to choose between a system that favors professional lobbyists or citizen activists, they would predictably choose the latter. Suppose you frame the question differently: Do you favor a more expensive, better-paid legislature or the current part-time, lower paid arrangement? You will find overwhelming support for the part-time approach. It is not acceptable to reward legislators for what is perceived to be a pattern of failure in dealing with social problems.

Consider a 1999 study comparing political and moral values of the 1960s and 1990s, in which author Robert Blendon and several collaborators found dramatic shifts in attitudes toward government (see Table I). Their data suggest a transformation of an American society that once accepted proactive government interventions into one that is highly skeptical of the public sector. The Blendon study depicts a political culture that is likely to be hostile to public policies driven from centralized governmental authorities and reliant on public funding.

As long as this unhealthy disdain for elected officials continues, there is no alternative but for the legislature to swallow hard and adopt a conflict-of-interest rule that admits that conflicts occasionally do exist and can be serious. Until such rules are adopted and enforced, there is no alternative but for individual legislators to insist on voluntarily removing themselves from certain decision-making contexts.

When employees or contractors of the Bishop Estate insisted on voting on the Bishop Estate bill with conflicts that were obvious to everyone, the dancers in our democracy took another long stride in opposite directions. As the public and the government look over their shoulders at one another, the romance of democracy has faded and there is no love or respect in their eyes. They still need each other, but a combination of pride and ignorance of the changes in society will make it harder to waltz again as one.

THE REPUBLICANS ARE COMING! THE REPUBLICANS ARE COMING!

The 1998 elections reflected public dissatisfaction with establishment politics. For the first time since statehood, more voters chose to vote in the Republican primary than in the Democratic primary. In part, this was because a very popular Republican mayor of Maui, Linda Lingle, was running for governor. In the Republican primary, she was challenged by Hawaii's longest surviving political force, Frank Fasi. Fasi served as Honolulu's mayor longer than anyone, ever, and ran unsuccessfully for governor first as a Democrat, then as the selfappointed leader of his own party, and finally, in 1998, as a Republican. He was seen by many voters as past his prime, but running to be a spoiler, intending to knock out Lingle in the primary, and make it easier for Democratic Governor Cayetano in the general election.

Lingle won the primary handily, and came within 5000 (out of over 400,000 votes cast) of beating Cayetano. Democrats, who have dominated state government at all levels since the early 1960s, had suffered an embarrassment and a near-death experience. While there were few incumbents who actually lost, one casualty was Judiciary chair and Bishop Estate attorney Terry Tom, who failed in his attempt to move up to a Senate seat. Democrats from across the political spectrum who survived 1998 gave a collective sigh of relief, privately noting that their hold on the hearts of Hawaii's body politic was wearing dangerously thin.

Table I. Public attitudes toward the role of government

Role of government	1960s	1990s
Trust government in Washington to do the right thing only some of the time or never	23%	66%
Big government is biggest threat to the future of the country	35%	59%
Government has gone too far in regulating business	43%	59%
Prefer smaller government with fewer services to larger government with more/many services	40%	59%
Would like government to do more to help minority groups	50%	37%
It is the responsibility of government to reduce differences in income	48%	30%

Source: Blendon et al., 1999

Another post-election casualty was House Speaker Joe Souki, who looked at the number of Democratic incumbents returning and publicly declared that "there was no message" given politicians by the voters. This attitude was apparently too much for even Joe's strongest supporters. Recognizing that the emperor had no clothes, he was quickly deposed by his long-term ally, Finance chair Calvin Say. Say was seen as a kinder, gentler version of Souki, more tolerant of diversity and democracy in the House, with fewer personal agendas, and with less inclination to cram them down the throats of colleagues. Since he became Speaker, Say has gotten widespread praise for his more democratic and open approach to running the House.

The 1998 elections left a few disturbing hints about the state of Hawaiian politics. In precinct after precinct where the Republican Lingle won, a clear trend emerged from the raw vote count: The most disaffected voters, who were also open to change, did not turn out in large numbers. In the Waikiki precincts where Lingle was strong, some voter turnout percentages were below 40% of those registered, with well over 1000 voters who declined to show up at the polls. On the island of Oahu alone, one can identify at least ten or more similar precincts that, if they had had an 80% turnout, would have changed the results of the gubernatorial election. This may mean that, like the trends in the other forty-nine states, Hawaii's voters are finding fewer and fewer reasons to vote, especially if they are already turned off by establishment politics. One national report indicated that the average turnout in the United States was 37%! Hawaii has not yet fallen that far, but we are on the way.

If the Democrats in Hawaii were uneasy over the 1998 elections, the year 2000 was nearly a revolution. In the State House of Representatives, Republicans found themselves with nineteen seats. Three Republicans filled seats formerly held by Democrats who either chose not to run or moved on to higher office, and four Republicans defeated Democratic incumbents in head-to-head contests. The new total of nineteen Republicans vs. thirty-two House Democrats is more than enough to force bills on to the floor of the House for embarrassing votes, and enough to block any procedure that requires a two-thirds vote. The mischief and contentiousness that ensued during the 2001 legislative session is just an omen of the partisan political environment to come.

The year 2001, before the terrorists attacks of September 11, would have been known as the year Democratic Governor Cayetano defied two public education unions and drove them to strike. It would have further been remembered as the year the governor refused to honor the agreed-upon settlement with public school teachers. The deep bitterness this evoked did not bode well for Democrats among those voters who chose to equate the behavior of the governor with the Democratic Party as a whole. This was true even as many Democrats publicly criticized the governor, seeking to distance themselves from his personality and policies.

Following the blow to the Hawaii economy caused by international terrorism, the governor may, if he emerges as a leader in a crisis, be able to rehabilitate his legacy. He is unlikely, however, to gain the kind of public acclaim as did the mayor of New York City.

There is speculation as to the impact of the tragic events of September 11, 2001, on the nature and stridency of politics. As America rallies behind its elected leaders, will this temper the kinds of partisan criticism associated with elections? Will challengers find themselves hampered by the public's unwillingness to listen to partisan debate? If so, how long will such a sensibility last?

Even if there is a public reaffirmation of political and governmental authority, Democrats in Hawaii will be more vulnerable than in the past. And all elected officials will be evaluated in terms of their ability to contribute to real solutions. In Hawaii, this will mean coping with another blow to the economy.

A PERSONAL ROAD TO POLITICS

When I was growing up, I could think of nothing more idealistic or beyond reach than a life of public service. Politics was the stuff of faroff heroes and villains: John Kennedy, Robert Kennedy, Earl Warren, Richard Nixon, Barry Goldwater. The civil rights movement, the environmental movement, the protest against the war in Vietnam, and the war on poverty dominated the news. They were inspiring to those who wanted to make a difference, but beyond the reach of the average young person. I was going to become a music teacher in a nice, safe, nonpolitical middle-class high school. I hung out at the band room in high school, practiced the baritone horn every day, and made it into Syracuse University's School of Music. My life was set.

The year 1968 was by far the most important of my life. That was the year I drifted away from music and closer to the passions of politics. I wanted to be part of the enormous changes that were sweeping the nation. I began working in local campaigns. The person who forced me to make a choice was Robert Kennedy. Like most people of the 1960s, I know exactly where I was when I heard the news of his brother's assassination (high school Spanish class). I can still feel the elation of listening to President Lyndon Johnson say in March 1968 that he would not seek nor accept the nomination for president again. I was excited and inspired by Bobby Kennedy's ability to articulate the needs of the physically, financially, and politically weak of our society. And I was crushed when he too was assassinated.

In 1968, I decided that even though I was about to emerge from music college with a teaching certificate, I had to find some more meaningful way to participate in Bobby Kennedy's public agenda. In 1969, I left the career I'd been preparing for and joined the Peace Corps, which taught me about myself and the world, and that we can adapt to more than we think. After three-and-a-half years on Cheju Island in Korea teaching English, I arrived in Hawaii as a graduate student in Asian history.

In 1973, still wondering if public life was a possibility, I joined Tom Gill's campaign for governor. Tom attracted people who still believed in politics as a noble pursuit. Many who worked in his 1970 and 1974 campaigns for governor were inspired to run for office. After three attempts, I was elected to the State House of Representatives.

LESSONS

Losing a few elections teaches humility and respect for the office. For twelve years I lived my dream: the chance to make a difference in the lives of real people.

The following are a few of my most important observations about the experience:

1. A state representative or senator has access into virtually every aspect of society because all of it might legitimately be a legislative concern. He or she has some responsibility to care about literally everything. This is one of the aspects of public life that sets it apart from the lives of most citizens. People in the private sector rarely have the time or the motivation or the perceived responsibility to be informed about such a broad range of issues.

2. You can be an outspoken and independent legislator. To a certain extent the electorate likes it. The media may rush to your door for a sound bite, but the public is often unable to identify your supporters and enemies when it comes to reelection. If you burn establishment bridges, you make enemies. Money drifts away from you and toward your opponents. Eventually they may gang up on you and find you vulnerable. You can be independent, but you've got to be willing to lose the next election.

3. Public interest in legislative work and even media attention are on the decline. It is increasingly difficult for the average citizen to have a complete picture of what a complex organization like the legislature is doing. Reporters seem to fall into two categories: those who are so new they lack even a basic understanding of the process of government, and those so jaded they tend to gravitate only to the most powerful people, the most dramatic issues, and the most cynical explanations. Their reports have an impact, and it is easy for the public also to become cynical.

4. The ability to bring people inside and outside of government to the table and talk is perhaps the most important and powerful aspect of being an elected official. Many believe elected officials have more power and influence than is the case. Because of this perception, legislators can facilitate a great deal of communication.

5. A strategic letter at the appropriate time can have a big impact. A letter to a state department head asking for information can create an absurd ripple effect of staff scrambling this and that way in the fear that someone's budget may be cut out of spite. Sometimes this exaggerated deference only encourages an unscrupulous legislator to throw his or her weight around. But because of this environment, it is also possible to use one's authority to get things done quite independently of passing a new law.

6. Networks of people who can give you information and tell you what is really going on are one of the most important aspects of a political community. Good information is the most powerful political force in a democracy. Advisors who will tell you when you are crazy or myopic or emotional or illinformed are worth their weight in gold. To be surrounded by boot-polishers is a tragedy for both the legislator and the community.

7. A great many players in politics are content to be participants in the status quo. This means that to push for change is to ask for trouble. One reason why this is so is that the public rewards the middle-of-the-roaders and is weary of the rebels. Rebels and visionaries are essential to progress, but their contributions are not always rewarded at the ballot box. A friend gave me the following quote I keep on my office wall to this day:

> It should be borne in mind that there is nothing more difficult to handle, more doubtful of success, and more dangerous to carry through than initiating a change in a system. The innovator has the enmity of all those who prospered under the old system, and only lukewarm support is forthcoming from those who would benefit under the new one. (Niccolo Machiavelli, 1513)

8. Often the knowledge and attitudes you bring with you to a legislative session are limiting factors. Personal growth in terms of real knowledge is difficult between January and

April. The flurry of bills and resolutions, all handled with only the most superficial review, means that only by increasing the number of eyes and brains does the system avoid total embarrassment and disaster.

9. Belonging is an important characteristic of the political community. Elected officials feel a strange bond, a common set of scars for having to face the election season again and again. It is a unique club. Once elected, it is just so warm and fuzzy to be part of the inner power group, a person of imagined influence, a person who sits in the room when decisions are made (or announced). To belong in this way is not the same as being influential. It just means you are not a threat. You will always get your crumbs, as long as you go along when it comes to the bigger issues that you might not care about anyway.

10. The government bureaucracy is filled with individuals who had to acquire credentials and jump through hoop after hoop to get their jobs, but who are never asked "What should we do?" before a policy decision is made. Often they are only told to implement this or that. Eventually some stop trying to be creative and energetic. Some lose their sense of urgency. They become demoralized. They punch the clock. They watch as seemingly incompetent, overpaid superiors mutilate their work. Occasionally their hopes are raised with end of the year brainstorming sessions and inspiring pep talks promising true partnership and respect, but ultimately their irrelevance in the eyes of the policy makers becomes apparent. In recent years, many public servants suffer because they are also despised by the general public.

11. In the Information Age (see Robert Audrey's The Third Wave), an industrial institution like a legislature is increasingly out of sync with society. It is big and clumsy at a time when the trend is toward small and efficient. Geographically based election districts obscure or ignore many of the most important bonds (our school, our work, our soccer teams, our artistic passions, and even our family ties) and overemphasize

a presumed affinity based on the necessity of a large number of people finding an affordable rental in Makiki.

12. Lately, the initiative to change policy has shifted out of elected bodies like the legislature and into the executive branch, the courts, and the private sector. Gridlock is common in many legislative bodies as they ironically reflect the ambiguities and diversity of the larger society. The public yearns for bold leadership, but the system is almost incapable of achieving the consensus it requires. The short-lived juggernaut of conservative policy created by the Gingrich era in Congress is a rare legislative event. In Hawaii, it is not easy for seventysix self-absorbed egotists (fifty-one House members and twenty-five senators) to agree long enough to pass a bill. It is a miracle that so many get through.

13. The attention span, cynicism, and knowledge base of the electorate during an election campaign are so small that last minute, emotional, single-issue campaigns have great impact. More and more voters are willing to make up their minds on the basis of one issue, one vote, one position, rather than the overall approach or political philosophy of a candidate. Consequently, the eleventh-hour negative attack is becoming more prevalent, more strident, and more dishonest. It is difficult to stay on the high road. If you don't respond to the negative attack, the public will accept it as fact. Is it possible that politics and thoughtfulness are incompatible? That reason and logic are incompatible with what seems too many to be a partisan food fight?

14. The public believes that being in the Legislature is so darn attractive that naturally politicians will do anything to keep their cushy jobs. Sometimes this is true, but for reasons other than personal financial gain. As I look around at my former colleagues, few have been able to translate their perks into prosperity. The aura of elected officials is exaggerated by sensational news reports about those who did abuse their power and face criminal charges as a result. They are the exceptions. It is fair to say, however, that some legislators

have become very comfortable with a life in which a little power, status, and fame overshadow their original goal of serving the general welfare.

1 | RUNNING FOR PUBLIC OFFICE

....

Politics is perhaps the only profession for which no preparation is thought necessary.

— R. L. Stevenson

The overwhelming number of citizens will never run for office. This fundamental democratic experience remains a mystery to many. It deserves some attention if only to understand the differences between the demands of an election and the real job of being a legislator.

WHO RUNS?

To be a successful elected public official requires optimism and idealism. You've got to visualize not only the role of a legislator, but also each step in a winning campaign. You've got to be tough and resilient. You've got to maintain the perception that you are confident of victory. You've got to admire and respect the democratic process enough to overcome the reality that the monthly or yearly wage is probably less than adequate to support a mortgage or a growing family. You've got to want to be successful enough to overcome the emotional and physical ups and downs of the competition. Though these character traits are essential, they are not always recognized or admired by the public.

There is a commonly used derogatory term for those who offer themselves as candidates: politician. This is just a notch lower than "lawyer" in the hierarchy of popular degenerates. (Q: How many politicians does it take to shingle a roof? A: It depends on how thinly you slice them.) Many citizens yearn for "better" people to offer themselves as candidates. Often those who do are accused of abandoning their moral values.

Where do they come from? Are they cloned in an ugly building somewhere in an industrial section of Oahu? Are they smuggled into state waters by unregistered Liberian oil tankers?

No, the reality is that a future politician probably grew up in your neighborhood. Seemingly normal and innocent on the outside, they secretly dreamed of making a difference in this world. Some are successful in their jobs or careers and "hear the call." Others might be urged by friends or professional colleagues to step forward. While the public may have the impression that most are attorneys, this is just not true. In 1998, out of fifty-one members of the State House of Representatives, only a dozen sported a law degree. In the twenty five-member senate, only seven were attorneys.

Some are propelled by an issue that affects them personally, like child abuse, or the condition of their schools, or saving a beach from over-development (Mike Wilson used his prominence in the Sandy Beach Initiative to run for mayor), or a woman's right to reproductive freedom, or a church's objection to Hawaii's moral decay. A minority is asked by one or more special interests to represent them. I've personally known politicians who fit any and all of these categories.

Do they have anything in common? Well, yes, of course. First, most of them begin with a picture in their mind of a president or governor or other high-level leader – a statesman – which implies a corresponding picture of what running for office might be like.

Second, they are quickly disabused of this illusion. Hawaii has very small legislative districts compared to many mainland states. To run competitively means you don't have to be a big cheese or even raise an inordinate amount of money. Most politicians start at a very modest level, not surrounded by a ready-made political organization. Few are independently wealthy or come from a famous political family. In fact, most new candidates find that they are on their own. While it is easy to get on the ballot, (only twenty-five signatures of registered voters are required) very few actual resources are provided by party organizations, especially for an unknown who may be openly critical of the establishment.

I was always surprised and amused at those who tried to paint all Democrats in Hawaii, especially new or independent candidates, as part of some establishment machine. There is a downtown business establishment, operating mostly as a nonpartisan defender and contributor of funds for the status quo and those who might represent it, but the only beneficiaries are the establishment-oriented veterans. Of course, the Bishop Estate during its heyday of political and economic influence created its own machine, and it was most closely associated with the Democratic Party.

Machine or party support for most new Democratic candidates is limited to providing a free breakfast after the primary, and, if you win, to printing your picture with about a hundred others in a onepage ad just before the general election. (I'm less familiar with the resources offered Republicans, but often their new candidates do not appear to be any better off.) In past years, Democratic candidates for the legislature were also awarded the "benefit" of participating in the unified campaign canvass.

The unified campaign canvass was often a drain on many smallfry, first-time candidates. To participate, you had to come up with a lot of literature (up to 5000 extra pieces) to be crammed into a plastic bag with brochures from five or six other candidates (senate, congress, city council, etc.), where it was likely to be lost in the shuffle or tossed out altogether once it was left on the doorknob. Next, you were asked to provide workers to stuff the literature in the bags, and then distribute it in your district. Finally, the date for the canvass was almost always a crucial Saturday just before the general election, forcing you to suspend all your other campaign activities for the sake of the well-financed gubernatorial or congressional campaigns. The idea of the unified campaign that mobilized all segments of the Democratic Party might have appeared somewhat of an overkill in the 1980s. However, as the influence of the dominant party declines, there is a sense that the withering of the unified effort reduces the energy and participation in party politics.

ON YOUR OWN

As a new candidate you are on your own to find a few loyal friends to devote more time than they intended to help you out. You must provide the organization, the content of your message, your professional looking wardrobe, your signs, your voter lists, your fundraiser committee, everything. For the first time you need to think about how to answer questions about issues you may never have heard of. Frequently the public makes few distinctions between issues at the neighborhood, county, state, or even federal level.

A new candidate seeks advice and support from former senator (and later lieutenant governor) Jean King

- Why can't we have a stop sign at this corner?
- What are you going to do about those loud mopeds?
- What's your plan to revitalize the economy?
- Do you support the building of West Oahu College?
- How do you feel about out-of-state union labor?
- Is health insurance too large a burden for business?
- Why does our park look so shabby?
- How do you stop releasing dangerous criminals?
- What services should we privatize?
- Do you favor the right to die?
- Why do I have to pay a conveyance tax?
- Why don't we tax the tourists more?
- Can't we protect our reefs?
- Why do you have to accept contributions?
- Should we ban smoking in all public places?
- Do you support traditional marriage?
- Do you support home schooling?
- What is your plan to save the public schools?
- Do judges deserve a raise? How about teachers?

If you are lucky, there are some seasoned veterans out there to give advice. Sometimes it's overwhelming or conflicting. Many people are willing to tell you to do this or that, as if you had money and twenty-six hours a day to campaign. Sometimes you are not sure they understand you as a candidate or live in your district. Sometimes you are just too new to grasp what they are saying.

Physical energy is one of the expendable assets that any new candidate must provide. It takes an enormous amount of focus and stamina to make 100 phone calls. Getting up at 5 a.m. to wave at commuter traffic loses its charm after a few weeks. Walking door-todoor at noon on a hot Saturday, sweating and trying not to look as tired and disheveled as you are - these are challenges that make planning and organizing a campaign even more difficult for the newcomer.

In the end, if you have two or three really dedicated campaign workers you are lucky. For the most part, the new candidate will run his or her own campaign, even if there is a nominal campaign manager. It is somewhat like opening a small store: If you want it done right, you do it yourself.

WHERE TO RUN

In 1984 I was elected from what I called the Freeway District, consisting of bits and parts of various neighborhoods left over from reapportionment. The right side was Kaimuki, my stronghold. The middle and left were toss-ups, and very transient. Up to 25% of the voters in this district moved between elections. After the 1990 census, this district was completely eliminated. The new district I ran from in 1992 consisted of part of my old Makiki precincts, Tantalus, and a small slice of Manoa.

While many if not most first-time candidates run from the district of their parents or current residence, others who are younger and more mobile have a choice. For some, one of the first tasks of a Jim Shon / Inside Hawaii's Capitol would-be candidate is to pick a district. Does the one you currently live in have the right profile ethnically or by voting temperament? If you are a Democrat, make sure that the district has a history of electing Democrats, and that the groups mostly associated with Democratic voting (e.g., Americans of Japanese ancestry over the age of fifty) are present in sufficient numbers. The public would be surprised how often politicians move to a more favorable electoral environment. (The guy who beat me in 1996 had never lived in our district until midsummer of that year.)

The Freeway District.

Voter Contact Services (VCS), a local firm, can provide a demographic profile of each district, with every voter categorized in every imaginable way. VCS will break down the area by age, by registered party, by ethnic group, by recent election results, even by the size of household. Data can be purchased and presented by each precinct to tell you where candidates of similar profiles have been strong or weak. If you are running against an incumbent, you can find out how he or she did in the last few elections, including the number of blank ballots if they ran unopposed (indicating voters who refused to support them even without an opponent).

For example, before the 1996 election I knew that 40.5% of the registered voters in my district were Caucasian, 22.8% Japanese, 18.4% Chinese, and 2.7% Polynesian. I knew that in the last general election in 1994, only 62.6% of the registered voters showed up at the polls. I also knew that in 1994, Clinton beat Bush by 47.2 to 37.5% in my district and that Republican Pat Saiki out-polled Ben Cayetano for governor by 39.5 to 30%. Almost 60% of all my voters lived in a one-voter household, and the largest age group were seniors over 65, representing 23.8%. All these data are useful in revealing the mood and inclinations of a district. A wise newcomer will look closely before leaping, and once a decision has been made, will use demographic data to shape an intelligent campaign strategy.

The next step is to try to plug into a network or web of resources, groups, organizations, or individuals you feel comfortable with in terms of issues, ideology, party, or whatever. I was an environmentalist, so I tried to get endorsements and campaign workers from that realm. I was also an educator, so I really wanted the support of teachers and professors. I favored leasehold conversion of condos, so I asked leaders in that movement to help. (Later, after becoming chair of the Health Committee, I sought out nurses, public health advocates, mental health associations, dentists – whoever overlapped my own positions.)

The difficulty with tapping an interest network is that sometimes they have few resources, and the volunteers they can mobilize are also needed in higher priority races, especially for "saving" a legislator who has really come through for them. (In later years, I was one of those who needed to be saved, and I'm sure there were some new candidates who received less help as a result of my vulnerability.)

Raising money is an unfamiliar and difficult task. You feel pushy. You feel like you are groveling. You feel like you've got to be nice to folks you need but really don't know. You have to sell and promote yourself. You must give the impression that you are a winner so that a contribution will not be wasted. To get started, you will need some cash just to print tickets and send out letters. A fundraising event costs even more, and several thousands of dollars must be invested just to break even.

I remember my very first fundraiser. It was held at the Club 100 hall on Kamoku Street across from Iolani School. The hall has one large room, and there was a smaller section off to the side where the regular members play pool and watch TV My event was held in the pool room, which was very small, and even then we did not fill the space. To add insult to injury, a few old-timers showed up during the event and started watching TV in the corner of the room!

A few years ago, I spoke with a new candidate who said his motivation was to improve Hawaii's economy so that his brothers could move back home from the mainland. He was filled with ideas and proposals and reforms - but none of this matters at all if few residents of the district recognize his name. They would not recognize it, let alone associate it with his ideas, if he couldn't raise enough money to penetrate the busy lives of citizens who are bombarded by infomercials, telephone solicitations, advertisements of every sort, and, last but not least, the literature of the incumbent legislator, his opponent. (He turned out to be very energetic and well organized, and was elected to the State House of Representatives in 1998 and reelected in 2000).

It is a common belief of many members of the public that one of the negative trade-offs of running for office is that everyone either knows or wants to know your private business. This may be true once you are established, but for the newcomer, the problem is just getting noticed and recognized. The losers in elections are often people who talked themselves into believing that they are famous because they are on the ballot, had a letter to the editor printed, or sent out one or two brochures. To run successfully, you need a resilient ego because it is going to be trashed again and again.

A final personal note: If you have a family, you simply can't run effectively without their support. My wife began as a de facto campaign treasurer. Later, when we had a young child, it was her tolerance of my absence that made it possible to continue. The presence of immediate family members in a campaign is noticed, as is their absence.

THE CAMPAIGN

In the world of electoral politics, there is a marvelous equality that imposes itself on even the most cynical of attitudes. The rich man, the poor woman, the condo owner, the small-apartment renter - all are endowed with a single vote, no more, no less. When you walk door-to-door in the most fashionable neighborhoods, you meet individuals who carry exactly the same political power on election day as the people who speak English as a second language. Lawyers and doctors with spacious homes have no more political clout than welfare moms and laborers crammed into small walk-ups near a noisy freeway.

When you wave and smile at passing cars, the 1999 Mercedes has the same importance as the 1979 Datsun. This reality challenges every candidate for public office to exhibit respect and attention to each and every resident of his or her district. I always felt that the idealism that is built into our political system demands an ever-vigilant attitude and demands that candidates for public office live up to a standard that in many ways is higher in politics than any other realm of life.

The vote is the secular expression of the soul. Many religions teach that each and every being is of value to God. To be a true Christian or Buddhist or whatever, the faithful follower must expand his or her self and somehow identify with the lowliest among us. A citizen politician who truly believes in democracy must reach out to each and every voter. Equality before God or the law is a challenge not all of us successfully meet.

On an even deeper psychological level, the needs of each citizen of the community also have equal merit. Of course, there is a huge difference between wants, demands, and needs, and being able to sort that out is what separates the statesman from the demagogue. Is it really possible to identify with all sorts of voters whose personal lives one might neither understand nor condone? Doesn't the decision to run for public office imply the setting aside of one's personal biases and preferences? And what of those who decline to vote at all? Do they also deserve equal consideration?

Our heritage, our ideals, and our system compel us to answer in the affirmative. Yet this almost impossible standard is undermined by the very same process, and the very same community in which we live. The tension between democratic principles, the ambivalence and contradictory needs or desires of a community, and the practical requirements of winning votes shapes political campaigning as we know it today.

I'll never forget visiting one home where the woman of the house was absolutely in favor of a mass transit system for Oahu. Just as she was finished offering her view, the man of the house walked up and warned me never to even consider supporting the proposed light rail system.

There are certain street corners in urban Honolulu that I try not to think about. When I pass by, a small part of my brain plays back hours of smiling at cars in the hot sun. Not only would I rise at 5:30 a.m. to say "hello" to early commuters (when all you can see are headlights), I would also plant myself in a visible spot just after 2 p.m. (when all you could see was the glare off the windshields) and wave until 6 or 6:30 p.m. These flashbacks go back to the mid-1970s when I was running in Waikiki (unsuccessfully). It is a part of political life that is taken for granted as necessary, and something I came to dislike more than any other aspect of public life at the bottom of the electoral totem pole. (It is interesting that although I was a state representative, dealing with statewide issues and laws, the electoral House districts are several times smaller than the Honolulu City Council districts. In fact, the state house districts are the smallest of electoral units.)

In the early days, many of us would play mind games with the cars – counting colors or types, and trying to predict patterns of behavior by the drivers. How many BMWs could you get to wave? The most enthusiastic responses, often from trucks, were probably from those people who were not registered to vote in your district, perhaps not registered to vote at all. We would marvel at Senator Anson Chong, who had the enthusiasm and technique down pat, shaka sign (the Hawaiian equivalent of "how-ya-doin'?" and thumbs up) and all. We chuckled at Steve Cobb, who saw sign waving as a military operation with his roving cell phone supporters reporting on enemy activity on other corners. Steve also had moveable messages he could put at the bottom of his sign, as well as lights for night waving. Dave Hagino was convinced that if they saw you at midnight they would never forget you. Calvin Say had a dragon. Rod Tam insisted you must stand next to the sign, not behind it. Some mounted radios and coffee mugs on the backs of the sign frames. This was still the age of innocence in sign waving, or so it seemed to me. Lately, it has become more routine, fighting the cynicism of the drivers. We all hoped and prayed that we would not be the cause of some accident through distraction.

On those days near the election when both sides had their troops out in force, you would always try to judge which group got the best response. You might compete for the best spots and the best corners. Sometimes this approached street theater, as when the doctors (who opposed me for supporting the nursing profession) would come out in white coats and stethoscopes for my opponent, and the nurses would come out in their hospital uniforms for me. I had banners that read "Hawaii's nurses support Jim Shon." They brought banners that said "Hawaii's doctors support "_____" (Every year it was a different name; what they had in common was running against me!) Some of this was fun, but most of it was drudgery. I am happy to live without the prospect of doing it again in the near future.

In 1996, on "Black Tuesday," the day the electorate invited me to take an extended and indefinite leave. It was my tenth election campaign, and one in which I probably exerted the least amount of effort since starting it all back in 1976. The motivation to walk doorto-door and wave signs at the commuting traffic was at its lowest ebb since I first was politically active. It felt stale, and I had for a few years thought how refreshing it might be to move into some administrative role where all I had learned about government and institutions might be put to some direct use.

Campaigning is nothing like governing. Total dingbats can appear oh-so-appealing and promising on the roadside. Their brochures might speak of leadership, vision, commitment, and community involvement. It may be true, but it may also be cleverly fabricated. In contrast, a wonderfully talented and honest individual can sometimes appear to be just another political hack. All successful campaigners have some understanding of the collective behavior of our citizens, and have learned to speak to voters' fears and hopes through imagery, symbolism, and self-promotion.

In 1989, a thoughtful political scientist, Kyosti Pekonen, wrote of the importance of personality and imagery in modern politics:

> The candidate's personal campaign does not so much project political plans as a public image: what he/she looks like, his/ her family, and most of all, his/her intellectual and emotional life. By their self-praise, they try to show that they are the best possible representatives. But representing what? Because every candidate must try to make him/herself necessary – at least in the citizen's political imagination – and because big political questions seem not to be forthcoming, the only alternative would seem to be self-praise and artificial, manufactured images. (*In Contemporary Political Culture*, ed. John Gibbins, 1989.)

The public, if such a collective noun can be used meaningfully, requires that a political candidate say what is popular and politically correct, and this can lead to an unconscious invitation to manipulate. Candid remarks that offend are often punished at the ballot box.

THE RULES OF ELECTORAL LIFE

There are a number of unstated rules of electoral life and successful campaigning in Hawaii. You might be successful dispensing with them, but you would do so at your political peril.

The first is sweat. Voters want to know you are working hard. If they see you every day when they drive to and from work, they know one thing: you really want their vote. They may not vote for you just because you wave signs or walk door to door, but without it, at least for a House seat, you are at a great disadvantage. A corollary of sweat is visibility. They want to see you for themselves, to size you up, measure your demeanor, hear your voice, see whether or not your smile is genuine, notice if you look professional or honest. In an age when there are so much cynicism and distrust, perhaps sweat and visibility are the only means of measuring a candidate.

Sign waving can be overdone. Intrusive and obnoxious overkill with thousands of mindless wavers at every intersection can turn voters off as well. But the chances are, whether we like to admit it or not, if the opponent is more visible, people will notice. They will comment: How come I don't see you as often as what's-his-name? Don't you care as much? There are also many voters who feel anyone who waves signs at cars is a subhuman species and does not deserve a vote. I would refer them to the several University of Hawaii professors who told me they first voted for me because they liked my smile.

The second rule, and this is a tragic one, is that negative attacks work. Now you might think that you and the public are perceptive enough to discount negative campaigning, especially if it is personal. I once thought the same. I was convinced that voters who knew me would not be influenced by it. I nearly lost four times because of this belief.

It was the year of the Willie Horton ads on national TV Willie Horton was a despicable criminal who somehow was released while Michael Dukakis was governor of Massachusetts. Ronald Reagan, who had released similar individuals while he was governor of California, made it a big issue. The Republican strategists made Horton-esque photographs available to many of their candidates in local races, and I had the bad fortune of drawing an opponent who was willing to use it.

Walking door to door is the most effective and expected form of demonstrating "sweat" and campaigning at the grassroots level in Hawaii. It is expected by the residents, and the candidate who shows up in the neighborhood more often is more likely to gain votes.

Picture a blown-up, close-up photo (nearly filling a full 8 x 11-inch glossy page) of a very dark, ominous individual holding the shiny blade of a long knife next to his face. The caption read: "Why Isn't Rep. Jim Shon fighting for our safety?" The brochure went on to say that I had done nothing to fight violent crime but that my opponent did care and had a plan of action. (The use of "plan" and "action" are quite effective apparently.) When this piece arrived in the mail, I was shocked. Not only was I depicted as somehow in cahoots with violent criminals, but the imagery itself was powerful. On reflection, I felt the residents of my district would see through the obvious PR smear. In fact, I was convinced it would cost my opponent votes. I was wrong.

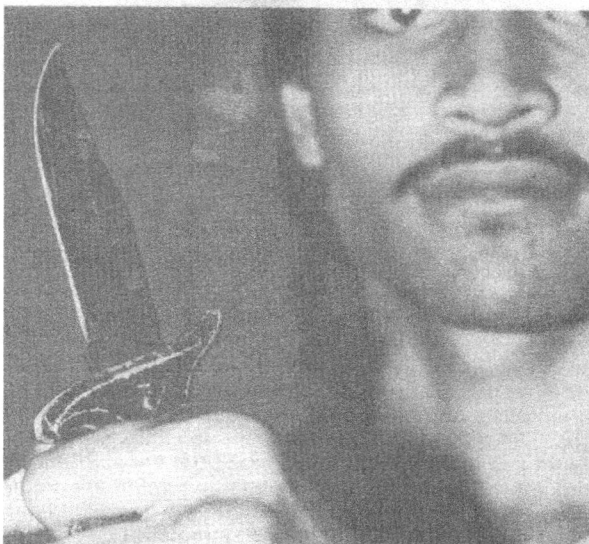

WHY ISN'T REP. JIM SHON FIGHTING FOR OUR SAFETY?

Clearly one of the most obnoxious pieces of campaign trash seen in Hawaii

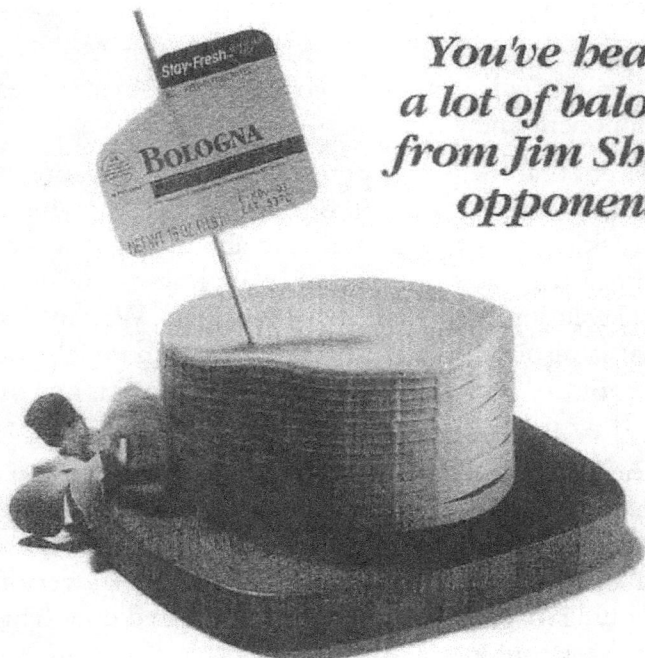

You've heard a lot of baloney from Jim Shon's opponent.

Now here's the TRUTH...

Occasionally I did fight back

The Willie Horton piece was only one in a series that year. Also arriving in every mailbox were reminders that I did not care about the mentally ill, the homeless, or the taxpayer. The crime piece was pretty common those days, but what angered me most was the attempt to convince the public that I did not care about mental health: "Why doesn't Rep. Jim Shon care about all of Hawaii's people?... Some of the most ignored citizens in society are the mental health patients... Why hasn't our present legislator, who is also the Health Committee... Chairman ever done anything about it? ... Our community and state cannot afford to keep a legislator in office whose inactivity shows a lack of concern to the most important issues facing our State."

Mental health had been one of my priorities while chair of the Health Committee. I had sponsored bills to increase funding, to create community-based services, to include consumers in decision making, and to lift Hawaii out of its dismal fifty-first in the nation rating. I had even been honored by the Mental Health Association, made up primarily of advocates and consumers of mental health services. My opponent knew this.

It was apparent that the primary ethical standard operating here was that if the public will believe it, one is justified in saying it. I am not so thin-skinned as to rant and rave about exaggeration. In private moments, I also question whether or not I have done enough to find practical solutions to serious social problems. We can always do more. What is dispiriting is the casual manner in which young politicians attempt to destroy an opponent's, integrity. It is one thing to say I failed. It is another to say I never cared.

The only way to counter this, I felt, was to put out my own series of positive brochures. Often I generated at least ten separate pieces of campaign literature in a campaign. It must have worked, because "landslide Jim" survived again and again, just barely. My very first piece, while running in Waikiki, was a poorly designed door hanger. Later, I became very sophisticated. My most successful venture was an annual cookbook. Somehow this connected with more people on a human level. (In 1996, the year I lost, I did not do a cookbook.) I have learned that if the target of an attack piece does not respond, he or she will suffer.

While I tended to spread my literature out over the course of a yearlong campaign, the more effective attack strategy was and is to bombard the voter almost every day for the last two weeks before the election. Ideally, a special leafleting on election eve would leave the voter with your mug and name in their minds as the last thing they remembered before entering the voting booth.

I wish I could explain why perfectly intelligent citizens allow themselves to be influenced in such a trivial way. Perhaps it reflects their deep cynicism, their sense that it doesn't really matter whom we elect since there is no candidate we can trust. It is one thing to insist that candidates behave in a more civil fashion, but it is almost impossible to uphold such a standard if the voters allow such poor electoral behavior. The only real check on negative campaigning is an alert and conscientious public.

The third rule is to recognize that citizens have less and less time for public issues and politics. In a state with just over a million souls, there are over 900,000 vehicles and nearly 300,000 TV sets. Voters are busy coming and going to the mall, to the child care center, to the school, to soccer or baseball or piano practice, or wherever. When they finally get home, they are too exhausted to rush through dinner in order to attend a neighborhood board meeting or a political coffee hour. They are bombarded with junk mail that competes for attention with political mail. They are pestered by telephone calls asking for charitable contributions. They stare at the news on TV, perhaps, and see mostly violent crime and deadly accident reports ("if it bleeds, it leads" is the TV news rule) supplemented by the new trend in extended weather news – even mainland weather! Investigative reports on serious issues are given two or three minutes in a half-hour news program. Thoughtful parents of young children do not encourage them to watch the news, because it will just expose them to the ugliness and corrupting influences of society. If you're a candidate and you don't get your picture on the front page of the paper or at least in the front section, the chances are you will not be noticed.

My friend the late Professor Ira Rohter (of the University of Hawaii Department of Political Science) often wrote and spoke of a new kind of democracy, one in which citizens gather nearly every night in town meetings to give meaningful input and even decide public policy for themselves. There is a part of me that wants to embrace Ira's rosy world of citizen activists, but it has little relationship to the day-to-day lives of our people. As the playwright Oscar Wilde said, "The trouble with socialism is that it would take too many evenings."

In my fantasy political world, campaigning would be as easy as keeping a schedule of small-group coffee hours where motivated citizens would gather to find out who you are and what you think, and to tell you what you ought to know. This may be the case for the larger races, such as governor or mayor, but for mere legislative seats, it is more difficult to get people's attention, even for short periods of time. Since few really pay attention until the last days before voting, the power of last minute campaign commercials and literature is enhanced.

My rule of thumb for campaigning in urban Honolulu was that if you did not somehow "touch" a voter at least three meaningful times, your efforts did not count. It might mean visiting their door three times, or a direct phone call, or some other form of personal contact. It might mean organizing a popular community event. Sign waving does not count as one of the three contacts. I marvel at new candidates who think they can get elected with just one brochure and one walk through the district. I'm not saying it can't be done, but it is rare.

Not long ago an environmental coalition brought a consultant in from the mainland to talk about effective political action. He offered this list of effective voter contacts, starting with the most effective and progressing to the least effective:

1. Candidate meets voter.
2. Candidate phones voter.
3. Candidate family member meets or phones voter.
4. Campaign volunteer meets voter.
5. Campaign volunteer phones voter.
6. Endorsing organization sends mail to member of an organization.
7. Candidate sends personalized letter to voter.
8. Campaign sends mail to voter.
9. Endorsing organization sends mail to nonmember voter
10. Voter reads newspaper endorsement.
11. Voter hears TV or radio ad.
12. Voter sees billboard, bus bench, yard sign, newspaper ad.
13. Voter bends down and picks campaign literature off front porch.

A fourth rule is that geographical neighborhoods with a true sense of community and the networks that go with it are becoming rare, certainly in urban environments. People sometimes move into condominiums to avoid contacts with others. The isolated refuge of a home or apartment is the reality of more and more people. They are increasingly likely to identify themselves as members of a profession, as employees of a corporation, as alumni of a high school or college, or as soccer moms and dads. It is getting easier for new candidates to just move into a district and not be terribly punished for being a carpetbagger. Longer-term resident candidates attempt to exploit the issue, but it strikes many citizens as irrelevant compared to questions like: "What can you do for me?" "Do you agree with me?" "Do you agree with me on this single issue?"

The relationship of the candidate to the electorate during a campaign is worth some serious reflection if we are to keep our democracy healthy enough to attract participation, both by voters and by those willing to serve.

LESSONS

1. Current politicians are the role models and inspirations for future candidates. Often voters gain insight into the values, attitudes, and opinions of candidates by looking at their mentors.
2. In a personality-driven electoral culture, the likelihood of a young, independent candidate being able to count on support from a political party or some other machine is slim
3. Neither the candidates nor the voters are able to match-up particular issues with a particular incumbent.
4. In the process of looking at voter profiles and talking with thousands of voters, candidates may be in the best position to understand the diversity of moods, attitudes, opinions, backgrounds, and inclinations of a particular district. Like a successful retail store that changes just enough with the times to always be profitable, incumbents know how to appeal to the voters in their districts.
5. To be successful as a campaigner does not correlate directly with being successful or effective as a legislator. The two activities are totally disconnected. On the campaign trail, the opportunities for thoughtful discussion are rare. Voters have only intermittent interest in paying attention to a small legislative race. Because they do not understand the day-today job of a legislator, voters are often unable to evaluate candidates by asking questions that are relevant.

6. Increasingly, the moral compass for ethical campaign tactics has been discarded. "If the public will believe it, I am justified in saying it" has become an all-too-common attitude.

7. It is not easy for voters to learn about candidates' real motives, characters, conflicts, biases, or opinions. Nor is it easy for candidates to learn about the specific opinions of their own voters. A professional poll will cost over $15,000. The political world, for all participants, is an anecdotal one, with rumor, innuendo, speculation, and unproven assumptions the currency of our democracy.

8. A successful legislative candidate is seldom in a position to reflect constituent views since there is no way of knowing what the majority may desire on any given issue. No matter how committed one may be to the role of mirror or representative of the people, most elected officials are forced into the role of steward or trustee. The nature of campaigning accelerates the transformation from mirror to trustee.

2 | A DAY IN THE LIFE

People who are first-time employees at the Capitol commonly report that they had no idea so much work is done during a legislative session. Even if they begin as cynical critics of government, they invariably take with them a much greater appreciation of the institution, the people, and the scope of the endeavor. Everyone should be a legislator for a day.

The day begins with the donning of the legislative uniform, which exists really only for men. Professional attire for women is generally similar for most work office environments in the white-collar world, but for men in Hawaii, only attorneys and legislators appear regularly at work in a suit and tie. (This is perhaps why so many believe most legislators are lawyers!)

There are many explanations for this occupational dress code. They range from long-standing tradition to a special sense of respect for the electorate. Pretentious self-importance has also been claimed. In any case, it is done. Occasionally the selection of the necktie might provide an additional opportunity to make a personal statement. (My favorite depicted a rain forest filled with wild animals – reflecting either the importance of the environment or the degree to which legislative life resembled a jungle or zoo, depending on who was Speaker of the House that year.)

On the subject of clothes and appearance, one of the first lessons of elected life is that you have become a public person. To appear in public unshaven or in unkempt clothes is no longer deemed appropriate by many. A sign of respect as well as political wisdom, neatness and grooming are not options but necessities. The longer you are in office, the more likely you are to be recognized in a grocery store or fastfood outlet. Your gestures and demeanor may well be measured against suspicions that all politicians are arrogant and aloof. Beware even of day- dreaming, for I once was told I lost a vote because I didn't smile at someone on the street. Those with their own bumper stickers and recognizable cars better be courteous drivers. It is clear that the public demands a higher standard of its officials, and rightly so. In an age when so many of our heroes have let us down, the community is rather unforgiving when a legislator is caught driving under the influence or misappropriating campaign funds.

When you arrive at the State Capitol, usually between 7:00 and 8:00 a.m., you are treated to your own parking stall, one of the two most essential perks for elected officials. The other, in my humble opinion, is a University of Hawaii parking pass. In the past, there were also free tickets to University of Hawaii sports events that eventually fell into disfavor with critics. Special perks are part of a bygone age where ethics were looser and there was a much warmer, more appreciative attitude toward elected officials.

THE CULTURE OF THE CAPITOL

Hawaii's Capitol was built at a time (1969) when there was still a sense of community pride in being a self-governing entity. Government, both nationally and locally, was viewed as a positive instrument for justice, economic development, and equal opportunity. This resulted in a structure that is both democratic and symbolic: pillars that look like palm trees, a pond and a mosaic piece that depict the ocean, House and Senate chambers that represent volcanoes, and chandeliers that evoke the sun and the moon. The open center is surrounded by walkways and railings that facilitate chance meetings, political celebrity watching, impromptu legislative business, and the feeling that one is a part of an important and complex process. In recent years, people began to take this ambience for granted until the legislature was forced to relocate temporarily for renovations. When we moved back, there was almost an audible sigh of relief and appreciation by those who missed this special building.

Buildings and architecture do matter. Democracy has enough problems on the personal level of human relations without structural barriers. Everyone knows the feeling of intimidation when entering a typical governmental, bureaucratic structure with their narrow hallways and mazes of identical doors. Spend a few minutes in the Federal Building in downtown Honolulu and the message is very clear: you don't belong here. Hawaii's Capitol is completely different. It facilitates the democratic process. It complements a culture of openness and aloha.

If you are a member of the State House of Representatives in Hawaii, you enter the State Capitol through two thick unlocked doors near the air-conditioning system in the basement parking garage (taking care not to step in the grease spots on the cement floor). You nod to Charlie, Frank, Barbara, Belle, Ronie, and the other long-time members of the House staff, who have been there longer than you and will no doubt be there long after you have gone. Confidently you stride through the lounge adjacent to the House chamber. The rug in the lounge always seems to have a musty smell to it. Opposite the elevator door is the minority (Republican) caucus room, which is furnished with a long table and comfortable chairs for special meetings of that group before or during the regular floor sessions. There is a similar majority (Democratic) caucus room on the opposite side of the House chamber. The private dedicated elevator requires a key. For most of my twelve years, any key would do, even the one to my gas tank. The elevator rises slowly as if to remind you that most of government lacks a sense of urgency. If you are impatient with bureaucracy, the elevator can annoy you every single day of the year. Energetic workers in the building, including legislators seeking to lose weight, might tackle the many flights of stairs to arrive at their floor. The stairwells are dusky cement shafts completely out of character with the beauty of the building itself.

On the third or fourth floor, your thick koa wood office door has your name on it, along with certain titles, the only one that matters being chair of some committee. If you are vice chair it means you have to prepare all the folders (with the proposed legislation and written testimony) for the chair. If you are assistant floor leader or hold some other insider title, it means you are completely unimportant. When you enter, your administrative aide greets you with a stack of phone messages. You probably won't respond to very many of them this morning because in fifteen minutes you must preside over your committee meeting, and you need to review any testimony that arrived before you did.

For many legislators, the selection of paid staff (one full-time, yearlong administrative aide, and several additional staff hired just for the four-month session) is their first experience as an employer. If you have a clear idea of how you want to behave, what role you will take in the institution, and what you want to accomplish, then choosing staff might not be so difficult. If, on the other hand, you really don't know much about being a legislator, then you might want to consult the insider veteran staff network, which tries to match up people looking for jobs with appropriate representatives.

My first legislative staff

Often, session workers are recruited from the previous year's campaign, which addresses the need to keep in touch with your district. When you become a committee chair, however, there is a much greater obligation, both to your colleagues and to the community. Your staff, their knowledge of the subject matter and the players in a certain field, and their competence to do legislative paperwork and meet short deadlines are resources that the entire community must rely on.

I believe that the selection of good staff is one of the most important functions of a legislator. As chair of the House Committee on Health for six years and (later) of the Committee on Energy and Environmental Protection for two, I was fortunate to attract energetic, intelligent, and competent individuals who were true colleagues and partners in the business of the legislature. (Their names are mentioned on the dedication page at the front of this book.)

I began my first legislative session with a staff of five: a woman who had worked for me as a delegate to the 1978 Constitutional Convention and whom I'd met during the 1974 Tom Gill gubernatorial campaign; a woman who lived in my district; a wife of a friend with whom I'd served in the Peace Corps; a knowledgeable environmental scientist and activist who was working on his Ph.D. in entomology; and a friend whom I'd met as a graduate student and who had a degree in political science and was getting his teaching credential from the University of Hawaii College of Education. Each and every one brought their own knowledge and a special connection with their own constituency. Each knew more about important issues than I. I knew I was lucky to persuade them to take a chance on the new kid on the block.

I never chose anyone because of their ethnic background, but some legislators believed ethnicity of staff could play a role in people's initial ability to trust or accept you. As a group, my first staff was rather a faithful representation of my past, the ethnic diversity of my district, and my current life. They were all bright, energetic, and highly motivated individuals who shared my philosophy and agenda.

Later, when I was chair of the Health Committee, I attracted graduates from the University of Hawaii School of Public Health, social activists, several graduate students, and a number of political veterans from other legislative offices and state government. I employed a nurse, a historian, an AIDS activist, a member of the American Civil Liberties Union, and a former Washington, D.C., employee of the Office of Technology Assessment. In twelve years, I hired thirty-one individuals who served as staff for forty-nine one- or two-year paid positions (eleven served during two or more sessions). I consider myself honored to be associated with these people, many of whom went on to important leadership positions in state government and the nonprofit community.

Many new legislators are rarely aware of how intense and pressure filled a four-month session can be. There is little time to train staff. My selection criteria were the following: they should know more about the subject matter than I (so that they increased the knowledge of the committee); they should know most of the key agencies and leaders in the field (so that they could expand and maintain the committee's contacts, especially when I was not available); they should know the legislative process; they should know computers; they should be able to write quickly and clearly; and they should share my goals and political philosophy. I was extremely fortunate to have found people who met these criteria and were willing to work in my office.

My office

In every session, the Capitol community is well aware of which offices are running smoothly and which are not. Some legislators are difficult to work for, and they end up hiring and firing people throughout the session. Others are secretive and share little with their staff, fostering a sense of isolation or irrelevance. A few are downright abusive.

So you chitchat with staff on your way into the inner sanctum, a private office that is bigger and better than 90% of the executive offices in the state. There is usually enough room for a small, civilized meeting, hundreds of which are required during a legislative session. The thick koa wood door is for privacy, because no matter how open you may be personally, many of the people you meet will need the comfort of confidentiality.

Most offices enjoy professionally hung artwork selected from the collection maintained by the State Foundation on Culture and the Arts. I usually brought in my own Korean and Chinese scrolls, but most legislators were content to display the state's offerings, many of which were abstract. Art has its place, and some legislators used their outer offices to display drawings from district schools. Representative Dave Hagino would occasionally feature a prominent artist's works, along with a special reception.

Your personal desk is a large one, usually with a long credenza in back of your comfortable chair. In spite of this luxury, there just never seems to be enough room for all the bills, correspondence, personal pictures, and computer hardware that go with the job. As sessions run their course, the offices become more and more cluttered with stacks of papers. The wall-to-wall carpets become hopelessly stained, requiring cleaning with a toxic smelling, sawdust like material that drives everyone out of the office several times a year.

In the early morning, the office has its own sonic environment: the fax machine is beeping and cranking, the phones are ringing, the coffeemaker is perking, and the three-ring binders are snapping as staffers insert all the bills and their subsequent committee reports in numerical order. People are talking on the phones, the heavy koa wood doors open and close with the delivery of mail or flowers or cookies (legislators seem to attract a lot of free, fattening snacks).

The phone rings before you can read all your messages. It is a constituent anxious to blame you for something you really had little power to affect, usually something in the morning paper. This call is followed by an appreciative lobbyist who is anxious to thank you for something you also had nothing to do with. It's normal since political and legislative life seems always to be filled with undeserving praise and unfair criticism. Usually it all evens out, but along the way, it can lead to a kind of intellectual corruption. You might find yourself accepting the perception of the public as reality.

It's time for your committee hearing. You put on your jacket, straighten your tie, grab your official folder, and stride confidently out the door toward the conference room. The hallway may be filled with lobbyists, citizen testifiers, and your colleagues. Insider familiarity and banter are the currency of hallway transactions and status. Whispered conversations, last-minute "crucial" information, and suggested strategies among committee members are the substance. Always at Hawaii's Capitol building there are the crowd-watchers who hang over the railing and respond to the call when the committee chair finally shows up.

The House chamber

In 1985, a number of freshmen legislators agreed to write their thoughts at the beginning and end of their terms in office. Former Representative Wayne Metcalf chose Valentine's Day as his day-inthe-life contribution:

> At random, I have flipped through my desk calendar to Thursday, February 14, 1985, the 22nd legislative day. It is St. Valentine's Day. On the day in which sentiments of love and affection are exchanged, the State House will hear a measure calling for reinstating the death penalty in Hawaii.
>
> 8:30 a.m. – Two of the committees I serve on are conducting public hearings simultaneously. After hearing testimony relating to the discharge of mental health patients, I will

move on to matters involving hazardous wastes in the environment.

9:30a.m. – I leave the hazardous waste hearing to meet with a professor from the University of Hawaii at Hilo who wishes an evaluation of the legislative intern he has placed with my office. I meet with the professor and return to the hearing.

A legislator's view

10:00 a.m. – The Committee on Energy, Ecology, and Environmental Protection concludes its hearing on eight separate measures dealing with the hazardous-waste problem.

10:15 a.m. – I meet with a lobbyist representing optometrists who are interested in a measure p ending before the Committee on Commerce and Consumer Protection.

There is a culture of deference at a committee hearing. The members' nameplates, personalized folders, and supplies of pens and PostIts await their arrival at the committee staff table. These items are delivered to the representatives upon their selection of a seat, as if picking up their own folders were a demeaning task. The chair's seat and nameplate are pre-positioned wherever he or she likes them to be at the conference table.

Bang! The gavel goes down, and the public hearing begins with the calling of the first bill and those who wish to testify. A hearing usually lasts several hours, punctuated sometimes with testy and challenging questions from the members. The chair's jobs are several: to get through the agenda, to help the committee identify the options for each bill during decision making, and to ensure that all the really important information is flushed out in the course of the discussion. Additional tasks might include keeping rival members from shouting at each other and ensuring that some form of consensus does emerge.

The reality is that most members have far less time to devote to the subject matter than the chair, and they are happy to defer to the chair's recommendations on most bills. Genuine disputes might be aired before or after the hearing, away from public or media eyes and ears. This confidentiality is much appreciated by colleagues, and it may result in a more civil and cooperative attitude later in the session.

It is now after 11 a.m. and time for the daily session in the House chamber. The House chamber has a red rug, a golden chandelier (the sun), and a huge red and brown tapestry behind the speaker's dais. The Senate chamber has a blue theme with a white (the moon) chandelier. The individual desks and high-backed chairs are connected in seamless koa wood arcs. Each legislator's place is marked in front by a marble like nameplate. (When I started, my name was carved. These days, stick on letters are used.) Each desk has its own hand-held microphone, a drawer, and a tray for bills and other written announcements, such as the order of the day (the agenda, which may include each bill or resolution to be acted on during that session). At times, this tray may be filled with a full 18 inches of stacked printed bills and their attached committee reports. Legislators drift in to begin going through the bills. During the period in which bills are introduced, it is a great way to get a sense of just what each colleague is thinking, and how much actual work they did since the last session.

After the roll call and opening prayer – "prayer?" you ask? Yes, notwithstanding the ban on prayer in schools, legislative bodies have retained this tradition. It tends to remind members of the larger picture, at least when the chosen minister does not get carried away. Some prayers are short and ecumenical. Others are long-winded and sectarian. (Their authors may believe that this is their only chance to save the souls of these poor, misguided politicians!) At times, the sectarian nature of the prayers becomes an issue, offending members who may not share their particular devotion. The military ministers seem to understand this point best, for they are accustomed to leading diverse groups in prayer. For several years, I sat next to the late Emilio Alcon, who would always share his opinion as to whether or not the minister should be invited back. The criterion was simple: Keep it short and sweet, and it was thumbs up; appear long-winded, and it was thumbs down.

There are different kinds of legislative floor sessions, depending on the rhythms and deadlines of the four-month calendar. Usually the daily agendas are empty and routine. Often they create opportunities for congratulatory resolutions or introductions from the gallery. Over the years, the congratulatory resolutions were abused, with some representatives using them as a kind of campaign strategy, bringing every possible business or school or person with a nice lawn down to the floor of the House. Thanks to Representative Sam Lee, I'm sure I've met just about everybody who ever lived in Mililani, the district he represented.

11:10 a.m. – The session begins. 60 sixth graders from Waimalu Elementary School are introduced along with a House colleague's aunt and grandmother. The House will also welcome a delegation visiting the Capitol this day to lobby for tougher sex abuse laws. Representative Kihano reminds members that it is Valentine's Day. Representative Tajiri, Levin and I present the University of Hawaii at Hilo Volleyball coach, Sharon Peterson, with a certificate and lei honoring her for being named the Quarterback Club's sportsperson of the year. Seventy new legislative proposals receive their committee assignments. By the end of the session, only four will have passed into law. (Representative Wayne Metcalf)

In my last few years, the House wisely began to limit the floor presentations to those of statewide significance, and only two or three per member per year. Yet these PR events do have a legitimate function for they are one way to connect the Legislature with the community, to invite the nongovernmental sector to the Capitol, and to acknowledge the contributions of a wide range of people. Leis are always given, and the special Hawaiian spirit of aloha permeates the chamber.

Another theme emerges: the interplay between the technical business of the Legislature, which is to attend to statewide problems, and its cultural and philosophical role, which is to foster and preserve an environment in which a community relates to its government.

At the one extreme, floor presentations can be seen as a phony, cheap public relations device intended to endear the politician in the hearts of the honorees. At the other, they can be seen as one of the most civilized and inclusive mechanisms of government, reminding us that Hawaii is a unique place and that we are all on this grand journey together. The sweet aroma of flower leis (a part of political life in Hawaii) and the stale blast of hot air (a part of political life in general) are always present.

In my twelve years in the legislature, there are only a handful of floor presentations I can remember offering. My favorites always included the chance to introduce a delegation of Koreans from our sister state Cheju Island because it gave me the opportunity to speak on the floor in Korean. Another was the day I offered two environmental congratulatory resolutions, one for a new process of laying gravel to resist ground termites, and the other to encourage efforts to keep the brown tree snake out of Hawaii. For each I had a visual aid: a jar of termites, and a pickled brown tree snake. Colleagues said these were among the grossest days they remembered on the floor of the House.

It's time for lunch, generously provided by the Friends of the Library as a device to lure legislators and, while they eat, to brief them on the needs of our public libraries. A large, unused committee hearing room has been reserved for the buffet and briefing. These kinds of luncheons are common, especially at the beginning of the legislative session. They represent two continuing benefits of elected office: flower leis and free food.

> 'Tis an old maxim in the schools,
> That flattery's the food of fools;
> Yet now and then you men of wit
> Will condescend to take a bit.
> —Swift

At first, there is something really intoxicating about all this attention. I've seen young legislators become mesmerized by it. They have gone from complete unknowns to instant celebrities, showered with appreciation just because of their job. Some are convinced it is because they are born leaders of society and will soon be drafted to run for governor. Over time, however, you come to realize that appreciation and manipulation can be two sides of the same coin. At this point, it becomes an expression not of self-worth, but of power. Some may believe they deserve the lei and the food because of what they can do for, or to, someone. It takes a healthy sense of humility to recognize what is really going on.

My wife has numerous stories about how people treated me with great deference, but not knowing who she was, paid no attention to her or, occasionally, were rude. Usually I was too busy to notice, but she did, and frequently reminded me that my apparent popularity had nothing to do with my dynamic leadership. The hypocrisy of those wanting to flatter the powerful will always be part of public life.

> 12:00 noon – The Hawaii Visitors Bureau is having its semiannual membership luncheon. There is also a lunch honoring Coach Peterson. I will miss both this day to prepare for this afternoon's Judiciary Committee hearing. (Representative Wayne Metcalf)

Back to the office to check on the staff and proofread drafts of the committee reports reflecting our morning hearings. A short meeting with lobbyists anxious to tell you why that particular bill you introduced would not be such a great idea is followed by a strategy session with your Senate counterpart on how together you can successfully get it passed. Your administrative aid in charge of district affairs tells you why the City and County of Honolulu refuses to put a traffic light on that dangerous corner. You outline the main ideas for a letter to the mayor and request a meeting with a key City Council member. (Did we get that memo out asking that the Finance Committee hear our bills? Can Representative Thielen get some more Republican votes against that anti-environmental bill? Set up a meeting later in the day.) Your committee clerk brings you the bad news that the majority attorneys have a problem with the amendment you made to that other bill. You quickly sign a pile of thank-you letters to constituents who wrote about this or that issue. Make sure our meeting with the department deputy is confirmed for tomorrow morning. And so on.

> 1:30 p.m. - The Judiciary Committee convenes in the Capitol auditorium to hear a single bill, H.B. 411, Relating to Capital Crimes. The testimony received on capital punishment ranges from arguments involving morality and theology to its deterrence value and cost effectiveness or lack thereof. The testimony received is overwhelmingly against reinstating the death penalty. The introducer of the measure thanks the chairman for hearing the bill, and the committee recesses. Capital punishment will not pass during the 1985 legislative session. (Representative Wayne Metcalf)

A half-hour late, you shuffle into a hearing of the Education Committee, of which you are a member. The Friends of the Library lunch is just starting to draw all the blood out of your brain, so you struggle to look alert. Perhaps you ask a question or two, to demonstrate that you are paying attention. The Education Committee's work is extremely important, and large numbers of people, including administrators, students, and teachers, may well show up, believing that their input will improve education as we know it. Unfortunately, 90% of the real decisions made regarding education are budget recommendations, and the Finance Committee, regardless of what the Education Committee might recommend, jealously makes those decisions.

To acknowledge these realities does not negate the value of the hearing. This is an opportunity to have a good discussion about how the schools actually function, and perhaps to work together to seek practical solutions. Not everything a legislator does can be measured by bills introduced and passed, by laws reconsidered and changed.

Another contradiction of legislative life is that the public often measures one's value as a legislator in terms of the authorship of bills and laws. Election time is when the loyal opposition often points out that "Representative Shon did not introduce a single piece of legislation to fight crime, or to solve the insurance crisis! Even worse, Representative Shon introduced over sixty bills and only ten passed!"

Such criticism is sometimes valid. Usually, however, it is irrelevant. When twenty nearly identical bills have already been introduced, why add another? Because if you don't, your opponent may just slam you for it. Often my Republican challengers used this tactic. This is ironic since, as a minority in the Legislature, they are the least likely to accumulate a record of bills successfully passed. More on this later, but suffice it to say that a day in a legislator's life may well include some anxious thoughts about how their personal bills have fared and how the distorted picture of success and failure will play in the next election.

If the legislator is chair of one of the larger committees, or is Speaker, all this business of getting credit tends to evaporate. Public attention is rightly focused on the value of their input and decisions, not on who technically introduced a particular bill. But for the less powerful and prominent, or for those who tend to have tight races, this gamesmanship over superficial credit can force legislators into unseemly efforts to demonstrate their effectiveness in authoring legislation.

The legislative day may end with a fundraiser. Many object to the holding of political fundraisers during the four-month session, but I always viewed it as an opportunity to schmooze and talk story with the Capitol community, especially those lobbyists and community leaders you did not have time to meet with during the day. Sometimes extremely valuable information is exchanged over the stew and rice.

> 4:00 p.m. – I have a meeting with the dental profession's lobbyist. From considering issues of life or death, I have moved to gums and molars in the space of only a few minutes.
>
> Dinner this evening is courtesy of former mayor Eileen Anderson's campaign committee, which is hosting a fundraising event at Aloha Tower. After a quick dinner of noodles, chicken and meatballs, it is on to a 6:00 p.m. hearing on Ocean and Marine Resources, followed at 6:30 by the joint committees on Labor and Consumer Protection, which will wrestle with Workers' Compensation reform. (Representative Wayne Metcalf)

The best thing about fundraisers for elected officials is that we always got in free, and, true to form, are honored with a nice flower lei. It is a time to relax. On the other hand, the food often was all too familiar, and after twelve years, it was difficult to get excited about it.

Over the years, some of us tried to spice this up. Representative David Hagino was noted for his innovative and creative fundraisers, one of which was held in the old Hawaii Theater before it was renovated. (Some of us were mobilized to provide a celebrity talent show.) I held "A Night in Korea" and "A Night in 1889" (complete with an appearance by Father Damien and that revolutionary scoundrel Lorrin Thurston). In later years, it was the music, a string trio or a jazz quartet, that I hoped would provide a reason to come. The main purpose was to raise money, especially from lobbyists, and the rest was just stale gravy.

Some candidates have the community organization, the connections, and the charisma to draw decent crowds whenever they hold a fundraiser. Others must rely on the Capitol community to provide a good showing. This can lead to coercive relationships: Show up or take the consequences. Some legislators did approach it in that way, but most relied on their own integrity and attitude to set the tone, not the month in which the event was held. Another consideration is that contributions tend to trickle into a campaign all year. Thus, the showing of a good crowd is often quite independent of whether or not lobbyists feel they have been coerced into buying influence. Notwithstanding this weak attempt to justify midsession fundraisers, I have concluded that if a restoration of public confidence in the Legislature is to be achieved, it would be best to hold these events outside the scheduled session from January through April.

> 10:30 p.m. – The Workers' Compensation hearing recesses and I return to my office. It is at this time, and during earlier breaks between hearings and appointments, that mail is read, correspondence answered, staff work reviewed and assigned, and preparation for the next day's schedule takes place.
>
> Typically, it is around 8:00 a.m. when I arrive at the Capitol and 1:00 a.m. when I return home in the evening. Home for me during the session is fortunately only a few blocks away. Home for others working similar hours means the long drive to Waianae or Kaneohe. (Representative Wayne Metcalf)

You end some days by hanging up your suit coat and tie, riding that slow elevator back down to your own convenient parking stall, and contemplating those hard cafeteria benches that await you at the neighborhood board meeting later that evening. This may be a time to reflect on the day's issues, meetings, agenda items, and so on. Even if there is time, however, there may not be the energy. If you have a family, and especially if you have children, the session may be fraught with guilt over the neglect of personal obligations. There are also nights when your mind simply will not quit, replaying this or that conversation, reliving this or that slight or honor.

"A Bill for an Act"

LESSONS

1. Legislative events may be interpreted cynically or idealistically. Often both terms apply.
2. There is a plethora of trivial symbols and niceties that the community is willing to bestow on its democratically elected officials. The challenge is not to take this personally, even if you feel it has been earned.

3. Political life is filled with undeserving praise and unfair criticism.

4. Every legislative day is a series of complex and challenging encounters, the meaning of which may be hidden, especially to the outsider.

5. Physical and mental stamina are important attributes for legislative life.

6. The Capitol environment is often so different and so insulated from the outside world that legislators can sometimes forget how wide the gap in knowledge, perceptions, and attitudes can be. The political miscalculation by the Senate in rejecting the renomination of the popular Margery Bronster for attorney general a few years ago is just one example.

7. The public measures of legislative accomplishment may be misplaced, and can distort legislative behavior.

3 | A YEAR IN THE LIFE

It is wonderful how little mischief we can do with all our trouble.

— Mandell Creighton

One of the differences between a new legislator and a veteran is the degree to which one understands and uses the rhythms of legislative life. From the intoxication of the electoral victory to the mysterious world of an organizational struggle, from the hopeful beginnings of the session in January to the intensity of the final weeks in April, there are patterns. Understanding them can enhance your effectiveness in influencing the legislative process. This rule applies whether you are a private citizen, a community advocate, a professional lobbyist, or a seasoned lawmaker.

ORGANIZATIONAL STRUGGLES

Before the November election, most candidates already have been approached to ask for their support of a particular leader who seeks the office of Speaker of the House or President of the Senate. For brevity's sake, this section will use the organization of the state House of Representatives as its basis.

The first thing to know about organizational contests is that they determine the character, direction, and product of the next two years more than any other decisions at the Capitol. Ironically, it is one aspect of political life that both the media and the public generally ignore. When a dispute erupts over leadership, media coverage is so superficial as to make it impossible to understand what is really going on, other than another food fight by petty politicians.

It takes twenty-six votes in the House (a majority of the fifty-one members) to elect a speaker. In Hawaii, because the Democrats have overwhelming numbers, a good-faith attempt is always made to get those votes solely from the majority party. As a practical matter, those seeking this job always try for more than twenty-six commitments because they never know whose commitment is solid or who might bolt to the other side at the last minute.

Over the years, there have been proposals to elect a speaker openly through a more democratic process. Committee chairs would also be elected by secret ballot following remarks and questions from the members, without all the wheeling and dealing that currently prevails. Because so much is at stake, both for the community and for individual legislative careers, such meetings are never held until the votes for one side are secure. Typically, this is accomplished by a major candidate promising certain positions of power in exchange for votes. Usually there are subgroups of three or four or more members who stick together and who may be led by one individual chosen to negotiate for the group. His or her job is to ensure that members of that group receive the committee assignments or leadership positions they desire. These groups may be based on ethnicity (such as Filipino), or on ideology (such as pro-environmentalism or pro-business), or on geography (such as neighbor islanders, who have been the most cohesive and persistent organized force since statehood).

The neighbor island delegation, thirteen strong in the House, stuck together because its members feared that they would not get enough for their districts if they were divided and overwhelmed by representatives from Oahu. Neighbor island delegates were also more closely knit and thus more vulnerable to influences from a powerful member from the same island. The former Speaker, Joe Souki, is from Maui, and most of the other representatives from that island were reluctant to join a challenging group because they are aware of the power and influence a Speaker of the House could bring to bear against them.

Occasionally neighbor islanders do find themselves on opposite sides of an organizational struggle. This occurred in 1996, when most of the Big Island representatives and one new member from a Kauai district broke the solidarity of the neighbor island group. Such events are rare, and they take enormous amounts of energy and effort to maintain. Oahu allies must be in touch on a daily basis to ensure that their coalition has not been eroded.

Calvin Say was once the newcomer.
In 2001 he was Speaker of the House.

The day after the Hawaii primary election, which is in September, there is a victory breakfast for both parties. At the Democratic event, veterans from both sides of a leadership struggle will be assigned to schmooze with the newcomers. By this time, many of the neophytes have already been called with warm congratulations, both by the frontrunners and by the challengers for leadership positions. It is wonderful to be the focus of so much attention, but it is also a little frightening. The front-runner, who may be the current Speaker or some other veteran, such as the Finance chair, will approach the novice as a father or big brother: kindly, gently, full of advice and respect. "It is time to think about joining the team, and the sooner you join, the better assignments you may get in January. So you'd like to sit on the Finance Committee, huh? Oh, you want to be on Education? How about a real leadership role, say vice chair of Education?"

The wise newcomers nod respectfully and say they really have to concentrate on the general election – "let's talk later, okay?" They will be reminded that once the train leaves it may be hard to catch a ride.

Before the general election, both the front-runner for Speaker and the challenger (if there is one) will try to demonstrate their support with donations of food, sign waivers, and friendly lobbyists with checks. The idea is to generate a feeling of obligation and trust. At the same time, all kinds of people - friends, work connections, or even church members - will approach the newcomer attesting to what a wonderful guy the Speaker really is, or why it's time for a change. Stories of admiration and abuse of power abound. The challenger will be characterized as selfish, inexperienced, and connected to a special interest, someone who cannot be trusted. Both sides will characterize themselves as reformers of the system, and as advocates for the democratic process with respect for all members. To a certain extent, this scenario will be played out with veteran legislators as well.

What is really at stake for an elected official choosing sides? First and foremost is their reputation for being fair-minded, consistent, and trustworthy. When they make a commitment, can you count on it even in the face of enormous pressure? If an individual says he will join a group and then turns around and joins the opposition in exchange for a position of power, people will remember for a long time that he is for sale - not necessarily for material goods, but for political capital. Even those who succeed in buying the vote will always wonder if a better offer later will change that person's loyalty.

Freshman legislators have little to lose, although they often do not realize this. If they challenge the Speaker, this can be forgiven later as the impulses of youth or ignorance. Besides, any winner in such a contest will do his best to befriend the wounded losers and convert them to allies in the next fight. Freshman legislators who choose to support the established candidate will, at most, be given the committee assignments they desire (which they probably would get anyway) and the position of vice chair of a committee, which allows them the privilege of preparing the hearing folders and sitting at the side of the chair, even during conference committees at the end of the session. They may even be assigned to the great Finance Committee, usually an assemblage of very loyal veterans and very inexperienced freshmen, all programmed to defer to the chair and his or her staff, some of who are more influential than most elected members. The Finance Committee experience is overwhelming for new members, and they are often reluctant to demonstrate independence or openly challenge the chair. The chair is usually able to provide just enough legislative crumbs for members to take back to their districts. A very strong dependency relationship often develops as the simple neophyte sits at the feet of the wise chair, learning how to govern Hawaii Nei.

Experienced members have much more at stake. Their pride, their sense of accomplishment, and their relationships with other members are all on the line. They are in a position, solely due to longevity, to compete for real power in the form of committee chairmanships. They can rise to positions of great influence or descend into political Siberia. Back in their districts, they know it is no longer acceptable to be the young learner. Voters who "invested" in the newcomer will begin to expect solid accomplishments, prominence, influence, bills passed, and so on. Those in Siberia know that the next challenger will argue that the incumbent is ineffective.

Since the Democratic revolution of 1954, Republicans had been in such a minority that they were regarded by many as irrelevant to this struggle. Because they would not hold positions of power, their independence and willingness to criticize came with few consequences. In the case of a stalemate, however, an alliance with a solid Republican group could be an option, as had happened in the smaller, twenty-fivemember Senate. In 1996, the House Republicans could have thrown their weight on the side of the challengers, but they chose to remain neutral, thus ensuring that Joe Souki and his lineup would succeed. It is assumed that they voted to keep Souki because they felt he would present an easier target in the upcoming elections, and would push for programs they would relish bemoaning in public. After 1998, when nineteen Republicans took their seats in the House, the possibilities for bipartisan involvement in organizational politics were significant.

The selection of a Speaker can involve intense discussions as to who will head the Finance, Judiciary, and Consumer Protection Committees. Veterans who are not viable candidates for these positions understand that their success or failure as chair of a lesser committee might well depend upon their working relationship and the orientation of the more powerful chairs. Are they open? Can I influence them? Are they fair? Are they corrupt? Are they too close to this or that industry or interest group? Are they going to kill all my most important bills? Are they mere puppets of the speaker? Are they competent? Are they respectful of committee members? Are they stubborn? Are they accessible? These are fundamental issues in determining legislative success. The credibility of a candidate for speaker can rise or fall with the proposed lineup for these key committees.

While these negotiations proceed, the media usually become preoccupied with describing a superficial struggle for raw power. Since both sides claim to represent reform and change, they are regarded with equal disdain or credibility.

I remember one leadership struggle in which a group a feisty dissidents were pitted against a more conservative faction. Among the dissidents were people who had, over the years, frequently challenged the leadership and the establishment through their speeches and votes on the floor of the House. When this was pointed out to one reporter, he said he didn't want to take the time to look into the record, he'd rather just report what people said about each other. In this environment, the unscrupulous are practically invited to exaggerate the past, for no one will challenge his or her stories.

Thus, an inherent part of the organizational struggle is the gap between the real-world experience of the contest and the public's perception of it. This is frustrating and threatening. Savvy and insightful reporting could bridge the gap, but reporters are unwilling to offend the potential winners. Their bread and butter is also access to the powerful. It is a small-town environment. Sharp contrasts tend to be melted into undifferentiated globs, making it difficult to tell the good guys from the bad guys, depending on your point of view.

When the dust settles, most members are so exhausted by the psychological and political pressures that there is a genuine desire to get down to business. Once someone has secured the necessary twentysix votes, the next step is appointing the committee chairs, vice chairs, and members. Even the losers will have private meetings with the newly elected Speaker. His (or her) role is to manage, administer, and govern the House, as well as exercise power. Healing is an important part of this process.

For the members, uncertainty over myriad details can now be cleared up. These include assigning offices and parking stalls, hiring staff, securing office furniture and computers, and beginning to think and act like a lawmaker. Presession hearings begin for key committees, or for those whose chairs have not changed. The people's business begins to descend upon the Capitol. There is much to learn, and there is much to do. There are so many people to meet for the first time, or for the nth time. Lobbyists and advocates begin to call for appointments. State departments that depend upon key chairs for support will invite members to tour this or that facility.

This is not to say there are no wounds, but that a great political burden has been lifted. Most members hope and pray their differences and unpleasant words can be forgotten, and new alliances formed. The Christmas and New Year holidays arrive, new staff appears, and a truce is declared.

Opening day

OPENING DAY

Many states celebrate the opening of their legislative sessions, but few turn the event into a public extravaganza of food, music, and flowers like Hawaii does. Families and friends gather amid desks covered in flowers, and the Islands' best entertainers regale all with song and dance. In past years, this was a genuine community celebration. Ever since the Gulf War, however, a subdued atmosphere has descended on the Capitol.

The Capitol on opening day used to become an agitated ant hill with lobbyists, friends, family members, staff, bureaucrats, and tourists forming an undifferentiated colorful stream up and down the stairs, jammed into the elevators, milling through the open halls, office to office, plate lunch to plate lunch.

The best-connected legislators always had a jovial Hawaiian combo with their ukuleles, guitars, bass, and lilting falsetto singers egging on one of the secretaries in a risqué hula. Thousands of invitations had been sent to loyal supporters and anyone who might be of use in the future to ensure that every possible member of the political community in Hawaii felt personally welcome. Those modestly active in community affairs would receive a dozen or more combination Christmas/ New Year/Opening Day invitation greeting cards or letters each year. These were obviously form letters sent out by staff and campaign workers; everyone knew this, but most felt good about getting them anyway.

It was a day for voters to have their pictures taken with an unrecognizable legislator piled so high with flower leis that only the nose and eyes would peek out above the crown of honor and admiration. The smell of plumeria flowers, the taste of Japanese hot mustard and raw fish, the texture of macaroni salad, and the sound of pop-top beer and soda cans made it difficult to believe that somehow this circus was a prelude to serious business.

It was, and still is, in its more subdued form, a very democratic and collegial day. Department heads smile to the department secretaries they never acknowledge on the job. Lobbyists for condominium developments joke with their environmentalist opponents. Advocates of every stripe corner weary senators and representatives whose only response might be, "call me during the week."

Everywhere are the young veterans, the experienced staff members, perhaps in their third or fourth or fifth session, hanging over the railings, watching, evaluating. On opening day, these treasured and trusted workers survey the new freshmen legislators as a drill sergeant appraises the new recruits. They seek inconspicuous corners and conduct muted discussions of what to expect in the weeks ahead, and who might emerge as candidates for leadership in the future. They have a lot to do with what actually gets done in this building, but very few ever achieve a position of recognized power. They live through their bosses, although the bosses change. They write the bills, fashion the language of committee reports, do the research, and try to push their elected mentors along the path of their hidden agendas. Late that night, after the large numbers of garbage bags have been bundled and placed outside legislative office doors, they will be busy at the computers, preparing for the next day's onslaught of paperwork.

The exuberant new freshmen have finally arrived on opening day. They are sworn in by the chief justice and have a first sample of sitting in their new desks surrounded by family and entertained by the best performers the Islands have to offer. Lofty speeches and myriad promises flow from the newly selected Speaker, his majority leader, and the loyal opposition. This is the only day the media will provide gavel-to-gavel coverage of their "business."

They are struck by the way their world has changed. Their job is not to sell themselves; their job, for the next four months, is to serve. It is a completely different psychological feeling from that of the campaign, and some never succeed in making the transition. They never stop campaigning. They can't just flip-flop like it meant nothing. Pride grows. They now belong to an exclusive club, a family. They are part of something bigger, an accepted member, one of the chosen elite. They have their own office and their own stationery. People who are twice their age and have twice their income are forced to defer. They will be treated with respect because of real or imagined power. Opening day evokes all these emotions and thoughts in the newly elected.

THE EARLY SESSION'S SPIRIT OF HOPE

From the opening day ceremonies in January through the first six weeks of the annual legislative session, there is a spirit that infects all who are part of the Capitol community. It is one of hopeful accomplishment. A constant stream of ideas flows to the majority or minority research offices for translation into bills. The Legislative Reference Bureau is abuzz with professional research and bill drafting as well. Departments and their planners are busy refining their proposals, which actually have been submitted up the chain of command months earlier, as has the budget.

There are some veterans who feel it is wisest to disguise their true agendas so as not to attract the attention of their enemies too early. Others lay out their priorities early for all to see. I was always among the latter, even though I realized that older political disputes with senate counterparts could came back to haunt my pet projects later in the session. The following is a memo I sent to colleagues when I was chair of the Committee on Energy and Environmental Protection. It was an early attempt to solicit feedback and proposals. It is illustrative of the ambitious nature of the early session environment:

January 4, 1996
MEMO
TO: House Colleagues
RE: Thoughts on the Upcoming Session

The following are a few preliminary thoughts on priorities for 1996. Please review, comment, add, and delete...

1. Energy

   a. Preserve the Solar Energy Tax Credit
   b. Encourage the Senate to pass our Energy Performance Contracting Bill.
   c. Tie DOE additional electricity funds to performance contracts.
   d. Enact a General Policy to phase-out all fossil fuels
   e. Require X% of All state vehicles to use alternative fuels.
   f. Try to prevent the High-Tech Development Corporation from nit-picking the Suntera Company out of the State.
   g. Allow other importers of oil to use Honolulu Harbor.

2. Environmental Protection

   a. Enact "Environmental Contract" legislation (includes DLNR "incidental taking" proposed amendment to Hawaii Endangered Species Law).

b. Encourage Senate to pass 1995 EPA creation bill, now in Ways & Means Committee.

c. Enact policy to promote conversion of ranch land to reforestation and habitat creation.

d. Enable DLNR to keep new innovative revenue sources.

e. Promote Aloha Aina Extension Service, Youth Corps, and Chapter 90 Volunteer efforts to accomplish DLNR mission.

f. Create a vigorous interagency Environmental Epidemiology Effort.

g. Revisit Island Carrying-Capacity Standards.

h. Require emergency Response Plans for all DOH regulated industries.

i. Adopt a contingency plan on the environmental future of the Ewa plain, with emphasis on soil conservation.

j. Require the establishment of an Environmental Special Design District for the Campbell Park/ Kapolei air district to ensure health and safety.

k. Review maximum environmental fines to determine deterrent value.

l. Require unannounced Hazardous Release Emergency Drills.

m. Ensure a mature Non-Point Source Pollution Program.

n. Pass Bill Dougherty's water quality monitoring bill...

If you think this agenda was ambitious, consider that it was offered in the context of an ongoing four-year dispute with Speaker Souki and many of his most powerful allies in the House. I was allowed to be chair, but most of our bills died soon after they arrived in the Judiciary or Finance Committees. If any did make it to the Senate, the powerful Ways and Means Committee chair, who had refused even to speak to me for eight years.

It is hard to describe the mad rush to introduce legislation in the first weeks of the session. It is complicated by the fact that even the most experienced lobbyists tend to wait until the last minute to walk through the doorway with their pet proposals. Reformers often insist on the wisdom of limiting the number of bills introduced. I, for one, always opposed this idea because it would mean cutting off access to the legislative process.

As chair of a major committee (Health, from 1987 to 1992), I was besieged by requests for bill introduction. Because the laws affect everyone in the state of Hawaii, proposals may originate from any island, organization, or individual. Virtually every citizen has a chance to have his or her own idea translated into a bill. In addition to being the channel for a subject matter committee, such as Health, there is an obligation to introduce legislation related to one's district, such as capital improvements for neighborhood schools or anti-crime bills that demonstrate one's concern for personal safety. I would commonly introduce from sixty to eighty bills each session. I would hate to have to tell someone with a great idea that his or her bill could not be introduced because a particular quota had been exceeded. These days limits on the number of bills that any legislator can introduce do limit access, in my opinion.

Contrary to public belief, it is not the large number of bills introduced that makes the legislative process hard to follow, since most are held at the first deadline and experience no further movement. What makes it hard is the large number of bills that do receive a public hearing. As a result, the first part of the legislative session is a mad scramble just to keep up with the hearing notices.

Every bill is sent to at least one committee, and often to two or three. This is called a referral. At the beginning of a legislative session, there is a deadline for the introduction of bills, usually a week or two into the sixty working-day calendar that makes up each fourmonth session. There is also a deadline for moving bills out of the first committee and on to the second or third. This is called the first lateral. The first referrals of a bill go to what is commonly called the subject matter committee, such as Health or Education. After the first lateral, they go on to Judiciary or Finance. The subject matter committees have about eight or nine scheduled hearings to deal with hundreds of proposals. Some of these are complex and deserve a lengthy period of testimony and discussion.

As a committee chair, I can remember sitting in my office surrounded by piles of bills, which I sorted according to general subject matter for thematic hearings. This was important as a courtesy for testifiers as well as coherence in making policy. The problem was that it took several days between the introduction of a bill and its referral. Therefore, I would never know just how many bills I would have in the committee until I had already allocated time slots in six or seven hearing days. Last minute bills, often of great merit, might well squeeze out others of less weight or importance.

One of the most significant bills written at the last minute was a measure to grant prescriptive privileges (the authority to write a prescription for a patient) to advance-practice nurses. The head of the local nurses' union and several lobbyists felt it was time for Hawaii to become the forty-seventh state to enter the twentieth century. It was near midnight, but the bill was prepared in time for introduction. As it turned out, it was the beginning of a multi-year, brutal legislative battle. At least three of my reelection campaigns were close calls due to doctors walking door to door in my district telling voters how I was threatening their health care (not to mention a few doctor's pocketbooks!). Nearly every legislative session, I could point to one or two such bills that trickled in at the eleventh hour. The local Island practice of being fashionably late is translated into deadline brinkmanship every February at the Capitol.

How does the timing of deadlines affect the public? If a committee chair had all the bills early in the session, he or she could make a master list of scheduled hearings to let everyone know what bills would be coming up and which ones would probably die for lack of time or support. This would also give colleagues time to lobby the chair to get their bills heard. Instead, as the first lateral deadline approaches, it is almost impossible to give adequate notice for upcoming hearings. The rule says 48 hours, but the actual notice might not arrive in the mail until after the hearing has occurred. The only real solution is to have a complete recess after bill introduction and before most of the hearings. But this would lengthen the session, and conservatives would complain of the additional cost.

One reason this does not change is the relatively small number of legislators who preside over an intense subject matter committee.

Members may have little insight into the frenzy of paper shuffling in some committees during February. The respective chairs of the Judiciary, Consumer Protection, and Finance Committees appreciate the way in which time filters out large numbers of bills.

By the second or third week of the session, the Legislature settles into an optimistic routine. Many bills are still alive, and every representative still hopes that this or that proposal will get a hearing. Memos flutter from office to office asking that the following bills be scheduled. Intense meetings occur to convince the chairs that not only should they hear the bills, they should accept this or that amendment.

THE PUBLIC HEARING

There is probably no democratic event more pervasive and indispensable than the public hearing. It is where most of the electorate has the opportunity to interact with their public servants. The public hearing is more than the exchange of views or testimony. It is a time when ordinary citizens can see firsthand the demeanor, behavior, and attitudes of a legislator. It can be a chance for a politician to get on TV or be quoted in the local newspaper. It is a cultural event. It is also one of the most misunderstood forms of democratic participation.

The first thing I learned to appreciate is that there is no one single kind of public hearing, but rather a plethora of related but distinct species. When you attend one, which kind you are actually attending may be determined by the type of proposal under discussion, the timing of the hearing, the location, the attendance by members, and the style of the committee chair, among other factors.

There is, for example, the genuine, problem-solving public hearing, which may involve one bill of modest importance and represents just one attempt to solve a particular problem. It may be authored by a representative or senator who does not need its passage for either electoral or personal status. This bill calls for no appropriation of funds, and it does not imply criticism of any particular department or program. If any of these criteria do not apply, the purpose and process change completely.

Modest proposals in the genuine problem-solving public hearing category might include:

1. Redrafting language that was too ambiguous or that created unforeseen problems encountered by an agency in its attempt to implement a previously enacted law.
2. Creation of a coordinating committee that all participants support, but which the enabling language has yet to be agreed on.
3. Giving more flexibility to the Department of Land and Natural Resources in its rulemaking for minimum net sizes regulating fishing.
4. Adding additional missions to an existing program that found itself acting beyond its technically granted authority.
5. Enacting a consumer protection law that acknowledges the economic activity of legitimate businesses but prohibits the activity of fly-by-night, shady, rip-off artists selling the same kind of service or product.

The genuine problem-solving public hearing will attract a small number of interested or knowledgeable individuals, often from public agencies, who offer their sincere analysis of a bill's strengths or weaknesses. Perhaps one or two citizens who can attest to the circumstances that gave birth to the proposal will present their case and offer generally positive opinions as to why the bill would help. Next, two or three departmental people may come forward who are intrigued by the concept but feel that the bill could be more effective if it were rewritten. Most of the key committee members are present, and there is healthy bipartisan questioning of the testifiers. The hearing is followed by a civil, nonideological discussion of how to make the bill work. The chair proposes a simple amendment that all can understand and gives the testifiers an opportunity to participate informally in the decision-making process.

The Public Hearing

All in all, it is a model of reason, problem-solving, and deliberative legislative action. All participants seem to feel they have made progress and created an improved proposal that will solve some genuine, but not earth-shattering, problem. Such hearings are boring for the casual observer who does not have the testimony before him, and the media never covers them. As a result, the public seldom learns about routine problems that the Legislature actually solves.

At the other extreme is what I would like to call the grand opera hearing. In 1987, just after I became chair of the Health Committee, my first meeting with Senator Bert Kobayashi, the Senate Health chair, was on the steps of the Capitol, right in front of the Queen Liliuokalani statue. We talked about agendas, and I said, "Hey, let's do fluoridation of drinking water this year!" Bert looked at me as if to say, "Are you nuts? Don't you know what a can of worms you are opening up? "To his credit, and in spite of his firm anchor in reality, he agreed it was worth a try.

Fluoridation became an issue that generated hundreds of passionate phone calls, a constant stream of lobbyists, and an incredible amount of community interest. It pitted the most recent scientific knowledge on the positive effects of prevention of dental disease, which was overwhelmingly in favor of it, against traditional

79

cultural sensibilities over water, fears of toxic reactions, distrust of the experts, and wild charges of conspiracies. I was forced to station my staff scientist, Dr. Steve Montgomery, right by the door to collect fluoridation testimony and intercept the passionate advocates before they entered the main part of the office and disrupted everyone's work.

The public hearing, held at the Capitol auditorium, was an amazing democratic event. Hundreds submitted testimony for and against. The auditorium naturally divided itself with supporters of fluoridation on one side and opponents on the other. Hour after hour of mostly redundant and predictable testimony was heard. It was indeed more of a democratic ritual, a form of drama, than a true public hearing. Questions by members were discouraged in order to afford all those who came to testify a chance to address the committee.

What we had created was an opportunity for each side to flex its mobilization muscles, to remind elected officials that their votes would be remembered, and to present some really interesting scientific and rhetorical arguments. At times, the grand opera type of hearing can generate information that might change a mind or two. Political pressure builds on the swing votes if it is close. The chair has to have a grip on where this whole thing is going, and whether or not the committee can reach a consensus around his or her approach.

At a standing-room-only auditorium hearing on gambling, Judiciary chair Terry Tom wanted to pass out a pro-gaming bill. He was one vote short. Pressure was applied to Representative Mike White, who was from Maui. Mike was hauled out time and time again during the lengthy hearing to have his arms twisted by majority leader Tom Okamura, Speaker Souki, and others. As a neighbor islander from the same island as the speaker, a loyal vice chair of Judiciary, and usually a solid vote with the leadership team, Representative White was under enormous pressure. He decided to stick to his conscience, which told him gambling would be a disaster for Hawaii.

Grand opera hearings are usually associated with issues for which positions are taken and solidified well before the event. These might include gun control, capital punishment, legalized gambling, same-sex marriage, no-fault auto insurance, and so on. The grand opera hearing is one that all the players feel they must attend and that the media is highly likely to cover.

In between the genuine problem solving and grand opera extremes, there are many variations. A hearing is supposed to gather input from open-minded citizen representatives, and often does. But personal agendas, ambitions, grandstanding, ideology, and partisan bickering can turn any hearing into a different cultural event. Misinterpretations of which kind one is observing can lead to disillusionment and frustration.

In mid-February, the first lateral sounds the temporary death knell of approximately 40% of the bills introduced. In1mediately, conscientious officials congratulate themselves if they had the foresight to also introduce the same bill in the Senate, or kick themselves if they failed to do so. In the latter case, there is always the possibility of reviving the content as an amendment to another bill with a broad enough title – a common occurrence.

One of the most challenging aspects of following the session is the number of bills with general titles: "Relating to Health," "Relating to Finance," "Relating to Education." You can amend a bill's content, but you can't amend its title. So it is wise to have on hand plenty of broad-titled bills just in case you need a vehicle to stuff your content into. (In 1996, Senator Milton Holt tried to outwit his colleagues by amending a bill titled "Relating to Licensing" to include his language banning same-sex marriage.)

Just keeping track of myriad topics is a daunting task for any legislative staff. The only way to do it is to track the committee referrals and make friends with those committee clerks who schedule hearings. Legislators find themselves shuttling from one committee hearing to another, feeling like ping-pong balls. (In 1985, I sat on six committees; four met in the morning and two in the afternoon. In later years, the number was reduced to four.) Fresl1men and others who are not chairs have a more difficult time because they really have no excuse to concentrate on just one area. The entire universe is their conceptual responsibility

The chairs, however, have a legitimate reason to focus on their subject areas, and only occasionally pay attention to their other committee assignments. They arrive at hearings late and they leave them early because they have crucial meetings in their own offices on esoteric subjects, such as the design of prescription drug labels for epilepsy pharmaceuticals, or the funding to recommend for this or that nonprofit service group.

The focus of the session narrows appreciably after the first lateral. The entire Capitol world awaits the endless Finance or Judiciary hearing notices, sometimes posted by the hour, with literally hundreds of bills on the agendas.

THE FIRST DEBATES

Though we cannot out-vote them, we will out-argue them.

– Samuel Johnson

Crossover refers to the time during which each house debates and votes to send its proposals to the other chamber. This is another puzzling exercise because many bills are written not for final passage into law, but as bargaining chips positioned for the conference committees at the end of the session. There are some legislators whose every word or action is merely a prelude to this climactic meeting of the House and Senate. With so much bargaining and posturing taking place, the debate at the first crossover sometimes may have a surreal feel to it. Many a speech articulates grave concerns, with the hope that this or that point can be improved when and if the bill goes to conference. The first debates are also the first opportunity for keen observers to discover whether there is a significant block of dissidents waiting to challenge or embarrass the majority faction.

Nearly every session in the 1990s featured a bill pushed by Speaker Joe Souki to legalize gambling in one form or another. A fairly progressive group of Democrats usually joined with fairly conservative Republicans to give these bills a run for their money. During four out of the last five years of my legislative life, one form of gambling was stopped by one or two votes at the first crossover. The debate was heated, and loyalties and friendships were tested severely.

It is at this time that legislative behavior is so often misinterpreted. When these bills come before the House, they must first pass second reading, and then third reading. Some legislators will support a bill on second reading, indicating their reservations. If the objectionable language persists, they may indeed vote "no," or threaten to vote "no," if the bill survives the Senate and comes back for a final vote at the end of the session.

The subtlety of this may be lost on the public, but it is the bread and butter of legislative life. No one wants to be the odd one out. It would be foolish to anger the powerful unnecessarily. If sincere concerns can be expressed without actually voting "no," this is seen as a legitimate way to follow one's conscience while remaining part of the team. Remember, it takes twenty-six votes to pass every bill, and every bill must be approved by every committee chair to whom it is referred.

The debate at the first crossover may well be the moment when simmering resentments, some left over from the presession organizational fight, spill over into an open rebellion on one bill. The trigger may be a trivial measure or a major policy issue. It is one time in the session when the legislative body, almost organically sensing a need to relieve internal pressure, allows itself the luxury of a rebellious prank. Two or three bills may attract as many as nineteen or twenty "no" votes. That is significant in terms of organizational positioning. Seldom does the media indicate that it has any idea of what has happened.

In 1985, when I was a freshman legislator spending much of my time on environmental protection, a bill arrived at first crossover which, in my opinion, deserved to die on the floor. With conservative fundamentalist religious fervor at its height, a neighbor islander sought to exempt a church located in a conservation zone from the permit requirements needed to put in a large parking lot. Because this was an area designated for special protections against development, I felt it was inappropriate to grant the project legislative exemption. And given our constitutional separation of church and state, the fact that a church was involved should have been irrelevant.

Pushing for the bill were several Republican legislators, including Hal Jones and Cam Cavasso, both strong proponents of legislating their own brand of Christianity into law. (Gallery observers could always tell when Cam was cranking himself up for a sermon. He would begin to rock back and forth, pressing his hands on the top of the desk. When he could not hold his moral indignation inside any longer, he would leap to his feet, and if recognized, bear witness to his faith in a sermon-like delivery. Once he even burst into song, chanting something about being morally wrong.) This was at the height of the national Pat Robertson for president movement when the Christian Right pretty much took over Hawaii's Republican Party.

The chair of the Committee on Water, Land Use, Development, and Hawaiian Homes was Representative Calvin Say, who cared little for the bill, but reported it out for a floor vote anyway. A concerted effort was made in our Democratic caucus meeting to get Calvin to withdraw it before the floor vote took place, technically recommitting it to committee. He pondered this move, but in the end decided to risk an open vote.

Those of us who opposed the bill had spent the better part of a day rounding up "no" votes, and we knew we were close. What we really needed was for a few of the eleven Republicans to come our way. I was the main vote counter, responsible for leading the debate on the floor. It was clear that Cam and Hal felt that this was a matter of moral principle, and that anyone who disagreed was behaving in a godless, heathen way. Fortunately, they did not represent the entire Republican caucus, which included, among others, Whitney Anderson, whose district also was home to some unpopular Hare Krishnas.

The debate dragged on and on, with neither side relenting. Finally, something I said must have evoked thoughts of strange and unwelcome religious sects imposing their will on Whitney's district, for he asked the Speaker for a short recess, and the Republicans went single file into their own caucus room. A half-hour later they emerged, and by that time Cavasso and Jones could count on the support of just one other Republican. The bill lost by one vote. It was one of the few times a bill was actually defeated on a floor vote - at the instigation of a freshman legislator, no less.

I was blamed, of course. That year, working in Hal Jones's office was a young and fervent staffer named Mark Au. The next three elections Mark came closer and closer to beating me. To this day,

I can trace much of my electoral grief to that one debate and that single vote on first crossover.

The first crossover in 1985 was part of the aftermath of the refusal of twelve Democrats to support Henry Peters as speaker. It was also the beginning of a growing effort that helped Richard Kawakami to unseat Peters after the next election.

THE AGE OF RESOLUTIONS

When the successful bills have passed to the Senate and vice versa, there is little to do but translate the rest into official resolutions. Those good thoughts that did not make it may be reincarnated as requests that this or that agency conduct a study of the problem. Resolutions are interesting because, in the absence of substantive legislation, the participants in the public hearings and the debate suddenly seize upon each and every phrase as if it was of enormous importance. Sometimes hearings on resolutions, which are mostly unbinding collective opinions, are the most rewarding in-depth discussions of the session. It is too bad we don't hear the resolutions first and then draft the bills. Those legislators who realize they will have little to show for their four months of hard work are suddenly passionately pushing meaningless resolutions that they hope their constituents will applaud.

The time of resolutions is a sort of session doldrums. It is also a crucial breathing space when serious work is done behind the scenes on the budget and larger bills, when posturing for the all-important conference committees occurs, and when a small group of conferees is appointed by each house leader to negotiate on behalf of their respective bodies.

THE FINAL CROSSOVER

Notwithstanding the empty promises made along the way, the second crossover, when amended Senate bills are voted up or down, tells a lot about individual and collective priorities. The session will soon reach its crescendo with the conference committees. Debate is lively and often laced with objections to violations of the spirit of consultation embedded in the rules. It is the time when last-ditch efforts of determined committee chairs to get their way materialize as objectionable last-minute amendments. Bills thought to have been dead for months somehow are revived with little discussion. Promises to deal with earlier objections somehow are forgotten. It's the time either to swallow hard and hope for the best or to stand up and be counted, with implications for future elections and organizational struggles.

The second crossover can sometimes be just as exciting as the first, but there is a fatigue in the air, and a sense that perhaps energy needs to be saved for the final struggles at the very end of the session.

CONFERENCE COMMITTEE AND LOYALTY

You can always tell which Representatives have made it their business to be ever loyal and quiet in the shadow of their mentors: They will be appointed to dozens and dozens of conference committees. Every chair who is responsible for representing the House's position on a bill in conference will suggest to the speaker the names of committee members who ought to serve on the five- or seven-member conference committee for a particular bill. Those who can be counted on to keep their mouths shut are often chosen. Those of an independent nature are left twiddling their thumbs.

Democracy aside, it is the committee chairs who wield the most power. Anyone willing to completely walk away from a bill and let it die is in the catbird seat. If you want a bill, you must get everyone to agree. If you don't want it, you need only get one chair to oppose it. The art is in not letting anyone know what you really want.

It is during this time that most legislators pretend to be important, though they are only spectators to a clash of titans. The system is inherently conservative in that many obstacles must be overcome before a bill is signed into law. I would introduce about sixty bills when I was chair, and pass over to the Senate perhaps twenty that I had authored. By conference time, I'd be lucky if fifteen survived. In the end, if a dozen of my personal bills became law, I considered it a good year. Legislators who were not chairs would be happy with two or three.

The Reverend Frank Chong, who presides over the Waikiki Health Center, has a keen eye and has for years maintained a "Yellow Pages" on the personalities and processes of the Legislature. He describes the environment during crunch time: "This is the time when tempers get short, memory fails, and people lose sleep. 'Disk Full; ' 'Not Enough Memory;' 'Your Program Has Just Performed an Illegal Act;' 'End Task Immediately;' and similar phrases will be heard quite often in the next three weeks."

In 1998, the biggest item on the legislative agenda was the Economic Revitalization Task Force's recommendations to revitalize the Hawaiian economy. These proposals appeared to hit the poor the hardest, and they stimulated a vigorous effort on the part of social service agencies. Frank Chong carried a stuffed bear named Bud to remind legislators to preserve the safety net. He also published a running commentary and report on the session, called Bud's Newsletter.

His detailed description of the conference committee between House Finance and Senate Ways and Means is as follows:

> When there is a disagreement, the Legislature has figured out a humane way of working out its differences. Each chamber chooses members from its ranks to form a team to go into battle. It is like an old-fashioned dueling contest, only rather than swords and pistols, it is with calculators and abacuses. There is a lot of formality and ritual.
>
> The staff is absolutely essential to the process. They remind the participants about rites and ritual, calendars and timing. They are also the ones who crank out the numbers.
>
> Imagine that you are present when Leonardo da Vinci begins to sketch his famous "Last Supper." Suddenly Salvador Dali takes over, and everything is rearranged, and different colors are added to the tableau. You now have an inkling of what the opening of the Senate Ways and Means (WAM) and the House Finance (FIN) Conference Committee is like.

The State Capitol has somewhat of an eerie feeling at night. As one drives down into the bowels of the State Capitol Building, it begins to get darker and darker as you enter the driveway. Suddenly the bright fluorescent lights blind your eyes. Except that the brightness is uneven since half of the bulbs are out in the turnabout, The parking lot is half full, and you park at the far end of the metered area.

You get into the elevator. Somehow at night it feels like one is in a virtual-reality video game like Myst, and the slowest elevator in Hawaii creaks and groans as it creeps its way to the third floor.

As you leave the elevator, you see groups of people leaning on the railing and lounging on benches. Familiar faces smile at you, and friends come up to hear the latest gossip. Bud is under your arm, and you explain to the uninitiated that Bud, the Budget Bear, is a symbol of how beaten up we have gotten. He has bandages all over. There is an uncontrollable response by most people to rub his head and to read his signs: "I can't take any more cuts; I've been beaten up enough;" and "Some cuts don't heal."

The door to the conference room opens, and everyone rushes in. There is a long table with chairs on both sides. It is as though a large dinner is being prepared, only in place of the usual candelabra, there are a varied assortment of microphones, and in the place of dinner plates, there are name cards and folders correctly placed ... for the various dignitaries. Protocol is important. The pecking order was established early in the session.

Finally, everyone begins to take their place. There is a subdued air of anticipation. One expects a Fellini-type surrealism to engulf the scene; instead, it begins to blend into a sort of black and white montage of mumble jumbo that is all in code.

Polite chit-chat pervades the room, and both of the families introduce each and every member of their clan, including the ones that are on the outer edges of reality.

The two heads arrive, and it is like a large state dinner where the host tells everyone why everyone has been invited.

Important assumptions are stated. The House will probably talk about the importance of an increase in the GET (general excise tax) in order to off-set the cut in income taxes needed to stimulate the economy. The Senate will say just about the opposite. They will say "no" to an increase in the GET and create more jobs to stimulate the economy. Their solution to balancing the Budget is to cut government jobs. They have targeted DOE administrators. Long-time Capitol watchers will tell you that this is about as bizarre as you can imagine since only half of the Senate is up for re-election. If this were a normal year it would be the Senate pushing for a tax increase and the House resisting since all of its members are up for re-election.

When they finally get down to work, they start at the beginning of the book of budget worksheets, organized by program area, and work their way to the end ....

AGR 101 ... AGREE ... DISAGREE ... UMBO ... and on and on and on. They will go through each item page-bypage and line-by-line. In the old days, it took almost thirteen volumes of paper. Today, it is much more condensed. In the future, it will all be on laptop computers. So while the exterior may have changed, the process is still the same. ...

When the Conference Committee works on the Budget, we want to have members of the Alliance, Community Revitalization Coalition, and Welfare Employment Rights Coalition (WERC) present to observe the deliberation. It is very important that we have representatives there to "witness" what is going on and to be available as resources.

Prior to the passage of the "sunshine laws" in the late 70's early 80's, conference committee meetings were closed, and not only was the public not allowed to testify, we were not even allowed in the room. When you think of back-room politics and cigars, it was true. Things did take place behind closed doors and away from public scrutiny.

During Conference Bud will be there, and we want to have a cadre of people wearing CRC (Community Revitalization Coalition) buttons so that the legislature is aware that we are there.

To be sure, there will be a lot of others watching to see what will happen to the budget. You will see many familiar faces, and now you will be able to match them with organizations and issues. Most prominent will be representatives from organized labor, especially from HGEA [Hawaii Government Employees Association] and UPW [United Public Workers]. Any attempt to cut government jobs will affect their membership. The visitor industry will be present since some of the ERTF proposals talk about an increase in the Transient Accommodation Tax (TAT or hotel room tax). The teacher's union (HSTA) and the University professors (UHPA) will also be there. If you go down one floor to the Senate Judiciary hearing room where the Judiciary Conference Committee will be holding its meeting, you will run into trial lawyers, insurance advocates, and perhaps some health and human services types watching for bills that affect their clientele.

Conference Committee is a virtual "who's who" of the political process. So keep an eye not only on content but also on process and people.

There is a conference committee for every bill that has not been agreed to by both chambers. Conference committees can meet any time. Most of them will not meet until April 17th (fairly late in the session).

We have found that once they start to meet, they go in spurts. Sometimes they meet for long hours, and sometimes they meet for a few minutes and then disappear. Sometimes they disappear to work out compromises, give staff a chance to run some numbers, get something to eat, or go home to sleep. Since none of this is on a schedule and since there is no 48-hour rule (for hearing or meeting notices) we have found it helpful to have a point person and a group of folks to be around ...

Bud will be the constant reminder to make sure that "this budget is for us." The official word is that they will not go past midnight, nor will they start before 8:30AM, but there are always exceptions. Rarely do they start early, but they often run late ...

Somewhere in the wee hours of the morning, staff members from two committees work out the details. A huge budget document is proofread and printed. Dozens and dozens of other bills, each with its own meaning, history, and scars, limp toward the finishing line. Compromise after compromise has drained a good part of the childlike optimism that characterized the early weeks of the session. When it is over, especially if you've been a chair, you do feel like a veteran. You're a little tougher, hopefully wiser, and probably disappointed in colleagues for whom you once had higher hopes.

Freshman Representative Wayne Metcalf reflected on the end of his first legislative session:

During the closing days of the legislature, action shifts from the committee hearing rooms to the legislative chambers. It is in those cavernous halls that the final drama of the legislative process is played out. Much of what takes place on the floor of the chambers during the first 50 days or so is of a procedural character, with little in the way of debate. All that changes during the last days as weary legislators gird themselves for the final battles. It is a time when the hours run long and the tempers run short.

The legislative chambers are conical in shape and are meant to represent the volcanic origins of the Hawaiian Islands. I rather suspect that the Capitol architect knew a good deal about human nature and the legislative process and something also about the geologic cycle of Hawaiian volcanoes when he chose the legislative chambers for his volcanic depiction.

To the casual observer of the legislative process, the floor action seems often to be one long series of delays as recess after recess is called. People in the gallery wait eagerly for debate to begin. Lobbyists and legislative staff are ready with their roll-call sheets. The delays often seem interminable. These frequent recesses, however, often only serve to mask frenzied behind-the-scenes efforts to convince or cajole a recalcitrant member into supporting or opposing a particular measure. While most bills decked (the official term for inclusion on the calendar for floor action) for final reading will pass, some will not, and tempers will flare, and feelings will be bruised on account of what takes place during these final days.

Then the gavel comes down for the final time, and suddenly the legislative session is over. One often reads of the legislature "winding down, "The legislature doesn't wind down. It builds during 60 legislative days, culminating in a crescendo of activity. Then suddenly all is quiet.

Members are left to ponder the successes and failures of the session, both individually and collectively. Each will draw his or her own conclusions. Thereafter, legislators must turn their thoughts toward resuming a more mundane lifestyle during the eight-month interim period. For myself and the other neighbor island legislators, this means packing up our temporary residences on Oahu, shipping automobiles home, and picking up the threads of what it is that we do in "normal" life.

Because of its intensity, there is a bit of sadness as the Capitol community realizes that there will not be another session quite like this one. Many staff will not return. If it is an election year, a good number of colleagues may also be missing.

The session ends with a somewhat emotional late night holding of hands and singing "Hawaii Aloha." Everyone is exhausted. They want to drift away and forget all the stress and grief.

I have searched without success to find written evidence to describe my first legislative session. The only document I could find was a letter I wrote to one of my friends in 1985:

Dear Larry,

My first legislative session is just over. It was four months of meetings, maneuverings, superficial reading, quick judgment, and little bits and pieces of contributions.

Crackpots like me seldom end up in the mainstream, and I quickly joined a group of so-called dissidents who opposed reselection of the current Speaker of the House. We lost and paid dearly for our rebellion. Most of our proposed bills did not get far, although it was possible to disguise the authorship of a few which led to success.

I managed to get my name in the paper at least a half a dozen times, was on TV a few times, and generally had more fun than I was entitled to have as a so-called "freshman." Even though I am quite familiar with the legislative process, the new chemistry of different people in the House and Senate always creates a brand-new environment that must be learned from scratch. Personal relationships are such a key to the democratic process that they are often in conflict with public desires for representatives who speak out.

In fact, probably the best strategy for the inside game, to be an effective lawmaker, is to shut up completely, never make public statements, and work completely behind the scenes. There is a prevailing sub-culture here that looks down on the public aspects of leadership and rewards the discrete. No representative wants to look bad, and open public opposition or debate is bound to make someone look bad.

The Insiders' Game is in direct contrast to the demand of the public who want to know what is going on, and who will tend to vote for people who have kept their names in the limelight. Constituents subconsciously demand, and quite legitimately I feel, that their representatives articulate their needs and desires in a public way. There is nothing more frustrating than to believe that no one in government shares your values or opinions, or that no one is out there "fighting" for the people.

This contrast between the inside and outside audience for actions creates a major tension in the legislative world. This tension shifts from time to time depending on the historical context. For example, some days there is considerable disenchantment with government in general, and the established government in particular. Here in Hawaii, the Democrats are on the defensive, and there is a growing belief that they (we) are without ideas or motivations to changes. In such a context it becomes even more important for progressive Democrats, reformers and do-gooders like yours truly, to be vocal and public. Otherwise, the opposition party, which really doesn't have much of an agenda except "Kick the bums out" tends to monopolize the public arena.

I am only beginning to sort through this experience. Personally, I had a great time and enjoyed the ability to get at least small things done, and to engage in conversations with folks who ordinarily would not give me the time of day. I'm just getting together my legislative report, which I'm enclosing. You must read this with the realization that constituents are not too crazy about reading a really detailed report, so this only gives a flavor of what happened - and there's plenty more info if they want to ask. I'll be walking door to door within the next month....

INTERIM WORK

When the session ends, the Capitol is like a ghost town. Senators and Representatives drift off to vacations and family obligations. However, even in a theoretically part-time legislature, come late spring or summer, you will find more and more legislators engaged in serious work. Sometimes this work involves formal hearings by one or more committees. Such activities will require the expenditure of legislative funds to pay for expenses of neighbor island members to attend. Official hearings will often be initiated during the regular session by the passage of a resolution, asking that a particular committee conduct hearing and write a report.

At other times, individual legislators interested in a particular issue will hold informal briefings or workshops. These are basically cost-free, and do not require permission from the House or Senate leadership. One of the most persist examples of this during my tenure was the work by Senator Suzanne Chun-Oakland and

Representative Dennis Arakaki. Together they kept alive a loose coalition known as the Keiki (children's) Caucus, and pursued other complex issues in the health and human serve realm such as welfare reform.

It is from May through December that some of the most important work is done. Complex legislative initiatives, such as no-fault insurance or civil service reform, will almost always require preliminary work. Highly controversial or complex proposals introduced without adequate preliminary work will almost always be tabled until such work is accomplished in the next interim period.

Because I was a full-time legislator during my entire career, each summer I usually participated in several interim projects involving entire committees or ad-hoc groups. Perhaps the most interesting and rewarding projects, however, were those I did on my own. I initiated a sister state relationship between Hawaii and Cheju Island, where I'd served in the Peace Corps. (Who said international relations was only the purview of the federal government?) I investigated oil spills at Pearl Harbor and wrote several white paper reports to my colleagues. If I took a legislatively sponsored trip or attended a conference, I wrote a detailed report. I conducted a survey on how the Peace Corps treated its returned volunteers.

One of the best things that happened to me as a legislator was the opportunity to work with Bob Grossmann, a former Peace Corps volunteer in Africa, who joined my staff for several sessions. Bob had been medically evacuated out of Benin (the previous volunteer had died!) filled with all sorts of exotic parasites, an issue that the Peace Corps and the health system seemed unable or unwilling to address. Because of his experience with tropical illnesses and the difficulty in getting appropriate medical treatment, we began to explore the flaws in the system. Bob and I discovered that the Peace Corps had never actually done a survey of former volunteers to assess any persistent health problems resulting from their overseas service.

We designed and implemented a survey for returned Peace Corps volunteers in Hawaii and found an astonishing number of lingering illnesses, many related to tropical diseases that hometown American doctors could not even recognize. (It will sometimes require ten or more specific tests to identify a parasite in the patient.

Only the medical experts who know what they are looking for and how to find it can do the job.) The documentation we received was truly moving, for some of the victims had suffered for many years, only to be told it was "all in your head." One respondent reported chronic diarrhea for over ten years!

Peace Corps administrators in Washington were also in major denial, and made some of the most ridiculous medical and scientific statements in writing to defend themselves. As of 1998, they refused to offer hepatitis B shots for volunteers serving in areas where it is prevalent. We were able to network with other returned Peace Corps volunteers across the nation who were also interested in health reform. At one point, we found that the national office had removed us from the official mailing lists because we had become an embarrassment for them. Ultimately we were able to improve the ability of returned volunteers to file workers compensation claims with the U.S. Department of Labor and to seek the services of specialists in tropical medicine. Bob was the driving force behind this, and I was proud to be along for the ride. The combination of his knowledge and intelligence and my position as Health chair made a difference.

A lesson from the Peace Corps study is that often things don't get done until someone decides to do them. It takes time but it doesn't always take more money. We certainly ran into resistance in Washington, where officials did not relish the obvious embarrassment of not taking adequate care of returned volunteers. By joining forces with the networks of former volunteers we tapped into throughout the nation, we helped to create an unstoppable movement for which there simply was no good reason for further resistance.

Our decision to do this study did not require anyone's permission, nor any appropriation. We did not have to drum up grassroots support, nor write myriad letters justifying our time and effort. This lesson is perhaps one of the most important realities of democracy: Legislators set their own agendas, and if you are willing to work hard, there is no telling where or when a meaningful contribution can be made. For government as a whole, this is perhaps a hint that many worthy actions are dismissed on the assumption that permission must be asked and received. This is a great fallacy. The first rule of public service ought to be: Do what you can do without asking permission.

LESSONS

1. The first decision of an elected official is which group or faction to join. This decision is seldom openly or intelligently discussed in public. The media tend to enjoy reporting what is said, but not what is meant. Yet this is perhaps the most important decision an elected official will make in a two- or four-year term because it influences not only the character of our government, but also the role that the official will play.
2. The early spirit of hope in a legislative session can easily be obscured by the manic pace of just moving all the paperwork through committees. At a time when the deepest thought is needed to frame and mold proposals, there is little opportunity to bring knowledge or intelligence to bear.
3. The legislative schedule diminishes the contributions of those who deal with proposals early, and exaggerates the roles of those who deal with them last.
4. Public hearings are often misunderstood. Some are opportunities for genuine input and debate. Others become dramatic spectacles where the actors posture for media attention.
5. Not understanding the rhythms of legislative life may result in misplaced effort on the part of citizen lobbyists. Uninitiated citizens tend to expend more energy early in the session, while veteran lobbyists tend to pick up their pace and intensity slowly, reaching their peak at the end, when most of the key decisions are made.
6. Much can be accomplished between sessions by taking the initiative.

4 | INTERNAL STRUGGLES FOR REFORM

. . . .

The boys in politics are those individuals who want position in order to BE something; the men are those who want position in order to DO something.

— *Eric Sevareid*

The struggle to control the State House of Representatives has, since the late 1980s, been undertaken with the primal understanding that legitimacy is achieved by being on the right side of legislative reform. It is as if Democrats sensed that the relationship of the public to their government was in jeopardy.

In 1992, when Danny Kihano retired as Speaker, a political struggle was rekindled that pitted Democrat against Democrat. The stakes were power and control of the House, its philosophical orientation, and its alliance with certain interest groups. This competition had its historical roots in dissatisfaction with Speaker Henry Peters and his Bishop Estate conflict of interest, Richard Kawakami's successful seizure of power in the fall of 1986, and the disarray that followed his untimely death early in 1987 while on a hunting trip.

The beneficiaries of Kawakami's organization of the House were a coalition of two main groups: neighbor islanders and progressives from urban Honolulu. Kawakami brought in Mazie Hirano as chair of Consumer Protection, Dwight Takamine as chair of Labor, Rod Tam as chair of Education, David Hagin a as chair of Water and Land, Wayne Metcalf as chair of Judiciary, Paul Oshiro as chair of Transportation, Romy Cachola as chair of Tourism, Dennis Arakaki as chair of Human Services, and Jim Shan as chair of Health. For Finance, he chose Danny Kihano as chair and Joe Souki as vice chair.

In subsequent years members of this group stuck together. There was in this lineup a distinctly liberal flair, as many prided themselves on their lack of attachments to the downtown power structure. Union support was strong. Big business was seen through skeptical eyes.

When Richard Kawakami died early in his first session as Speaker, a rapid succession of meetings took place to ensure that the current lineup and orientation would remain. Majority leader Tom Okamura, having paid his dues in leadership roles, felt he should have been speaker. So did some of his closest allies, such as Carol Fukunaga, Dwight Yoshimura, and Calvin Say. But it was not to be Tom's time in the sun. Kihano was chosen and quickly elected by the caucus. The losers were left to brood and plot for the future.

By 1992, the tension between groups in the Democratic caucus was at its height. Joe Souki, who had been a member of the Kihano faction (and who had to be defended repeatedly because of his heavyhanded tactics) made his move, cut a deal with Tom Okamura (each promising to deliver his followers in order to gain power), and gobbled up votes of enough Democrats to secure the speakership. There was never any attempt to include the inner core of urban liberals in any organizational lineup. Hagino, Hirono, Tam, Hiraki, Takamine, Amaral, Arakaki, Shon, and others were "exiled to Siberia."

Our candidate for speaker that year was Peter Apo. When we lost, Peter issued the following statement on November 6, 1992:

> It is apparent that my bid to lead the House will fall short of the necessary votes, and so I am withdrawing as candidate for the speakership.
>
> I would like to express my deepest appreciation to those courageous legislators who joined me in the effort and laid everything on the line, asking nothing in return.
>
> We shared a common notion that the quality of legislative decision-making was directly proportionate to the quality of the process and sought to make substantive changes to the way we do business. We shared the common belief that restoring public confidence in the collective

institution should be a matter of highest priority - and that the quality of our decisionmaking is only as good as the process itself.

We sought to bring about meaningful structural changes in the way we do business, beginning with the notion that we should organize around ideas rather than people, and that the assignment of responsibilities should be triggered by those ideas rather than the traditional approach of trading votes for positions.

While it is clear that the House is not yet ready for that style of leadership, we are very encouraged that our effort provided a meaningful forum of discussion for structural change, and that it has captured the attention of the body as a whole.

The centerpiece of our effort called for a flattening of the hierarchy, whereby the power would be more evenly distributed amongst the members, and particularly in the lateral transfer of authority from the Speaker's Office to the larger body.

We envisioned a leadership structure that was based on a linking of arms rather than top-down management.

We are interested in providing all members of a standing committee with a formal, and more democratic, appeals process that would serve as a check and balance to the autonomy of a chair by creating a Rules Committee.

We are interested in creating an atmosphere on the floor that encourages debate on the issues during Second Reading, especially for bills with a lateral referral.

We are interested in providing gavel-to-gavel1V coverage of public hearings on high-profile issues.

We are interested in having more women serve at the highest levels of decision-making.

We are interested in bringing more sunshine to the operating budget by making it a subject of informational public hearings.

We are interested in having more public hearings in communities that are affected by legislation.

The laundry list goes on and on. We are cognizant that we are not the crucible of all wisdom and need to reach out to the public for help in solving problems. We are interested in putting a human face on this institution, the Legislature.

The good news is that members on both sides of the speakership battle recognize the need for change, and we believe that you will see some of those changes reflected in the new organization. To that end, we believe our effort was a success.

Well, this was hardly a revolutionary document. Joe had won, and we had lost, and you could interpret this as just public posturing by the losers. But this mild-mannered document was only the tip of the iceberg. One of the reasons we opposed Souki was because we feared he would refuse to change the House in ways necessary to restore public confidence in our democracy. The principal changes after the 1992 leadership fight were that we did increase cable TV coverage of our proceedings, and we did require a recorded vote of members present in a committee. The media heralded these as wonderful breakthroughs. Others, myself included, felt they were fairly superficial, and would ultimately mask the continued manipulation of the process by a small group of power brokers that included Judiciary chair Terry Tom, Finance chair Calvin Say, and Speaker Joe Souki.

Our fears were borne out in the coming years. Violations of the spirit of a democratically run institution were common. In May 1995, the following memo was circulated among Democratic House members. Each item identified an actual event or problem. The questions posed were just a polite way of suggesting, "why don't we do it this way?"

Item #1: A Committee Report and Bill are reported out of a committee in a form not approved by that Committee in their decision-making vote. This actually happened with the Workers Compensation Bill in 1994.

Question: How do we deal with a bill that hits the floor [of the House for a vote] in violation of our own process? What commitment do we have to rectifying this kind of error? [The answer by the leadership was to ignore allegations of the discrepancy and support the unilateral actions of the Chair of Judiciary.]

Item #2: While we do vote publicly on bills in committee, a minority [of committee members] in attendance can determine the fate of a bill, in contrast to the old system when a majority of signatures [by members] was required. Also under the old system, all members could review both the final language of a bill and the language of a committee report before signing off, which could be crucial in Judicial reviews. [Courts often look at committee reports to interpret original legislative intent.]

Question: Would it not be possible to consider open voting on the motion to circulate the committee report and bill, thus combining the strengths of both approaches? [This would create an open, recorded vote, but still require that the final movement of the bill out of committee be subject to the signature of a majority of members, which would also be a public document.]

Item #3: A Committee guts a bill and inserts content which upsets a major constituency. The public hearing was on a completely different, benign bill. The emerging bill is far more significant, and it is argued that most testifiers did not speak to the substance of the final version. This actually happened with the Leasehold Conversion Bill.

Question: Does the House have a policy to discourage such actions which place the institution in an embarrassing light and which break faith with public expectations? Should we not insist that totally transformed bills be given another hearing? [Actually, for so-called "short-form" bills, those with only a title and no content, we did require the amended bill with new content be referred back to committee for a hearing. Thus, the House recognized the principle, but refused to apply it when a bill that did have substance was completely changed.]

Item #4: A pro-health, anti-smoking bill is passed by the Health Committee but radically changed by the Judiciary Committee without prior concurrence by the Health Chair or Committee. [Prior concurrence refers to the requirement that the previous chair, on behalf of that committee, must review and agree to the changes.] This actually happened in the now famous Smoking Bill, which pre-empted the countries' ability to regulate smoking.

Question: Should we not find ways to insist that committees are respected and prior concurrence becomes an expected feature of our process? Should we not distinguish between what a second committee Judiciary or Finance) can actually tinker with? Are there limits to the preemption afforded by a second committee?

Question: This bill added a major pre-emption of county government. We do have a committee set up specifically to deal with this: Intergovernmental Relations. When the content was changed, should not the bill also be referred to that committee? In other bills, if you were to add funding to a non-funding bill, it would certainly be re-referred to Finance. Why are not other committees given the same status and respect? [The Intergovernmental Relations Committee was not chaired by a close ally of the Speaker.]

Item #5: A similar situation arose with the dermatologists bill, which emerged at the last moment to include "medical specialists" as primary care providers [meaning that virtually all specialists, including dermatologists, could circumvent a system designed to have a generalist first refer patients to specialists, an amendment that had not been considered in any hearing or previous proposal]. It was amended without any discussion with the Health Committee.

Question: Should the previous committee have a veto on amendments that violate the general consensus of that committee? [This is the same problem applied to yet another controversial bill. The Speaker supported the second chair to make the amendments. Not all bills are changed in the second committee, and sometimes these changes are minor. However, major amendments undercut the integrity of the committee system.]

Item #6: A committee chair is told she may retain jurisdiction over a bill only if she agrees to pass the bill in the form dictated by the Speaker [who was anxious to support the Governor's request for a high-risk Medicaid "provider tax"]. [This actually happened in 1993 over a human services bill (the so-called ProviderTax) that attempted to count new tax money as a state match to attract more federal dollars, which would be used to pay back those taxed, where Health and Human Services Committees, chaired by Representatives Suzie Chun Oakland and Julie Duldulao, had voted to kill the proposal earlier.]

Question: Under what circumstances and by what process should leadership or a policy committee be permitted to over-rule the legitimate jurisdiction and decisions of a committee? Should these instances be brought before the Caucus?

Item #7: In the previous two years (Convention Center Bill, Kahoolawe Bill, Clean Water Bill), as in others, last-minute bargaining ran up against the inflexible deadline at the end of the session, causing either an extension or the death of key bills. (This happened with the budget bill again in 1998.)

Question: Even if the Senate does not agree formally, should our Conference Committee chairs set earlier deadlines for good-faith bargaining to ensure deliberative, quality work that can be written up in time for decking? [Decking is the delivery of the bill to the House Clerk for formal addition of a bill to the Order of the Day for action on the House or Senate Floor.] Is there any reason to encourage the brinkmanship that seems to disgust the public and lead to more back-room deals without true participation by Conference Committee members?

Item #8: It is common practice that only committee chairs determine the "House position" in Conference Committees, and that only chairs speak during the conference. Membership on these committees becomes less meaningful as the years go by.

Question: Should we not encourage Conference Committees to meet prior to their negotiations to get the true sense of members' positions? While this probably could not be a hard and fast rule, is there no way to make participation more meaningful?

Item #9: Most of our citizens work during the day, and this is when we have hearings. They can never attend our public hearings when held during the work day. In the past, efforts to take hearings to the public, at schools at night or on weekends, on a regular basis, were resisted and finally shut down. Recently, only occasional weekend hearings at Mabel Smyth Auditorium speak to this problem. Most citizens still are locked out by the timing of hearings.

Question: Should we not encourage and facilitate the regular holding of hearings in the community? Obviously, this is not possible with all bills, but with the big ones it is possible. Shouldn't every committee chair report to the Caucus how they plan to make their committee more accessible to the public?

Item #10: Parking is also a constant problem for participants. There has been no concrete commitment on the part of DAGS (the Department of Accounting and General Services, which administers the Capitol parking area) to make it easier or less expensive for the public to attend Capitol hearings.

Question: Could we not be more aggressive and encourage public participation by insisting that DAGS respond to this need?

Item #11: It has long been common practice that whatever budget is recommended by a committee is treated by Finance as only a suggestion. There is no inherent structural respect for the priorities of a particular committee.

Question: Would it not be possible for the Finance Committee to respect the priorities of the subject matter committee as long as they remained under the ceiling of the administration's proposed budget? Would it not be possible to clarify what policy role Finance has for prioritizing funds as long as they are within the overall financial plan?

Question: Would it not be possible for the first version of the House Budget Bill to be an assembly of the various recommendations of the subject matter committees? This way, the Conference Committee with Ways and Means would at least have on the table all the priority programs identified in extensive hearings by those subject-matter committees. It would also show respect to all those who testified at those hearings, and for all the members of the committees who participated in discussion over recommendations.

Item #12: In 1993, House Finance and Senate Ways & Means staff contacted members of the Administration to inform them that certain cuts in personnel funds were specifically directed at the position of individuals who had work with a specific legislator in the past [one who had not supported Speaker Souki]. While this effort was somewhat unsuccessful, it raises certain questions as to how far political retribution should go.

Question: Is it possible formally to adopt a policy that discourages the unfair punishment of staff who may have worked for a particular legislator? Is it not in our interest to protect staff and encourage good people to join the legislative process without fear that future government job opportunities may be jeopardized? [This issue was in regard to three people who had worked for me, had gone on to gain government jobs on their own, and who resisted attempts by certain legislators to interfere in the workings of a particular department.]

Item #13: Following the reorganization of the House in 1993, at least one committee chair openly and repeatedly stated that bills introduced by a member of the losing Democratic side would never get a hearing in that committee.

Question: Should we not discourage exclusionary policies and personality tiffs? Should it not be a part of our legislative culture to heal wounds and respect the participation of all members?

It is obvious from this list of grievances, which was circulated to all House Democrats, that members were well aware of the alleged abuses of power and violations of procedure. Many of the bills cited were the subjects of long and heated debates in the Democratic caucus as well as in private offices. What was done in response to the issues if not the memo? Nothing. The environment of intimidation and the satisfaction with the way things were operating prevailed. Speaker Souki tended to dismiss such criticisms as mere red herrings, attempts to sow the seeds of revolution among the ranks. Perhaps more important was the fact that only a minority of the members felt strongly about such violations. They tended to excuse the Souki regime and its bullying tactics with, "that's just his style."

What was the outside view? The media were clearly not interested in the legislative process except when it might provoke a fight. Even citizen watchdog groups cultivated a conveniently short memory. When Souki instituted the recorded votes in committees, Common Cause Hawaii gave him an award. And whenever he appeared both decisive and effective, he was often praised in editorials as one of the best legislators, as one who got things done.

I have known Joe Souki since we both served in the 1978 State Constitutional Convention. I have always respected his basic toughminded intent to do what he thinks is right for Hawaii. As Finance chair, he initially was helpful in supporting some of my initiatives. We had an early history of working together. I enjoyed his crusty sense of humor. He came up through the ranks by working with the poor of Maui.

I also grew deeply disturbed by his increasing disdain for the democratic process and his coziness with powerful interests, such as the Outrigger Hotel chain and the Bishop Estate. I once described him publicly in a newsletter to my district as "well-meaning" but a "control freak." I don't think we have ever spoken harsh words to each other in person, but both of us knew in the last few years that I was committed to a fundamental change in the House and that he was not part of that scenario. Joe Souki is a tough survivor, one who will not hesitate to turn against a fellow legislator if he feels it is necessary to stay in power.

THE FAILED COUP OF 1996

The group grew cautiously, aware that less than a full commitment to challenge a sitting and powerful speaker was a bit like jumping off a cliff without knowing what was below. Those invited were initiated through a tedious process of discussion over specific reforms. We did not want our revolution to be just about power, although the abuse of power was the central issue. It had to be about positive change that would empower individual members to use their energy and talents to solve problems without fear of control, censorship, or retaliation.

A major breakthrough was the decision of Dwight Takamine (from the Big Island) to join the movement. Dwight represented a number of things that gave our group more legitimacy. He was a neighbor islander. He was a respected chair of an important committee. He was also a bit more cautious than some of us.

A major debate raged over whether or when to invite freshman Ed Case (from Manoa). Ed was brash, opinionated, and just as frustrated as the rest of us. But Ed also came from a very establishment law firm. He did not fit into any of the usual categories of comfort for us liberal, mostly union-oriented reformers. Many of us liked and trusted Ed, but it needed to be a collective decision. The group had to be sold collectively before any invitation was issued.

The debate over inviting Ed Case is typical of the kinds of deep skepticism that politicians must nurture for survival. Those of us who were veterans of previous attempts to overthrow the establishment can remember all the hard work and good feelings we had when we campaigned for Len Pepper, and then learned after the fact, "Oh by the way guys, I committed to the Speaker yesterday." I have always liked and enjoyed Len's friendship and contributions, but I can tell you there were many of my colleagues who will never forgive him for using our resources and jumping ship without a blink of an eye. There are other examples I could cite from past political history, but the point is that you can't always trust what people seem to be saying. They may not know how to say "no" to anyone, and in the end, they burn a bridge or two because they were open and candid.

Politicians ask who is close to another person. Who do they confide in? What are their deepest inclinations on issues we care about? Do they have a track record of holding up under the enormous pressure, real or imagined, in a leadership fight?

You cannot imagine the paranoia that surrounds the planning of a political revolution. On the world of the Legislature, dethroning a sitting Speaker or Senate president does amount to a kind of palace revolution.) We feared that spilling the beans as to what we were up to could be dangerous when talking to someone who was still on the fence, someone who might see it in their interest to run to the Speaker and ingratiate themselves by spying. As far as we knew, our conspiracy was still a secret well into July.

As the group expanded to include Scott Saiki (representing Moiliili), Eric Hamakawa (representing Hilo), Mark Takai (representing Aiea), David Tarnes (representing Kona), and others, we agreed on a sequence of conversations that would be required before we'd pop the question. First, a general informal gripe session would test a potential member's level of frustration and willingness to express dissatisfaction with the current leadership. Next, we would analyze as a group the candidate's statements and known circumstances: What does this person really want? Is this person really interested in reform? Are there ulterior motives, such as who can deliver the most important committee chair or leadership position? At what point would we as a group be ready to make certain selections?

The final process hinged on a request for absolute confidentiality as to what would be revealed in the next meeting. If the candidate was comfortable with that, a small delegation, including at least one person who was relatively close to the candidate, would set up the meeting, lay out what was happening, and ask him or her to join.

We were attempting to organize the House in a way that had never been done before (at least in our memory). In the past, a fairly respected, ambitious, seasoned, and powerful member would decide to become Speaker. A small group would be recruited, not as equals but as lieutenants. From the start, the challenger would offer specific positions in exchange for support.

In our process, we studiously avoided the slotting of people to specific committees or positions. It was deemed part of the old style, what was wrong with Joe's group. The most ardent advocate of this approach was Alex Santiago. Alex had for years sneered at all our attempts to effect change because they "played the same game." He imagined an idealistic, dreamlike scenario in which all House Democrats would enter a caucus completely uncommitted. Individuals would express an interest in this or that position, including the speakership. We would civilly debate their respective merits. We would be objective. We would be idealistic.

While many of us liked and admired Alex, we told him his approach was basically unworkable. I was reminded of a bumper sticker I saw near the University of Hawaii: I Brake for Hallucinations!

Over time, Alex had his arm twisted, his back stabbed, and his idealism trampled by the establishment. Eventually, he become one of the conspirators, but he never lost his vision for a better process, and he often chided us in meetings when he felt we were imitating the enemy.

There were serious discussions of alternative speaker candidates. Within the group, we had Ken Hiraki and Annelle Amaral. Dwight Takamine would have been a great candidate, but he was unwilling to spend the necessary time away from his home on the Big Island. Potential Speakers from outside the group included Representative Paul Oshiro, who was one of the most deferential, even-handed committee chairs throughout his career; Representative Ron Menor, known for his hard work on consumer issues and his willingness to take a stand; and Bertha Kawakami, currently vice chair of Finance, and generally well liked by most members. All these people had a reputation for fairness, and they were not known for trying to punish those with whom they had a disagreement. We recognized that Oshiro, Menor, and Kawakami might have greater appeal than any of the members of our group. Subtle and not-so-subtle overtures were made, but all three remained cautious and unwilling to risk falling on the wrong side of a leadership struggle.

It is important to recognize that even those who we had the most conflicts with, namely, Joe Souki, Terry Tom, and Calvin Say, were not thought of as villains. Many in our faction liked them personally. We were all Democratic colleagues who had experienced unique and intense times together.

Our dispute with the leadership was over policy, process, and vision. Personally, there are very few legislators for whom I did not have some admiration, some appreciation of the fact that they tried to do what they thought was right for the community. One measure of any politician's success is making a difference.

In early September 1996, we held a meeting with over twenty house members and candidates for seats who had a better than even chance for victory. This meant that Joe could count on a mere fifteen or sixteen votes.

Here's my personal list of members in our Democratic faction (those not-yet elected are identified as "candidate"; all the others were incumbents): Annelle Amaral Dennis Arakaki, Eel Case, Iris Catalani (candidate), Elaine Cohen (candidate), Pam Fergeson-Bray, Mark Forman (candidate), Nestor Garcia, Eric Hamakawa, Ken Hiraki, Mike Kahikina, Marilyn Lee (candidate), Mina Morita (candidate), Devon Nekoba, Marcus Oshiro, Scott Saiki, Alex Santiago, Jim Shon, Nathan Suzuki, Mark Takai, Dwight Takamine, Roy Takumi, and David Tarnas.

We were also hopeful that Mike White and David Morihara from Maui would consider joining us in the near future, as would Len Pepper. Romy Cachola and Jun Abinsay were sitting on the fence.

In addition to struggling with a certain number of internal rivalries for the next speakership, this increasingly confident group continued to write and rewrite concept papers on legislative reform. This process was not a new one. The freshmen elected in 1994 had started their own written dialogue among themselves. For two years, memo after memo was circulated. I contributed my share, while others lobbied in personal meetings and through faxes and even e-mail. As far as I could tell, the media had not the slightest idea of what was going on, and certainly showed little interest in the notion of reform. They, like the political community that traditionally gathers at the Capitol, were mesmerized by whoever was most powerful and saw no reason to go out of their way to detect the musings of those from "Siberia."

One idea that was hotly debated was put forth by Ken Hiraki and others: that we should not shrink from asking the Republicans to join our effort to change the House. A corollary of this idea was that if Joe needed them, he would seek Republican votes for his own survival. Before the general election, they represented a small but significant swing bloc.

The Democratic primary was not kind to us. Iris Catalani lost her race against Terry Tom, and Mark Forman was defeated by Lei Ahu Isa. The Catalani-Tom race was well covered, and even the media seemed to understand that there might be important implications if one of the Speaker's closest and most seasoned supporters lost.

Then came Black Tuesday, the general election of 1996. Many people think its significance was that a few liberals who supported controversial issues like same-gender marriage were thrown out. But more fundamentally, the election crippled the reform movement in the House. Losers from our group included incumbents Devon Nekoba, Annelle Amaral, Len Pepper, and yours truly. Up and coming new faces who were defeated by Republicans included Pam FergesonBray in Waikiki and Elaine Cohen in Kona. A number of swing or independent members who had been sitting on the fence quickly joined the Speaker's faction. This left the reformers with just sixteen, while Joe Souki had twenty-three. But you will recall that in a House of fifty-one members, it still takes twenty-six votes to elect a speaker or pass a bill. Joe Souki was three votes short. There were now twelve Republicans, and if they were really interested in a new regime, they could well have joined the Hiraki group and elected a new speaker. They were asked, and they declined. "I do not see how we can support Hiraki, despite his promise to open up the legislative process," said Republican Paul Whalen to the Hawaii Island Newspaper *West Hawaii Today.* The report noted, "Hiraki could wrest the leadership of the House with the support of the 12 GOP representatives."

In the end, they went with Joe. Why? For one thing, some had become quite cozy collecting their crumbs from Speaker Joe and Finance chair Calvin Say. They really were more comfortable with the accommodations they had made. But the real reason, in my humble opinion, was that Joe Souki and his style of leadership held out the most promising scenario for Republican criticism, and ultimate success in the next election. Plain and simple, Speaker Joe Souki and his lineup would be better targets. A reform group led by Representative Ken Hiraki would have been harder to attack in November 1998. I think of this when I read Republican criticism of Democratic legislation. They really did have the chance to make the House a better place for them and for their agenda. They chose to play a political game instead.

As a typical postscript to the last few years, in the 1998 Democratic primary, Hiraki faced a challenger who, reliable sources said, had met with Speaker Souki to receive support in order to "knock off" Hiraki, who has been a thorn in the Speaker's side.

LESSONS

1. Leadership struggles often create strong bonds that may endure for years, and hold the key to collaborations and coalitions in the future.
2. Most factions vying for power characterize themselves as agents of change and reform.
3. Many legislators become sincerely absorbed in this dialogue, which tends to melt away once the contest is decided.
4. Members of the Legislature are increasingly aware that the operations of the House and Senate are somehow out of sync with the needs of our democratic society. However, this

may not extend to a conviction that reform is needed to do a better job, rather than to appease the growing restlessness of the electorate. The defeat of Attorney General Bronster a few years ago by the Senate and the subsequent public outrage is just one example where the inside political culture and the outer community appear to live on different planets.

5. It is extremely difficult to organize a rebellion. Members are reluctant to jump on just any old bandwagon, knowing tl1at failure will bring isolation and punishment. (In the book *Shogun*, Toronaga interrogates the English pilot Blackthorn on his lack of loyalty to his superiors. Treason and disloyalty are capital offenses. "When is treason justified?" he asks, expecting to trap the Westerner into an incriminating statement. Blackthorn responds with the only answer that could save his life: "When you win!") It is even more difficult to organize a reform movement that seeks to change the relationship of legislative leaders from top-down authoritarians to collegial facilitators.

6. Occasionally, the minority party will have an opportunity to play a pivotal role in the selection of a Speaker or Senate president. This poses a difficult dilemma because to contribute to the selection of a leader also means to accept some responsibility for his or her subsequent behavior. The minority may well prefer to stay at arm's length and retain greater moral authority to criticize the majority party. In the case of the 1996 struggle, the minority Republicans in the House actually did have the power to change the leadership, but chose not to. As the Republicans gain numbers, power, and assertiveness, expect Democratic factions vying for power to flirt with bipartisan coalition building.

7. During election campaigns, the various factions will seek to gain an advantage by supporting or opposing sympathetic incumbents or new candidates. A sitting Democratic Speaker may well decide that it is in his interest to encourage or outright support a Republican in order to eliminate a troublesome Democrat from a rival faction. Discreet meetings, which are often hard to keep secret, are held on a bipartisan basis to

maneuver for the next leadership vote after the elections. Support or opposition, especially in terms of contributions, will be delivered through the medium of friendly interest groups or lobbyists who are close to this or that faction. (In 1996, lobbyists close to Speaker Joe Souki were active in contributing to my Republican opponent. In fact, the chair of the Campaign Spending Commission says he has documents indicating that the Bishop Estate conducted an illegal poll in my district to determine my relative strength and ways to bring upon my defeat. According to the chair, about ten days from the election I was "well ahead." In the final days, it is suspected, a great deal of generally invisible attacks were mounted to eliminate that lead.)

5 | MAKING POLICY

....

A blind, fortuitous concourse of atoms, Not guided by an
understanding agent.

— John Locke

I n twelve years at the State Capitol, I cannot think of even
one elected official who did not want to make a difference in
the lives of others. To be responsible for influencing the lives
of hundreds of thousands of women, men, and children is among
the fondest of legislative dreams. This ambition may be mixed with
desires of political longevity, fame, immortality, and appreciation by
certain interest groups, or just good old-fashioned idealism. Self-
interest sometimes overwhelms our "better angels," but given the
right environment and encouragement, legislators have been known
to rise to the occasion.

The making of policy, fundamental policy that can indeed affect
thousands of lives, is most easily seen at the constitutional level.
Article I, the bill of rights of our state constitution, contains some
of these lofty ideals:

- Section 5. No person shall be deprived of life, liberty or
  property without due process of law, nor be denied the equal
  protection of the laws, nor be denied the enjoyment of the
  person's civil rights or be discriminated against in the exercise
  thereof because of race, religion, sex, or ancestry.

- Section 6. The right of the people to privacy is recognized and
  shall not be infringed without the showing of a compelling
  state interest...

These policies are so fundamental that they affect every member
of society. Their presence or absence would make an enormous

difference in all of our lives. There are other policies in our state constitution that merely reiterate governmental powers or programs for which there is a consensus. These include:

- Article IX, Section 2: The State shall have the power to provide for the treatment and rehabilitation of handicapped persons.

- Article IX, Section 4: The State shall have the power to provide for the security of the elderly by establishing and promoting programs to assure their economic and social well-being.

- Article IX, Section 8: The state shall have the power to promote and maintain a healthful environment, including the prevention of any excessive demands upon the environment and the State's resources.

Often it is through proposals to amend this basic constitutional document that legislative debate reflects most faithfully the philosophy and principles of our democracy. The present will of the people (now represented by media polls) is measured against the long-term relationships of each citizen to the community as a whole.

Making a difference by making policy, whether openly or behind closed doors, is the meat and potatoes of legislative life. But it is also elusive. The public often demands that we concentrate on the mundane problems of life - traffic lights, criminal penalties, targeted tax breaks, neighborhood school improvements - all of which can also make a difference, but to smaller numbers in smaller ways.

In 1996, a graduate class in the University of Hawaii College of Education invited a legislator to address them on the subject of how educational policy is made. The first questions back to the class were "What do you mean by policy?" and "What makes you think policy is rationally made?"

One example comes to mind in which educational policy was indeed on the line. In 1996, the pressure was building to do something about disruptive students. The teachers were fed up, and the idea of reducing the mandatory age of attendance from eighteen to sixteen was gaining momentum. Representative Jun Abansay summed it up:

> The police and the courts are concerned that crime may increase as sixteen-year-olds with no skills and few job prospects go out into the community. They also point out that many of these students come from dysfunctional families and need some time to mature, focus, and find themselves. Sixteen is too early an age to give students the choice to make a decision that will affect their entire life. On the other hand, many lawmakers, Mr. Speaker, and I feel it is time for something to be done to improve the learning environment because educators have stated that the current system does not work. Educators talk of constantly having to spend many hours disciplining disruptive students who do not want to be in class, and it is believed that most of these students have already a record of truancy. As a result, educators claim that the quality of instruction is lowered and good students are being denied the education they deserve. I feel it is unfair for students who are serious about learning to be forced to be in a non-conductive environment with constant disruptions. It makes learning more difficult on their part.

An opponent of this idea countered, "This bill says that every sixteenyear-old has the opportunity, if you want to call it that, for the State to give up on them, for them to leave school, for whatever reason – pressure from parents to go out and get a job, whatever ..."David Stegmaier, the Education Committee chair rebutted by quoting teachers: "We urge passage of House Bill 2515, which would allow students who want to learn to do so. Those who do not want to learn in public schools would be free to learn from the school of life."

At issue was a fundamental perspective as to what the purposes and limits of public education are. Obligations to all comers were being tested by the reality that some who needed it most were the most difficult to accommodate. It was, in part, also a debate as to the nature of government. Yet most of my colleagues did not perceive it as a struggle for the principles of equal opportunity. It was approached as a practical response to an ongoing discipline problem. If the last two years of one's youth were not the responsibility of government, what other implications might that have for our community? This was indeed about fundamental policy making. Most issues at the State Capitol are not.

On May 4, 1998, the *Honolulu Advertiser* printed a story that identified nineteen policies established by the Board of Education for all the public schools in Hawaii. There was a measurable attempt to implement or monitor only six of these. These attempts to change the direction and culture of Hawaii's public schools were generally adopted with no specific deadlines for implementation and no additional resources to gather data and determine their impact.

Some of these Board of Education policies involved significant issues. One required that a student's grades be based on state standards. Another called for character and ethics to be taught in each grade. Smaller enrollments for new schools, a plan to recruitment new teachers, and programs for the gifted and talented were also on the agenda.

The Hawaii State Department of Education, the only statewide public school system in the United States, is often criticized for its top-heavy centralization. This is true for administrative lines of authority, but where the rubber hits the road, in the schools and in the classroom, it is hard to find any coherent sense of direction or policy. Each district office has its own approach. This is filtered through the school principal, who sets the tone and level of innovative engagement for the school.

Following review by the principal, there may be further screening through the school community based management councils recently established for each school. Once we reach the classroom, the teacher reigns supreme. Anything that requires a change at this level is extremely difficult to execute with any confidence across the board.

The prevailing overall policy is that students shall have a very wide range of options and electives. This means that many graduate without meeting the minimum requirements for entry into the University of Hawaii at Manoa's programs. A high percentage of students attending Hawaii's community colleges need significant remedial work. They have not been forced to achieve entry levels for college in their core courses. Instead, they have been invited to pursue their own paths, even when they are too inexperienced to appreciate what they may need in terms of high school courses and performance.

This is the real policy: We will not impose anything on the principal, the teacher, or the student if we can avoid it. As a result of this general policy, whenever a specific goal is adopted by the Board of Education, it is by implication of lower priority than the overall objective of maximizing flexibility and choice in terms of curricula development, coordination, and articulation. In spite of being the most administratively centralized school system in the United States, Hawaii's single public school system is ironically too operationally decentralized to be effective or to be subject to many of the so-called policy determinations made at higher levels. Paperwork is imposed on all from above. Curriculum and course selection remain inconsistent from school to school.

"Policy" is one of those much-abused terms that are used too often to elevate a mere decision to a serious level of consequence. A policy is a mega-decision that, when followed, provides guidance and direction for myriad subsequent decisions. To be a policy, a decision cannot be trivial or personal or short-lived. It is not enough for advocates to intend for it to be of significant influence; it must in fact be significant.

Some policies can actually be made by one person or one commission, at one moment, given enough power and given the ability to ensure it is implemented. Other policies evolve over time, are hardly noticeable until they reach a critical mass of consensus, and may be difficult to identify with a particular author. Perhaps the best way to understand these distinctions is to appreciate what happens when there is a policy change, and when, despite the best of intentions, there is not. Occasionally, a major policy is changed, and hardly anyone recognizes it.

In the 1960s and 1970s, Hawaii's labor leaders pursued an agenda of social benefits for the working people of the Islands. They wanted mandates, such as unemployment insurance, workers' compensation, and employment-based health insurance. This last benefit was not passed until 1974, and although there was heated debate, not too many of the legislative movers and shakers even appreciated what they had accomplished. The passage of the Prepaid Health Care Act was indeed a policy change and one that would eventually have ramifications throughout the United States during subsequent debates over health care reform.

In the 1980s and early 1990s, it certainly was the intent of several governors and the Legislature to pursue energy self-sufficiency and a conversion to cleaner, renewable energy sources. Agencies and commissions were created, plans were formulated, and myriad generic policy statements were inserted throughout the Hawaii Revised Statutes. This might have been comforting on paper, but it can be argued that the state of Hawaii never did adopt these as functional policies. The various departments steadfastly refused to participate in recycling, conversion of lighting to energy-efficient fixtures, and performance contracting to reduce the state's energy needs. The University of Hawaii at Manoa has been the largest single user of energy among state institutions, yet when it came time to build faculty housing, the use of efficient designs and solar hot water heating was not part of the agenda. In fact, the university has been so disinterested in saving energy that it had to return federal matching funds for energy conservation because implementation of the project was delayed too long.

For years, the Legislature attempted to integrate the use of solar hot water heating into the state 's housing program. Some progress was made in persuading the Hawaii Housing Authority to cooperate in the installation of solar systems on the roofs of housing projects, but when it came to the newly built housing on Oahu, state planners refused to incorporate solar systems. A bill was passed. The utility companies, which used fossil fuels, objected. The governor, without consulting with the state's own energy experts, vetoed the bill.

What all this means is that despite the enactment of legal and enlightened policy statements, implementation may be sabotaged by lame, if not hostile, administrative decisions. Paper policy is not real-world policy. Thus, although the Legislature was able to exercise influence up to a point, it had very little power in a proactive sense. The Legislature does have the power to prevent change through its checks and balances, but it can implement change only by partnering with many other players in the democratic game.

A few years ago, a dedicated environmentalist used the following analogy for the enactment of laws that, in his view, thwarted the desires of developers to pave over the state. Developers are like ants that have found a picnic lunch, he said. They proceed to carry each morsel single-file back to the nest. Their efforts are discovered, and a log is placed in their path, creating confusion and disorientation. For a time, the log accomplishes its purpose. But eventually the ants figure out a way around it, and the struggle begins anew. The log is a new law, a new policy. Chances are, in a democracy, the law's effectiveness will be limited, and future generations of legislators will be called upon to solve this problem "once and for all."

An excellent example of an unstated policy has been the state's unwillingness to offer health insurance to an entire class of workers, generally known as casual or emergency hires.

When a department needs someone to perform a task, often the existing position descriptions or minimum qualifications simply do not fit. Until the job description can be changed (estimated to take two generations of bureaucrats), the department is forced to hire that person as a so-called emergency hire.

According to law, if you work for the state for more than three months, you are entitled to receive benefits. However, the state has found a way to subvert even this modest attempt at policy. Buried in the rules is a definition of a month: thirty consecutive days. Each department is required by another internal policy to technically fire each emergency hire every thirty days to ensure that none of them receive benefits. Some 3000 workers in the early 1990s were subject to this real-world policy.

At the same time, the state of Hawaii was telling all who would listen that we had virtually universal health insurance coverage, and should be considered a model for the nation. The Legislature did pass a bill providing health insurance to the emergency hires, but Governor John Waihee vetoed it. "It's not as pathetic as it seems," said Health Director Jack Lewin, who was clearly embarrassed his boss's veto.

The policy of promoting universal health insurance had come head to head with another less well understood principle of many labor-generated laws: the attachment to the work force. New state workers were not given the same benefits as permanent employees because they were not yet firmly "attached" to the state's work force. Here, a labor principle that is applied to a wide range of employeremployee relationships, not to mention union memberships, came in conflict with a newer goal relating to health. In this case, collective bargaining rather than health was the arena in which the goal or principle was shaped.

Thus, in spite of numerous formal commitments to universal health insurance, it is clear that this was not a high priority policy of the state of Hawaii. And now we arrive at an important feature of public life: Idealistic goals often masquerade as enlightened policies. The setting of a goal is not the same as changing a policy. And the changing of a policy is not the same as the setting of a priority, which is only one among many conflicting policies.

During the 1970s, Governor George Ariyoshi led the state on an ambitious pursuit of rational planning. The state plan was a collection of smaller, departmentally driven plans. Each departmental plan might have numerous sections, all with their own goals and objectives. Little attempt was made to reconcile the priorities of one department with those of another.

We wanted economic growth, and we wanted environmental protection and energy self-sufficiency. We wanted a secure safety net for the poor, and we wanted a leaner, more efficient government. We wanted an educational system second to none, and we wanted jobs in the tourist industry that often required very little education.

In order gain the acceptance of diverse legislative perspectives, state planning had to back away from being specific and from directing budgetary priorities. Each department and each parallel legislative committee was left to be a free-floating advocate for policies and priorities that usually clashed with another department's agenda, at least in terms of competing appropriations.

In the state 's educational system, power and authority are distributed in many different places. A teacher has some discretionary power, as does a school principal. The Board of Education also has some power, but so do the governor and the Legislature. The agesixteen compulsory-schooling law is one example where a particular kind of power had traditionally been placed with the Legislature.

There is no confusion about this, as is often claimed. Everyone knows that the Board of Education can require three credits of science to graduate, or impose a 2.0 grade point average in order to play in the band. Everyone knows that the Department of Education has no money unless it is appropriated in a bill passed by the Legislature.

Within the administration and under the governor, there are many key agencies that also influence what happens in our schools, such as the Department of Budget and Finance (B&F) and the Department of Personnel, and Accounting and General Services (known as DAGS). Each of these departments has its own view of the Department of Education. Each may feel that it is better equipped to implement, if not make, policy. If DAGS doesn't want your school repaired this year, you will have to mount a full-scale march on the governor's mansion to get it done. If B&F won't release the funds for your new innovative drug prevention program for teens, that will be the end of it, unless you can get the governor to intervene and override his department head.

Under these institutional circumstances, it is not always meaningful to say that policy is "made." I have a useful analogy that may explain how you know when a policy is changed. In the novel *Jurassic Park*, the hero finds himself in the back of a cave filled with dinosaurs. They are all facing the opposite end of the cave, which opens toward the ocean. Suddenly, through some mysterious instinct, all the dinosaur heads turn in the same direction. (The author explains this as a primal kinship analogous to the migration instinct of birds.) Imagine that each dinosaur is really a different agency or program or decision maker. It is when all heads turn in the same direction that policy has changed.

Something like this has happened recently with so-called privatization of public services. A few years ago, it was merely a shrill cry from some business leaders and conservative ideologues. But today, virtually every department, every decision maker of consequence finds the need to address privatization. This doesn't mean that they support it, only that it is on their agenda and cannot be ignored. From library books to health services to landfills - outsourcing is the latest panacea.

It is clear that this represents a potential change in the culture of government, perhaps even larger than a policy. Where did it come from? Who started it? Who controls it? If we are not yet all moving in the same direction, we are at least contemplating a mass migration.

As part of a larger governmental culture, the Legislature, by virtue of its diverse base and peculiar mixture of promoters and resisters to any particular change, is not always in a position to influence that culture's direction. In fact, it more often than not will insist that no clear direction be apparent. This is called compromise or balancing or being fair to all.

Many legislators dream of that moment when their revolutionary idea, brilliantly translated into a legislative proposal, will emerge from its final committee and gain overwhelming praise and support. It is a time to bask in glory, knowing that society will never be the same, that generations to come will benefit. It is a common dream and a rare event.

Most legislative bills are modest proposals to solve modest deficiencies in the system. Perhaps this or that office is a bottleneck; let's give it an additional secretary and a new computer. Perhaps a particular crime, such as Peeping Tomism, slips through the cracks and is not treated with the gravity it deserves; let's increase the penalty from six months to one year for the first offense. Our kids need more help in coping with the pressures of modern teenage life, such as drugs, sex, depression, and low self-esteem; let's create a peer-education program in some of the schools, led by an additional resource teacher. The incidence of HIV is increasing in Hawaii; let's give some funds to a private nonprofit organization for case management of those with HIV or AIDS.

The above bills were among those I fought for, and I would argue that they made concrete contributions to real people. I would even like to think of them as policies, but that would not be accurate. While it is often only the Legislature that can initiate major policy change, it is also true that the public demands that the Legislature deal with every day and even mundane issues that affect their lives.

Making a difference comes in many forms, some dramatic and some trivial. It is the responsibility of the Legislature to juggle these different tasks, both collectively and individually, and make a goodfaith effort to accomplish both.

Just as the political culture is shifting certain functions out of government to the private sector, there are times when legislative ambivalence and gridlock may require a shift to a more favorable governmental arena. In the 1950s, American policy making on civil rights moved out of the conservative Congress to the courts. It was the judiciary that forced desegregation of our schools. It was the judiciary that outlawed electoral laws designed to weaken the power of minorities, such as literacy tests and poll taxes. Only an independent judiciary can ensure that the Constitution is not ignored by the public mood.

In Hawaii, persistent failures of our legislative priority setting and policy making have been the neglect of conditions within our prisons and funding for mental health services. In both cases, the federal government and the courts stepped in and forced the reallocation of public funds. In the case of mental health funding, Hawaii must now comply with the so-called Felix-Waihee settlement agreement, which is overseen by the judiciary. Judicial, not legislative, requirements provide adequate screening, planning, and treatment for child and adolescent mental health. This is becoming a significant burden on the state budget. It could have been avoided had we used a portion of our budget surplus to address the issue before it became a crisis. At one point, I concluded that only the intervention of the federal government's Department of Justice and the courts would delivery needed services. The following letter was one of the early initiatives that ultimately led to the setting of priorities by higher authorities.

Mr. Arthur E. Peabody, Jr.
Chief, Special Litigation section
Department of Justice

Dear Mr. Peabody,

As a Hawaii State Legislator, and former chair of the House Committee on Health for six years, I would like to request that the Department of Justice take a more active role in pressing Hawaii to improve the Children's Mental Health System.

SPECIFICALLY, THAT YOU REQUEST OF THE COURT A CONSENT DECREEANDTHE ESTABLISHMENT OFA FEDERAL PANEL TO OVERSEE HAWAII'S SYSTEM.

The Department of Justice MUST look beyond the narrow interpretation of the settlement agreement - beyond just sixteen beds. If you remain passive, the children will have no future in Hawaii.

I do not make this request lightly. A federal panel will clearly cost us more money, but there is no alternative. While there are periodic public statements by the state administration that mental health will receive a higher priority, there are no indications that the immediate future will be anything but dismal.

The following realities call for your intervention:

1. As an institution, the State Legislature has never placed children's mental health as a high priority. Yearly proposals from the House Health Committee have fallen on deaf ears. The current Speaker of the House is the former Chair of the Finance committee, which has never been sympathetic to the cause. The current Chair was last year's Vice Chair of Finance, and supported the Chair's rejection of increased funding. This is all in spite of two members of the House co-chairing a task force on children's mental health. (It should be noted that the State Legislature recently approved a budget that required numerous cuts in Health and Human Services while appropriating over $100 million in CASH construction projects that could have been funded with bonds. Thus, it is clear that Health and Human Services were not a high priority in the 1992 budget.)

2. The state administration has repeatedly submitted budgets that have been embarrassing in their ignorance of and support for children's mental health. The Department of Health must justify each and every penny to an oftenhostile Department of Budget and Finance. Elaborate, cashfunded construction projects have taken precedence over human needs, even during times of staggering surpluses. During the summer of 1992, when a downturn in revenues required the restriction of appropriated funds, mental health was not give a high priority. They were required to take an across-the-board cut just like everyone else. THERE IS VIRTUALLY NO INDICATION, BASED ON BUDGET PRIORITIES, THAT THE CURRENT ADMINISTRATION ADEQUATELY APPRECIATES THE NEEDS OF CHILDREN AND ADOLESCENTS WHO SUFFER FROM MENTAL ILLNESS. THERE IS NO INDICATIONTHATTHEY APPRECIATETHE IMPORTANCE OF PREVENTION OR EARLY INTERVENTION.

3. Both executive and legislative approaches to budget cutting adopt the policy that extra funds for program needs must come from WITHIN the department in question. Only extraordinary circumstances will add funds to the overall departmental ceiling. What is likely to occur is some additional funds will be transferred to children's mental health and that adult mental health services will suffer

There is no coherent plan to maximize Medicaid dollars to increase mental health services and resources. Unlike other states, Hawaii insists on funding Medicaid reimbursable services with 100% of state funds, leaving no incentive to the departments to "chase after" the federal match, which goes back into the general fund. There is no indication at this time that either a special fund will be created or that the additional funds generated by a yet-to-be- developed billing system will be returned to mental health. Thus, the failure of the Hawaii mental health system to maximize federal dollars is not seen by the Administration as connected to inadequate funding.

4.   Your own Department of Justice has been less than helpful. For several years, our Task Force on Children and Adolescent Mental Health has submitted a comprehensive programmatic plan for funding. It is far more detailed than the very general guidelines issued by DOJ, which seem to be preoccupied with building codes. If we are to be successful, we need you to think more programmatically, and to support, or constructively criticize, efforts of community advocates such as the Task Force.

In numerous communications with DOJ, we have been told of a lack of interest in the broad range of services required of an effective children's mental health system. We have been told you choose to narrowly interpret the settlement agreement.

If you have believed the pronouncement t11at Hawaii will improve if you just give us a little more time, you have been duped!

This is not because there are not sincere people trying their best, but because the basic structure of our funding system does not take into account the urgency of the situation. Mental health in general, and children's mental health in particular, are just two of the many programs asking for more.

5.   In recent years, the administration has responded to recognized emergencies by introducing emergency appropriation bills, and lobbying hard to get them passed in the first few weeks of each regular legislative session (we meet from mid-January throughout April) This approach could be taken with children's mental health. The absence of such a sense of urgency will only mean business as usual.

You should recognize that if the usual timetable is followed, and even if the administration and the Legislature agreed to put significantly more resources into children's mental health programs, no new money would enter the system until late summer or early autumn. This means a major setback for those children and their families who need help today.

I am calling on you to act immediately. You cannot count on the State of Hawaii to suddenly "get religion" for an issue it has been sweeping under the rug for years. The same key players are still calling the shots. Their attitudes have not changed. Children need help NOW.

I would respectfully suggest plans be made to request a consent decree and the creation of a federal panel to take control of the system on February 1, 1993, subject only to legislative action on an administration-sponsored emergency funding bill moving quickly through the House and Senate. Absent that, the best thing that could happen would be for the Department of Justice to step in and do the right thing. Thank you for your attention to this matter.

It is impossible to determine to what extent such a letter contributed to the ultimate involvement of the courts, but following the receipt of the letter, there was an intense dialogue between Justice Department officials and Hawaii's nonprofit mental health advocates. We could feel the wheels beginning to turn. I'm convinced that without this little push, certainly others would have forced the courts to take control of the children's mental health system. Yet it was, I know, a contributing factor to the raising of federal and judicial consciousness necessary for real progress to be made. The lesson, however, lies not in the substance of the letter, but rather in the shift from legislative to judicial initiative. Just as the United States in the mid-1950s was a land in which many legislatures were incapable of taking on segregation, today's budgetstrapped state legislative bodies almost beg for the outside judicial system to force them to do the right thing. Children with serious behavioral problems are still a tiny minority imposing on the sacred realm of the public school classroom. Mental health is a symbol of the recurring need for the shift in activism from legislative to executive to judicial, wherever times and circumstances require action that seems impossible to achieve. The lesson of children's mental health, then, is that a threebranch system of government not only balances power, but also allows for the evolution of policy and priorities in the face of gridlock.

LESSONS

1. Policy is an elusive concept, and an even more elusive accomplishment.
2. There is a significant difference between an intended or paper policy and the real world. Just because someone passes a law does not mean it will be implemented as a policy.
3. The making of governmental laws or rules is only one of the ways that policy can be developed or changed. The culture itself has many unstated rules or traditions that can overwhelm the efforts of a single institution or legislature. You need to ask: "What is the underlying, consistent principle or rule of thumb that seems to be operating?"
4. The arena in which policy can be made may well shift from issue to issue, and historical time to historical time. It can be argued that the greatest influence on public policy has shifted from legislative bodies to the courts. Recent books on the Supreme Court argue that one of the underlying agendas of the current Court is to restore some policy-making power to the legislative branches of government.

6 | PRIORITIES AND THE ECONOMY

Any man can be in good spirits and good temper when he's well dressed. There ain't much credit in that.

— Charles Dickens

In 1993, the Legislature voted to freeze welfare payments. The same year, we funded a Hawaii state race car to promote tourism, a new sports arena, a convention center, and several golf tournaments. The House also supported a lottery.

Setting priorities is one of the most difficult of tasks for a democratic body because there are so many constituencies with so many different agendas. If the Legislature ever could be an absolute mirror image of the thoughts and priorities of the electorate, it would probably behave the same way.

Sometimes there is a stark contrast between the long view and today's immediate needs. It is not always easy or appropriate to be a loyal team player when priorities run amok.

On the twenty-sixth legislative day of 1993, I rose in frustration to reject the proposed priorities brought to us by the Finance Committee.

A young single mother enters the town meeting with her ten-year-old daughter and one-and-a-half-year-old son. She listens attentively to the report of this 1993 legislative session. It's question time. "Representative;' she begins, "you cut me off from my assistance. I'm a working single mother – a working, single mother - and I need the support to pay for childcare. If I lose state support, I'll have to quit my job."

The Representative answers, "But look, we're giving you race cars to promote tourism. In twenty years, your son will have a great job."

"But Representative, my daughter needs money for a summer program so that I can continue to go to school. She needs that now."

The Representative answers, "But look, in about ten years, there'll be this wonderful convention center out there. Prosperity is just around the corner in a few years."

"But Representative, I can't even get health insurance now. You know that SHIP program [State Health Insurance Program] ... They've frozen enrollments this year."

The Representative answers, "Ah, but you can stay healthy following the professional golfers on their tour."

"But Representative, if I can just keep support and complete my training at the community college, I can get a better job."

"Don't worry, here's a lottery bond. This is your ticket to prosperity."

Mr. Speaker, the contrast here is between long-term, well-meaning efforts versus the need today - now. The contrast is between whether or not we believe that someone who is working and yet not well off should be encouraged to keep working to get off of a system. The contrast here is whether or not we will even ask those who are best prepared financially in the society - the wealthiest - through our income tax system, to make a greater contribution before we ask those who are at the lower end, and indeed, are about to slip off and not pay taxes...

These remarks were not well received by my colleagues on the Finance Committee. Later that same session, I voted against the budget bill, the ultimate act of defiance. It was a budget based on the so-called welfare freeze, the inadequate funding for children's mental health, and the lack of relief for medically underserved areas of the state, to name only a few of its deficiencies. But it was a typical budget, a little tinkering here and there, a few more dollars for tourism, and the Legislature pats itself on the back.

When it comes to money, the Legislature is a middle-of-the-road, conservative animal. This is not to say that it is shy about appropriating funds, rather that powerful, established interests tend to get the lion's share, including the state administration.

An alternative view is that the physically, financially, and politically frail of our society deserve special consideration. But this is the minority view. Not long ago, I was at a neighborhood party and fell into a conversation with another Democrat (who had once run against me) over the size of government. Another friend asked, "What should we do about the homeless?"

"Now this is where I differ from you," he explained. "You believe that there are no limits to what government should do, and I disagree;' meaning that trying to respond to homelessness was symptomatic of an insatiable appetite to expand government beyond its appropriate bounds.

I asked my two neighbors what percentage of the federal budget they felt probably went to welfare. Both, one a liberal, the other a conservative Democrat, guessed about 20%. They were surprised to learn it is only 3%. But that is the nature of today's middle-of-theroad party - ready to accept impressions and myths rather than facts. That assisting the homeless would be somehow beyond the appropriate scope of government for moderate Democrats would have surprised me once, but not anymore. It is one reason why I do not miss the Legislature each day of my post-electoral life.

In March 1997, the Reverend Bob Nakata, a leader among advocates for the poor, wrote a challenging article exposing the pubic myths surrounding welfare. Nakata's research revealed that the public tends to believe that welfare perpetuates generational government dependency (where in reality two-thirds of the welfare mothers studies did not grow up on welfare, and most leave the system within one year), that welfare women had more children (when in fact their birth rates have dropped at the same rate as the national average), that most people on the dole were too lazy to work (when two-thirds of these people were children and most of the adults were working but could not earn enough to support their kids), that teen mothers were a big factor (when only 7.6%

of welfare moms were younger than 18), and that welfare costs were bankrupting the federal budget (when all federal spending on AFDC, food stamps, and Medicaid for the poor make up less than 3% of the federal budget). Bob Nakata was elected to the State Senate in 1998.

Governor John Waihee (1986-1994) will probably be remembered most for turning a healthy state surplus into an ugly deficit. He is often spoken of with contempt by citizens who are convinced he had no priorities or respect for the common person. Many of his harshest critics are also unhappy with the state's school system. It is ironic that the two areas where Waihee added the most public workers were in education and health care. They might also be surprised to know that for several consecutive years during Waihee's administration, he proposed and we passed tax cuts. Of course, you could argue they were not enough. You could argue we really did not need more teachers or programs to fight the spread of $HN I$ AIDS or additional funding for mental health.

It was during this same period that Hawaii's private sector was intoxicated by the so-called bubble economy. Billions were invested in our state. The visitor industry overbuilt its Waikiki hotels to the point where they had to compete for the location of the proposed convention center for fear that their competition's empty rooms might be the only ones filled. The unholy and unseemly struggle to secure the site near this or that hotel concentration was, in my view, a direct result of the esteemed private sector not having any more wisdom than government at the time. We actually had the chance to let an Asian investor build the thing for free. But a close examination of the initial policies controlling our new convention center can provide the answer why this was not to be.

In spite of all the public tours of the Hawaii Convention Center, many voters would have been surprised to learn that the people of Hawaii were not welcome to use the facility. It was strictly reserved for off-island convention business. And its facilities were not to compete with our existing hotel ballrooms (as in Outrigger). In 1998, a local businessman who promotes musical events asked if it might be possible to hold a concert in the convention center at a time when there were no other bookings. The answer was an emphatic "no."

This initial policy was particularly galling because, for several years, concerned legislators had pestered the people in charge of design to ensure that the center would be acoustically well built so that the Honolulu Symphony and other musical groups could use it as a venue. The Honolulu Symphony is often prevented from playing in the Neil Blaisdell Center Concert Hall when the City and County of Honolulu rents it out to higher paying acts, such as "The Phantom of the Opera." And why not stage an opera at the convention center?

Here is an example where the private sector not only prevented the private building of a facility, but it also managed to prevent that facility from adding to the competition for local users. This is worth remembering the next time you hear people singing the praises of the perfect, pure, and always superior private sector.

The ideal size of government is unknown. In a small island economy, so easily influenced by big outside investors or lobbyists, a strong state government may be needed as a counterbalance. What other entity would be able to mitigate the effects of unbridled and careless development that aims at short-term profits and have little interest in the long-term quality of life in Hawaii?

Today the politically correct explanation for Hawaii's economic slump is the large size of government. It should be noted, however, that the state government was larger when the economy was booming a decade ago. Our local economy is responding to megatrends in the global and national market place that we have little or no control over.

Domestically, we have witnessed the decline of our main agricultural industries: sugar and pineapple. Unemployment in these sectors has been accompanied by a prolonged downturn in the construction industry, with jobs declining from 34,000 in 1991 to 24,000 in 1996. The military, once the number-two industry in Hawaii, shank from nearly 46,000 jobs in the late 1980s to only 36,000 in 1996. Civilian hires also dropped, going from 20,000 to 16,000 during that same period.

The impacts on our state have been dramatic. The overall civilian labor force has declined, while unemployment rose from 2.8 to 6.4%. Medical payments to the poor approximately doubled ($ 207 million to $428 million), as did monetary payments ($114 million to $212 million) and social service costs ($14 million to $50 million). In the past two years, the percentage of Hawaii residents without health insurance has grown from an estimated 4% to over 10%. Visits by uninsured patients to community health centers grew from 47,600 (17% of all center visits) in fiscal year 1996 to 59,700 (21%) in fiscal year 1997. Meanwhile, the economic viability of many nonprofit organizations, such as the community health centers, has been weakened.

As the gap between government revenues and government expenses continued to grow, Hawaii was forced to embark on dramatic cutbacks in program support in the areas of health and human services. New hiring was frozen. Mid-level professionals, including attorneys and white-collar workers of all kinds, were suddenly unemployed.

Perhaps the biggest impact has come from the foreign economic scene. In 1991, Asian investors were pumping as much as $2.6 billion into Hawaii each year. By 1995, this was down to less than $100 million. Japan, Hawaii's largest outside investor, suffered from over $450 billion in bad loans, and both the yen and the Korean won declined in value. Visitors from Asia not only declined, but more importantly, they stayed fewer days and spent less money per visitor per day.

A Governor's Economic Revitalization Task Force, made up chiefly of establishment economic movers and shakers from Hawaii's corporate world, most notably did not include members of the health care industry, which is today Hawaii's second largest industry after tourism, nor representatives of small business or private nonprofit organizations.

The task force collected data indicating that the per capita state corporate income tax revenue in Honolulu was $40.12 as compared with the U.S. average of $110.83, and that Hawaii ranked forty-sixth in corporate tax burden. Their conclusion: Lower our corporate taxes!

Being the great power brokers in our state, they did not want any competition from government. The national average of state and local government full-time employees per 10,000 population is 521 , while Hawaii had 564. However, 42% of them were from the staterun public education system, the only one of its kind in the nation. If you subtract these employees, you end up with a number considerably below the national average.

A few years ago, University of Hawaii professor Noel Kent wrote a book titled *Hawaii under the Influence*. Kent argued that Hawaii has always been subject to strong outside influences on its society and economy. Lobbying money that might be a pittance in California can have inordinate influence in our state, or in a particular county. We should have a healthy fear of these outside influences, operating as the proverbial big fish in a small pond. This is why flirtation with organized gambling is so dangerous; it can bring enormous amounts of political and financial influence to bear on a relatively small number of politicians. In our most populous county, Honolulu, only five votes on the city council are needed to make policy, six to override a mayoral veto.

Back to priorities. The Governor's task force found that our tax structure created a much lower impact from our excise tax ($583 versus $834 for the national average), much lower from our property taxes ($967 versus $744), but much higher from our income tax ($2759 versus $1854). There was some justification for such a distribution. In a state with a high cost of living, you would not want to extract an inordinate amount from basic housing. Housing costs too much as it is. Perhaps we should keep our property tax rate relatively low.

The following is an article printed by the Honolulu Star-Bulletin in which I explained this perspective:

Throwing Away Our Wealth

What's wrong with this picture? In 1996, Alexander and Baldwin made its largest investment in the history of the company - $178 million. It allt went to Guam. In fact, lots of Hawaii-based businesses actually expanded their number of employees. Maui Land and Pine, Theo. H. Davies, Fletcher Pacific Construction, and ABC Stores each added at least 100 workers. In all these examples, the investments were made out of state. The Economic

Revitalization Task Force and the State Legislature are determined to grant tax breaks to Hawaii's largest firms and wealthiest individuals. The assumption is that they will use the extra cash to improve our economy. However, the August 1997 issue of Hawaii Business quotes Bank of Hawaii economist Paul Brewbaker as noting, "Many in the *Hawaii Business* Top 250 credited their growth in 1996 to expansion outside the State."

Hawaii Congressman Neil Abercrombie recently lamented that even when they guarantee business to local firms for Department of Defense contracts, they often subcontract out to mainland companies.

So when you provide extra tax relief to these large firms and upper-bracket individuals, think twice. Their investment strategies rely heavily on compensating for Hawaii's lagging economy by investing elsewhere. You can hardly blame them if they find they can make more money off-shore, except, and this is important - they are the same folks who insist that by giving them a break, it will help us here at home. None of the proposals require that the tax relief be utilized in Hawaii. There are no mechanisms to reward firms after they have created more jobs here with a tax break. NO, the approach is, We'll hand it over, and hope for the best. And the record shows that the wealthiest companies have exported their investment capital.

I am not surprised that the hemorrhaging of Hawaii's capital has not been recognized as a serious problem by the gurus driving our revitalization bandwagon. A simple but poignant example will illustrate our collective myopia.

The City and County of Honolulu insists we will all be better off if we collect generous rents from out-of-state musical production companies, like Phantom of the Opera or Miss Saigon, while shoving the Honolulu Symphony out of its home. Whatever the rent for the auditorium department, the bulk of the receipts collected will leave Hawaii in the pockets of the producers, the imported artists, and the promoters. These funds are always collected from local residents since the Hawaii Visitors Bureau still has not found out how to market such events to visitors. Each time a large and expensive musical comes to Honolulu, the local artists suffer. Few if any are hired for the show, and whatever performances they have already scheduled must compete for the dwindling discretionary dollars of local audiences.

When our officials celebrated the outstanding concerts by the Rolling Stones, few thought to observe that well over a million dollars left with Mick. The local promoter got some, and the Aloha Stadium got some. But because we did not think to aggressively market these concerts to visitors, the bulk of the money came from local fans. Governor Cayetano said we always benefit economically from such shows, but that is not the case.

We have perhaps forgotten a very basic principle of economics: You can't prosper if you don't keep your wealth here long enough to use it.

There is recently a virtual mania to cut government employees. Yet we know they are the same folks who shop at Liberty House and who pay mortgages to the Bank of Hawaii. The Bank of Hawaii took some of these government paychecks to buy 21 branches of the California United Bank, and it added four more branches in Arizona to boot.

Perhaps it is because I am not an economist that I ask the naïve question: How many defaulted mortgages from those dastardly government workers can the local financial community absorb? And don't government workers tend to spend most of their incomes here in Hawaii? Perhaps they use this for Rolling Stones concerts or Miss Saigon, so maybe it doesn't stay here long at all. But most government workers we know do shop and invest in our state. And when a civil servant buys Kona Coffee at Foodland, or jewelry at Maui Divers, the person behind the counter does not sneer at the cash, Oh, this is government money, we're not interested. Cash is cash, and all companies are glad to have your business.

The point here is that we should place a high priority on those actions and jobs and smaller businesses that tend to keep capital and wealth in the State. While it may be wise in the long run to reduce the size of the government work force, in the short term, we seem intent upon punishing those who use their wages to support our economy, and reward those who look for greener pastures.

The University of Hawaii brings in millions into our state. The School of Public Health and the other excellent research departments are doing their part for our economy and creating good, clean, information-age jobs in the process. Yet we seem to think it wise to cut them back. There was even a state policy to discourage departments from seeking outside federal grants. Why? Because of a fear that in the long run we might become dependent. But this attitude has left us at a great disadvantage vis a vis other states, which see nothing wrong in securing their share of the federal pie.

Even our most Hawaiian of organizations, the Bishop Estate, has chosen to take a huge portion of their investments off-shore. They are the largest landowner in Michigan! What about Maui or Molokai? What about Waianae? What about jobs for OUR people?

I would modestly suggest that we pose the following questions when evaluating any new proposal:

1. Does it bring revenue into the State?
2. Does it support existing jobs or create new ones?
3. Does it keep money in our local economy long enough to benefit Hawaii's people?
4. Does it sustain or destroy services essential to a healthy community?

I do not envy legislators this session. Most of our economic woes were not created here. But we can either exacerbate or alleviate the problems if we don't pay attention to keeping capital working for our people. It is the middle class and the smaller businesses that deserve tax relief simply because they are more likely to spend it in Hawaii.

Actually, Hawaii has a tradition of responding to human needs. When the federal government cut back on block grants in the Reagan years, our Legislature expanded so-called purchase-of-service contracts and grants in aid to private nonprofits from $5 million to a peak of $100 million. Now that is an example of privatization! When we had a surplus, the primary growth in government workers was in the Departments of Education and Health.

Currently the public holds those years of spending in contempt. Many seem to feel there was a greedy building of civil service empires by those all-powerful unions. (This is ironic because so many of the new hires were not welcomed by the union system, and some were even denied health insurance.) It is the size and cost of government, suspected to be unrelated to actual delivery of services, that irritates many citizens of our state. Yet, when you get down to specifics, you find a much more ambivalent view of what we should be doing.

Hawaii's up-and-down experience with surpluses and deficits, and intensified by the current economic doldrums (influenced by Asia), it was, in the fall of 1999, nearly impossible to argue that the working poor (let alone the mentally ill or the homeless) should receive more services.

The highest priority for today's society is a reduction in the size and cost of government, regardless of the impact. It is an article of faith that the over-extension of the visitor industry a few years ago in Waikiki will not be repeated again by the private sector. It is an article of faith that giving more money to those who like to invest outside of Hawaii will suddenly result in more investments in the state. It is an article of faith that corporate wealth will uplift those on the lower rungs of the economic ladder to more than compensate for their higher relative tax burden.

There is a difference between priorities and ideology. Ideology says that the best way to provide services to the weakest among us is through government workers. Priorities say to use whatever works, just get it done. Ideology says you should reduce government and promote the private sector at all costs. Priorities say that there is such a thing as a healthy economy, and that it is made up of both the public and the private sector, which need to be in appropriate balance. Ideology says cut taxes for everyone, especially the rich. Priorities say that taxes should not be onerous, and that they should be distributed in ways that are fair and promote a healthy of economy.

LESSONS

1. Balancing the budget is not the same as consciously setting priorities.
2. There are dramatically different views on what those priorities should be, especially when established interests are pitted against the needs of the weak or poor.
3. Economics has its own language, and it can be applied either to the individual trees (i.e., organizations) or to the entire forest (the economy of a community). These are two very different kinds of analysis, and they are often greatly confused. Debates over the size of government, as opposed to the health of the economy, must take into consideration different kinds of data and apply different values.
4. Those elements of the society without powerful electoral voices have great difficulty penetrating the inner sanctum where budget priorities are set.

7 | INSTITUTIONS

The intangible duty of making things run smoothly is apt to be thankless because people don't realize how much time and trouble it takes and believe it is the result of a natural and effortless unction.

– A. C. Benson

Governor Ben Cayetano, a life-long Democrat who has benefited politically from the support of public unions and the many civil servants who work in Democratic campaigns in Hawaii, declared at the beginning of the 1999 legislative session that civil service reform needed to be placed high on the public agenda. He even proposed a bill that would have required the current system to "drop dead" at a specific date in the future in order to stimulate goodfaith efforts at reform.

It is unclear what Cayetano had in mind, other than some modifications to collective bargaining that would make other internal reforms of the bureaucracy easier to accomplish. His point man on this project, Mike McCartney, was a former legislator who ran Cayetano's campaign and who was closest to those who thought in terms of collective bargaining, but not necessarily in terms of how institutions behave or work on a day-to-day basis.

Political scientists tend to believe that the structure of a system (a constitution, an organization chart, the rules of bureaucracy, etc.) is the primary determinant of behavior. This belief reinforces a rather academic preoccupation with abstract analysis, model building, and other ivory-tower distractions. You can publish articles about such things, but seldom will anyone who actually participates in politics ever read them, let alone respond to them.

A January 1998 article in the journal *Health Affairs* ("The Role of Health Services Research in Developing State Health Policy" by Andrew Coburn) commented on this gulf between the university and legislatures:

> The universities we visited had little formal interaction with state legislatures. What relationships existed tended to be informal. Most of their project-related work, however, was with executive-branch agencies. Several explanations were offered. First, the nature and time frames of university-based research and analysis do not easily fit the legislative process, in which issues must be addressed quickly and where decisionmaking tends to be politically charged. Second, there is often a significant skill deficit on the part of academically based faculty and researchers when it comes to understanding and effectively working within the legislative process. Legislative staff noted that university faculty often lack the patience for the sometimes-tortuous process of legislative policy making. It also was noted that some faculty and researchers harbor negative attitudes toward legislators, whom they may view as uninformed, incapable of understanding complicated technical issues, political hacks, or worse. Likewise, legislators may see academics as "ivory tower" analysts with impractical or irrelevant ideas and recommendations. Concerned with maintaining control of information or of relationship with legislators, legislative staff may resent the involvement of academics in the policy process.

Politicians, on the other hand, tend to see the world through personalities and power relationships. Who has charisma? Who has the most powerful friends? Who has leadership skills? Who is popular and moving up? Who is ambitious? Who is mesmerized by their own self-image? When it comes to motivation, personal needs, such as kids in college, a wife who wants more time spent with the family, a mortgage, or anxiety over retirement benefits, are what the political world talks about when trying to figure out what someone will do.

Personality politics drives our current legislative governance system. This means that for many a politician, the focus is not on how a government of agencies, programs, and departments is organized as much as the idiosyncrasies, strengths, or weaknesses of administrative leaders or bureaucrats. If there is a relevant context to explain bureaucratic behavior, politicians will first look to friendships, alliances, family connections, and personal needs before examining the actual environment in which they work. Or, they may not look beyond the organizational flow chart to determine what is really going on. When a mayor or governor wants to shake things up, look for changes in agency directors: musical chairs, who is in, who is now out.

It is no wonder that the politicians and the political scientists seldom have anything in common except for mutual contempt. But to understand what is going on, either in a private company or in a public agency, both perspectives are essential.

Agencies, departments, programs - these are the essential building blocks and tools of governance. If you don't examine how they work and how they fail to work, you are unlikely to be able to influence them in a positive way. You are also unlikely to know what is really needed and what is bloated bureaucracy. If you want a smaller government, you still need to know how to make it work.

Each year the legislature polishes the fictitious apple of downsizing by freezing or eliminating existing vacant positions. The result, observed Director of Health Dr. Larry Miike, is that you move from a large inefficient organization to a small inefficient organization. Like going on a starvation diet, you lose both fat and muscle. You do not get stronger. The positions that are vacant at any point in time may actually be the most important, left empty because a very senior or expert civil servant either retired or was lured into the private sector. The notion that all empty chairs are examples of waste is absurd, yet this is one of the most common ways to achieve savings. You really wonder if those people freezing or cutting the vacant positions know or care what functions those positions serve.

Another related and equally counterproductive approach is the elimination of positions within an agency in the belief that the deadwood has been culled out of government. In Hawaii's system, with its tradition of influential public sector unions, those who have been axed have the right to replace, or "bump" another less senior worker in another agency. The result is that a host of programs are saddled with workers who have transferred in or who have been bumped, with no knowledge or interest in that program's operations. The workers who got transferred might well be the brightest, most enthusiastic part of the team, yet it is only seniority that counts. (It is ironic that former University of Hawaii president Kenneth Mortimer, who allowed the School of Public Health to slowly wither on the vine in the hope that it would fade away, could theoretically have had his own secretary bumped by the more senior executive secretary to the dean of the School of Public Health!)

If you are going to cut positions and you don't want demoralization and incompetence to spread throughout the public bureaucracy, you've got to change the bumping system. But legislators have not chosen to do this. The result is another shell game that cares little for whether or not the executive branch of government has the morale or the appropriate mix of expertise to accomplish its missions effectively.

In my twelve years in the House, I participated in numerous meetings, hearings, and decision-making events designed to force or encourage a particular agency to change its behavior. Unfortunately, very few participants attempted to understand the culture of a particular agency, the institutional context in which it existed, or other structural factors that were not driven by individual personalities. I'm not proud to say that I was often just as guilty as anyone else in not taking the time to delve into the workings of a particular agency, nor did the legislative schedule permit such analysis before laws relating to that agency were introduced. It is one reason why I felt the need to be at the Capitol all year around.

Individual personalities are important, but they are not the whole story. In the Legislature itself, abuses of power are often dismissed as personal style, as if the choice of that style were simply not a matter for debate. Oh, the chair is a bully because that's just his style. Nothing you can do about that! The fact is that the Capitol is so preoccupied with the personal relationships inherent in a legislative body or a political system that legislators are often unable to recognize the influence of structure on operations.

A recent example of this was a change in Hawaii's procurement laws. It was assumed that departments had too much flexibility in awarding outside contracts. We had glaring examples in which favoritism and conflicts of interest determined where the money went. Distrust over individual discretionary power within the bureaucracy led the Legislature to dictate an even more cumbersome system. So, when the media, and to some extent the public, congratulated us on the new amendments, those in the trenches just rolled their eyes in frustration. They knew that rather than ensuring a better system, the bureaucracy had just added more inflexible red tape.

Why did this happen? Legislators and others assumed that the bureaucracy behaved like the House or the Senate, that is, that individual personalities and agendas would negate the best policies and allow our government to drift toward a form of cronyism in the awarding of contracts. In a truly corrupt system, ways will always be found to deliver contacts to the favored few. There is no substitute for integrity. We all want some sense of accountability. No legislator welcomes another ugly headline about corruption, perceived or real. It is a black eye for everyone, and it makes the public even more cynical.

Our dilemma is that when we seek to achieve a vague sense of accountability by creating stricter rules, we may be sacrificing efficiency and common sense. We insist that there be a thorough review at all levels before significant government purchases are made. This sounds sensible and accountable, but when it is applied to items like new computers, it becomes absurd.

It was often the case that by the time the original specifications to purchase new computers for a state agency were finally approved, the technology (hard drives, programs, memory, capacity, speed, etc.) identified in the original purchase order would be out of date. Practically every six months computers get cheaper and better. Nevertheless, bean counters at every level, diligently following the new rules, would insist that any change in the original specifications will require significantly more paperwork and a new round of approvals. One suspects that in a system that offers little respect for its members, the only way to assert one's value is from time to time to simply say "no," and force the petitioner to jump through the hoop again.

If a program had the flexibility to change the purchase orders easily, it would actually get more computer power for the dollar. But that would be at odds with other goals, such as preserving a strict hierarchy of approvals, usually by people who have no understanding of the tasks required.

MEANINGFUL CIVIL SERVICE REFORM

"Civil service" is a catchall term for a wide range of issues. One of them is accountability, which is translated in the bureaucracy as approvals. To get a letter, purchase order, contract, or trip approved may involve as many as a dozen state workers including secretaries, deputy directors, directors, and even the governor. If we are going to reform and rejuvenate government, we will need to look more carefully at such processes and why they fail. There are three kinds of meaningful review: for clerical or grammatical errors, for micro policy content and clarity, and for consistency with broader policies or the identification of trends. For each of these, there is an appropriate match-up between a civil servant with appropriate authority and the task at hand. When a deputy director spends time on grammar or minor rewording, it is a waste of time. When a budget analyst unfamiliar with programs essentially vetoes a deputy director's policy decision, the system is out of whack. When a governor spends time approving travel requests, more important work is neglected. All of these occur regularly in Hawaii's state government. More importantly, there is a ripple effect of demoralization, the sapping of enthusiasm, and the befuddlement of priorities throughout the state system.

What the system needs is bypass surgery. What is clogging the organizational arteries? There are at least eight chronic diseases we dare not ignore: memory loss, the pride of forms, desk-top parking, loss of urgency, black-box bafflement, grassroots demoralization, micro/macro confusion, and fear of failure.

By memory loss I mean the demand to resubmit the same information two or three times. The Department of Budget and

Finance was notorious for this, seemingly unable to locate the same program justifications submitted a few months previously. Legislative committees do it all the time. Even within departments, a logical filing system seems beyond some offices.

Related to memory loss is the pride of forms, the demand that the same data be reformatted. At the University of Hawaii, to order a pencil in one department requires two different secretaries or student helpers to manually convert one requisition form to another, each of the two offices defending its form. Taking into account the time required to order a box of pencils, it costs far more to order them through the UH system than it does to go down to the store and buy them.

A third disease is desk-top parking, which means that your pet project is put in a miscellaneous limbo pile with no expectation of ever being moved to the next desk. Personal relationships with the occupant of the parking desk have been known to determine the fate of such a document. Desk-top parking is allowed to clog the system because there is no expectation or even knowledge of timely movement due to the loss of urgency. There may be crucial lapses in federal funding or other important negative consequences, but the system cannot penetrate the piles or hold the pile-holder accountable for parking. What the system needs is a tracking mechanism that tells everyone how long a document is sitting in one place. Institutional parking tickets might be in order.

Black-box bafflement refers not only to the time but also to the place of a document's disappearance. Often it is impossible to find out exactly where a document has stalled. Attempts to locate it may take longer than would a meaningful review.

Grassroots demoralization results when workers know that an unqualified person is reviewing their substantive work. At the other extreme, an overqualified supervisor may insist that the grass roots workers can't even write simple letters that don't need correcting. This situation arises because the system is hierarchical and fosters the myth that the higher an official ranks, the more knowledgeable and competent he or she is. (One department director insisted he knew best how to arrange the desks in every office!) This is not a team approach, but an ongoing put-down of talent. Many civil servants have jumped through numerous academic and experiential hoops minimum qualifications) to secure a position, only to find that the job they have accepted is limited to carrying out someone else's policy. With no chance to give meaningful and timely input, they would be shocked if they received a phone call such as, "Dick, we need to make such and such a decision. I know you've been working on this problem. Could you take some time and make a few recommendations to guide our thoughts? Send your comments directly to me. I appreciate your knowledge and attention to this. *Mahalo.*"

Another example of demoralization comes when an office says it needs such and such a worker, but the state's personnel department cannot write a job description before the year 2020. When the description is finished, it will not be what the office required. This is why so many so-called emergency hires appear in the system: It is the system's way of getting the job done in the face of mindless conformity.

Macro/micro confusion reigns when a system cannot determine the appropriate level of attention. If the governor is not spending most of his or her time determining the broad directions, visions, and so on of the state, who is? If high-level departmental officials spend their time scribbling minor edits on each page of a document, rather than molding departmental policy, then who is doing the larger job? And if lower level employees know that whatever they write will be edited and reedited for no good reason, then how much responsibility and pride can they take in their work?

Permeating the entire system is a fear of failure. If you are uncertain about what your job entails or what direction you should go, then delay, delay, delay. Cover your *okole* (Hawaiian for backside) with unnecessary reviews. Some people think that just passing around a document is the same as a meaningful review. This is not so. We should be asking ourselves, "given my job and other responsibilities, why am I looking at this?"

One reason for unnecessary reviews is that the system is unable to track, even with the aid of computers, the ebb and flow of work. It cannot spot trends or anomalies. It should not be necessary for the governor to approve all travel requests in order for someone to track the overall travel expenses. Let people in the lower levels decide whether something is justified. If the approvals are too numerous, then ask departments to prioritize, or give them a limited travel budget. Why waste the governor's time on a matter like this?

Our political and administrative system reflects a high level of distrust. Within a department, there is a personnel officer who is suspicious of every request for more staff. He or she does not believe that any suggested job description is appropriate. Requests for more program funds are viewed in a similar fashion, "Oh, there they go again, carried away with empire building. "The public may be surprised to know just how antagonistic various parts of the government are to new programs, let alone new approaches. Hiring competent new people is not an easy process. Citizens tend to feel that everyone in government is devoted to bringing more and more friends to the public trough.

The inordinate amount of time it takes just to gain a department director's approval of a new budget item could have been used for productive work. It sometimes appears that most of a public employee's time is spent just shuffling paper to and from offices within the system, a practice that is designed to ensure accountability. Bureaucratic fear of mistakes leaves many wading through a foot of molasses, while the Legislature and the public are demanding they sprint.

Once a budget request has been approved by a department, the real battle for new funds begins. The Department of Budget and Finance (B&F) will receive and review all requests. B&F analysts, often having more power than the directors of major departments, begin with the assumption that most requests are not justified and a department is once again seeking an easy way to accomplish its mission. The conservative culture of budgetary distrust extends beyond the final approval on the part of the Legislature. Indeed, the funds cannot be released until yet another request has been approved, this time by B&F.

There is no doubt that well-meaning public officials all along the way sincerely believe they are holding agencies accountable to a higher standard, thereby ensuring that each dollar is spent in the manner intended. Skepticism can be healthy, but hostility is counterproductive. In reality, the pursuit of superficial accountability has little influence on the way public funds are actually expended. The use of state funds has more to do with quantifiable justifications, the shuffling of paper, and covering one's backside in case something goes wrong. The more the public and the Legislature demand improvement, the more the system responds with layers of plausible deniability for those who mess up.

The budgetary process requires programs to identify quantifiable "performance expectations." I once worked in this system, in the Office of the Marine Affairs Coordinator, and I can remember many occasions when agencies just pulled these numbers out thin air. It is not so much that they intended to deceive anyone. Rather, they felt that the exercise was meaningless. Not every program can be judged by counting things: the number of brochures distributed, the number of people in audiences during presentations, the number of fish cultivated with government subsidies, the number of meetings held to count things for the Legislature.

Legislators tend not to look at the budgetary outcomes, except when there is a sensational failure, such as an outrageous case of child abuse that has slipped through the system. The tendency in such cases is to require more reports, more paperwork, and more bureaucratic review. These are substitutes for having the experience or knowledge to recognize when a department is doing a good job. I do not mean to say that bureaucratic strategies are never appropriate, but rather that there is an over-reliance on them due to a lack of understanding of what really goes on in a department day to day.

Recently, our legislative auditor's office has gotten high praise for critical reviews of this or that program. However, much of this analysis is in terms of discrepancies between the written guidelines and the daily operations. It is as if a game were being played to see if the auditor could catch a program failing to cross all the t's and dot all the i's. The University of Hawaii's College of Education was criticized because its faculty did not all recite the same mission statement. (I doubt if the auditor's staff would have passed that test!)

Sometimes legislative audits are able to pinpoint genuine weaknesses in the system. The audit of the state's Medicaid managedcare health insurance system was such an example. But just as often, the audits represent a paper analysis with little sense of the living and breathing organism that is an agency. In 1999, legislative auditor Marian Higa was a feisty and generally popular individual who was appreciated for her willingness to take on the executive branch with sharp criticism. Yet her audits were not in themselves helpful blueprints to improve the workings of agencies.

Dr. Lawrence Miike, former director of the Department of Health. complained about this attitude in a letter to the editor:

> ...While the auditor continues to rip into departments about their alleged management shortfalls, her office chooses not to take into account the institutional restraints under which departments such as mine operate. These restraints include a burdensome personnel and collective bargaining system. which is impacting state functions far more than it was intended to. The Felix court monitor stated as much when it wrote, in a recent report to the governor, that the DOH had instituted important changes to the children's mental health program and that "resistance and barriers in the civil service system presented a number of obstacles to rapid and smooth implementation."
>
> In response to what I see as shortfalls in the auditing process, I have the following modest proposals.
>
> For the legislative auditor: Take our exceptions to your reports seriously and do not dismiss them as kneejerk defensive posturing. Establish a framework of analysis which identifies the limitations under which managers such as yourself operate, and where the "system" impedes such managerial actions. Hold us accountable for what we can manage, not for everything wrong in the system.
>
> For the Legislature: Direct the legislative auditor: 1) to conduct her audits within the framework suggested above and 2) to conduct a study on "system" constraints, including the original purposes of the restraining components of the system, which has evolved since then, and what needs to be done. (Honolulu Star-Bulletin, May 18, 1998, p. B-3)

The culture of the Legislature is personality driven, which ironically leads to cookie-cutter structural "fixes." Bureaucratic red tape is mistaken for accountability, and distrust is a substitute for intelligent review.

Who knows how agencies work? Well, many bureaucrats do, and they can often use legislative or even high-level administrative ignorance to maintain the status quo. The civil servants who must navigate the system on a daily basis may well be the only experts on its operation. They are unlikely to step back and question the overall structure and operational basis of the rules they live by. Or, if they do question the rules, they may be unwilling to sacrifice their careers in order to point out their department's shortcomings. And, it should not be forgotten, if you are relatively successful in using the rules to your advantage, even if you dislike them, you are less likely to welcome big changes.

Technical expertise at all levels is sometimes a substitute for open communication and objectivity. If you can't understand the jargon or the technology, how can you judge its value? A few years ago, I was embroiled in the controversy over electromagnetic radiation presumably generated by the Coast Guard's OMEGA submarine tracking system on the windward side of Oahu. The new H-3 freeway was being built nearby, and the state Department of Transportation was forced to use an expert consultant to evaluate the potential health risk caused by OMEGA. The guy they chose made a living out of writing positive reports for the Coast Guard, demonstrating in inaccessible language why there was nothing to fear. It was obvious to me that if he had found potential problems, his career as consultant might be over. My conclusions were the result of several years of personal interest and investigation into the subject. Most of my colleagues had no basis on which to question such a technical report.

To understand electromagnetic radiation issues, you need to dabble in physics, cell biology, magnetism, cancer studies, epidemiology, statistics, and the broad spectrum that extends from radio waves to ionizing radiation. The experts, be they from Hawaiian Electric or the Coast Guard or wherever, are fond of saying that a particular level of radiation is within a certain acceptable standard, without mentioning that the standard referred to is a level intense enough to burn the skin, that is, to generate considerable heat. But for the most part, my concerns revolved around very low levels suspected more of accelerating the growth of cancer cells, an outcome that is much harder to quantify. I learned that you really couldn't trust an expert not to obscure or even intentionally deceive.

A 1996 study by researchers at Harvard University examined this issue of trust in relationship to the receptivity of legislators to technical information. One legislative staff member from Florida noted:

> A member is much more apt to be persuaded by the same piece of information if it is coming from a trusted staff member or a trusted lobbyist from the executive branch or a trusted lobbyist from the private sector, a trusted trade association, a trusted constituent, a trusted personal friend whom they believe has expertise and credibility in that area than receiving that same identical piece of information in a written report from some third-party organization, even if that third part may have a national prominence and reputations in that area. (Megan Jones, David H. Guston, and Lewis M. Branscomb, *Informed Legislatures: Coping with Science in a Democracy*. University Press of America, Inc., 1996.)

Expertise, when applied to a bureaucracy, shows up when the departmental accountant simply says to the new department head, "Oh, we can't do that." Perhaps it can be done, but the new guy on the block, unfamiliar with the wide variety of strategies open to an administrator, will just shrug his shoulders and move on.

The top governmental administrators, if they are recruited from the private sector, often lack an appreciation of how to get things done in the new environment. They may even lack the knowledge of how to make themselves look good through accomplishments rather than PR. Department heads in Hawaii are usually brought in from the outside, chosen perhaps because of their success in another field, such as law, medicine, politics, private business, or whatever.

When Dr. Jack Lewin was state director of health, it was common knowledge that many of his innovative initiatives were being thwarted by his own internal bureaucracy. Some of his deputies, who also shared his sense of urgency and "damn-the-paperwork, let's-getit-done" approach were also victims of institutional sabotage. I can recall vividly one session when Dr. Hank Foley was deputy director for mental health. He specifically wanted an appropriation to be directed to a nonprofit organization to deliver services. I just happened to be in the Finance Committee room as the final budget was being constructed by the committee staff. There was the Department of Health's fiscal officer telling the Finance Committee staffer to ignore her boss's decision and to do it her way. Words like treason, sabotage, and insubordination came to mind.

I wish I could say that none of these conflicts had anything to do with ethnic or racial bias. But the fact is that the selection of an impatient mainland *haole* (Caucasian) administrator was perceived as a challenge by a bureaucracy made up of Asian, Pacific, or otherwise "local" sensibilities. Style and race can indeed generate resentment in Hawaii. Any newcomer with an aggressive agenda and a sense of urgency must expect the departmental "tribal staff" to resist. If you add other cultural and ethnic factors, the gulf between the new team and the old veterans can be huge.

You might ask, "Aren't these folks professionals? Why would they let such subjective factors influence their actions?" Well, professionalism is in the eyes of the beholder. On the one hand, loyalty to the director could be seen as a highly professional trait. On the other hand, loyalty to the statutes or the official rules, not to mention a personal understanding of the mission of the agency, might require negating the personal agenda of a new administrator. If department heads are ordered by the governor to do something civil servants believe is of a political nature, they may well feel that they are standing up for the professionalism of their agency by resisting. Recently, a department head was reassigned to a lower position in another agency. One factor, suspected of influencing the governor, was a petition by workers in his former department asking that he not be reappointed.

I do not mean to suggest that continuity among staff is undesirable. One of the most persistent difficulties we have in dealing with an agency is staff turnover and the inevitable need to bring new employees up to speed. In my former job, funded by a federal grant, we were amazed at how high the n1rnover rate was, both in the federal executive agencies and among congressional staffers. All of our paperwork and personal explanations needed to be repeated again and again.

Aesthetics may also play a role here. I'm talking about the image people have in their mind of a well-functioning agency. Some may see a beehive of activity, organized chaos, like the newsroom of a large metropolitan newspaper or a campaign headquarters, with everyone on task and with few hard-and-fast rules to get in the way. Others may visualize the efficient and timely flow of paper, each worker generating the right forms filled out in just the right way, and someone always staying late to write those progress reports to the Legislature due twenty days before the beginning of each session. Still others may see a mega-system, believing that rules and organized structures must be respected to be consistent throughout the entire system. To break or bend the rules here or there might actually mean a lack of fair treatment for workers who do not have the good fortune to work in a more flexible, less rigid agency. Labor laws and contracts play a role here, but for the most part, I'm talking about the movement of paper and the willingness of people to focus on the product rather than the process. Predictability may be seen as a virtue by minor functionaries and a vice by newly appointed department heads bent on change. There is something to be said for all these views, but reconciling them within the public workforce can be a daunting task.

In 1992, Michael Barzelay authored a study of the bureaucratic model titled "Breaking through Bureaucracy." He outlined what most citizens imagine to be the internal workings of a large agency:

> Specific delegations of authority define each role in the executive branch. Officials carrying out any given role should act only when expressly permitted to do so either by rule or by instructions given by superior authorities in

the chain of command. Employees within the executive branch are responsible to their supervisors...

Experts in substantive matters - such as engineers, law enforcement personnel, and social service providers - should be assigned to line agencies, while experts in budgeting, accounting, purchasing, personnel, and work methods should be assigned to centralized staff functions...

Barzelay identified two essential elements that bedevil all large organizations: the decentralization of substantive expertise and the centralized control of budgetary and other central administrative control functions that are needed to implement any decision. In other words, the accountant can veto the dreams of the technocrat.

This is pretty dry stuff, yet it deserves the closer scrutiny of all policy makers. Remember, all these rules came into being at a time when big city political machines turned government into a spoils system. There is a lot of criticism of government today in that vein, but by comparison, today's state departments are squeaky-clean.

The professional bureaucratic ideal was described in 1946 by Max Weber, who saw merit in mechanistic clockworks of a system: "Precision, speed, unambiguity, knowledge of the files, continuity, discretion, unity, strict subordination, reduction of friction and of material and personal costs - these are raised to the optimum point in the strictly bureaucratic administration." So said Weber, and since then, his model of the objective and almost inhuman organization has persisted as the presumed alternative to cronyism and the subjective abuse of power.

Every organization of any appreciable size is commonly depicted with a chart consisting of a series of vertically connected boxes. This suggests that bureaucratic life is an essentially vertical relationship. Those who live and work in such environments also understand that such charts rarely describe how the organization actually works. There is a tension and a contradiction between the formal hierarchies and the informal functions. Not only are there informal networks and nodes of power and influence, the actual policy making may be too complex to rest on the shoulders of a single chief executive officer or CEO at the top.

As Lord Chesterfield once wrote: "You must look into people, as well as at them." A legislature needs to find ways to look more deeply and analytically into the agencies that form the building blocks of government.

LESSONS

1. Politicians tend to focus more on the individual personalities in a bureaucracy and less on the organizational structure.
2. Accountability can be poorly understood; this may result in counterproductive strategies being crudely imposed on the bureaucracy.
3. Organizational arteries are clogged by eight chronic diseases: memory loss, the pride of forms, desk-top parking, loss of urgency, black-box bafflement, grassroots demoralization, micro/macro confusion, and fear of failure. If reforms do not address these habits, real change is unlikely.
4. Technical knowledge is difficult for legislators to use appropriately.
5. Sabotage of distrusted new management is common.
6. Don't expect an organizational chart to tell you how an agency really works.
7. You must look into people, as well as at them.

8 | OUTSIDE THE BUREAUCRATIC BOX

••

Put things in their places, and they will put you in your place.

– Arab Proverb

A 1996 Harvard University study1 examined the impact of science and technology on state legislative functions. "The general incorporation of technology in our everyday life has meant that it's a factor in a lot more decisions," explained a staffer from Florida. "The issues that Florida faces as a legislature are exceedingly complex, and traditional structures simply don't adequately address the kinds of complex problems that we have to find solutions to," added a colleague. "Biotechnology is nothing my father ever dreamed of when he was in government, whereas now it's a big deal,' said a legislator from Wisconsin. Telecommunications was also mentioned as a highly complex issue about which legislators now need technical assistance in order to make informed decisions. "Legislators need to know such things as different bandwidths, what they can carry, the difference between copper wire and fiber optics, and what software technology is the best and not the one with the most political clout," explained a legislator from New Mexico. The Harvard study noted the following persistent technological issues facing all branches of government:

- Economic development: technology transfer; defense conversion; tax reform; trade issues, including gateway to North American Free Trade Agreement (NAFTA); biotechnology development; space port development and single-stage rocket technology; industrial extension service; technology incubators; mining technology; impact of technology on workers' compensation; strategic state planning and economic forecasting.

- Environment protection: water quality and quantity management; ambient air quality; wildlife and fisheries management; wetland protection; oil field cleanup; highand low-level radioactive waste storage/disposal; solid waste management; underground storage tank leakage; waste tire recycling; environmental trust fund; lead screening; asbestos removal; pesticide regulation; ozone layer depletion; biological diversity; land use; comparative risk assessment.

- Health care: telemedicine; cancer prevention; genetic engineering; licensing of genetic counselors; prison health; surrogate motherhood; disabilities research; medical technology development; infectious waste incineration; HIV testing; mammography equipment regulations; abortion.

Megan jones, David H. Guston, and Lewis M. Branscomb, *Informed Legislatures: Coping with Science in a Democracy*. University Press of America, Inc., 1996.

Time and technology are intertwined, conspiring against thoughtful policy-making and executive initiatives. As issues become increasingly complex, it is painfully obvious that state agencies are ill equipped to resolve them.

No-fault auto insurance reform was a difficult political challenge for government in Hawaii, but next to the health needs of a demographic tidal wave of baby-boomers who will soon become senior citizens, insurance reform looks simple and straightforward. As society becomes more complex and our population more diverse, it is fair to ask whether our current governmental structures are capable of meeting the challenge. Can government solve complex problems? What happens when you have a ticking time bomb and an appropriate response that never seems to arrive?

There is no way to avoid the megatrends facing our society because of our aging population. We can see these impacts in the growth of the aging population, their composition and status, the cost of delivering their health care, and the costs of assisted-living arrangements, especially in Hawaii.

ELDERLY POPULATION GROWTH

There has been significant growth in the percentage of the U.S. population that is over age 65. There were 16.7 million Americans in this age group in 1960, 25.7 million in 1980, and 33.9 million in 1996. Consider these future projections:

- By 2000 there will be 34.7 million.
- By 2010 there will be 39.4 million.
- By 2020 there will be 53.2 million.
- By 2030 there will be 69.4 million.

The Graying of Hawaii

	1990	2000	Change
United States			
Total Population	248,709,873	281,421,906	+13%
Median Age	32.9	35.3	+7.3%
Age 65 and over	31,241,831	34,991,753	+12%
Age 85 and over	3,080,165	4,239,587	+37.6%
Percentage 65 and over	12.6	12.4	
Percentage 85 and over	1.2	1.5	
Hawaii			
Total Population	1,108,229	1,211,537	+9%
Median Age	32.6	36.2	+11%
Age 65 and over	125,005	160,601	+28.5%
Age 85 and over	10,397	17,564	+69%
Percentage 65 and over	11.3	13.3	
Percentage 85 and over	0.9	1.4	

Source ; Honolulu Star-Bulletin table of U.S. Census data.

In 1900, 40% of the population was under the age of 18, and only 4% was over the age of 65. By 1980, these percentages had shifted to only 28% under the age of 18 and 11% over the age of 65. By 2030, it is estimated that 21% will be under 18, and 22% over the age of 65. The percentage of Americans 65 and over has more than tripled in this century (from 4.1% in 1900 to 12.8% in 1996), and the number has increased nearly elevenfold (from 3.1 million to 33.9 million.)

In Hawaii today, 11% of the population is over age 65. According to the state's Executive Office on Aging, more than 34% of the state's population is made up of baby boomers who will begin to join that group of older adults in the year 2011. There will be 380,000 such persons living in Hawaii, more than three times the current number.

COMPOSITION AND STATUS OF THE ELDERLY

There is also a dramatic shift to the very old, those over 85. In this population group, there is a corresponding rise in chronic ailments, as well as in impairments impacting the activities of daily living (ADLs). These include the ability to perform common chores of personal hygiene, the ability to prepare food, the ability to communicate (eyesight and hearing loss), the ability to walk, the ability to remember important tasks and information, the ability to take one's medicine on time, and so on.

In 1987, it was estimated that 5.9% of the population aged 65-69 had at least one ADL difficulty. This number rose to 7 .9% for ages 70-74; 11.5% for ages 75-79; 18.6% for ages 80-84; and 34.5% for those 85 and over.

After 65, with an average 17 years left to live, 6.5 of those years (or 38%) are expected to be spent in a highly dependent state, meaning either nursing home care or a home-based equivalent. At age 85, with an average of 7 years left to live, 4.4 years (or 63% of the remaining time) will be spent in a dependent state. These trends are expected to peak in the first few decades of the twenty-first century as the socalled baby-boomer generation ages.

THE COSTS OF HEALTH CARE FOR THE ELDERLY

The federal government has seen an unprecedented growth in its health care programs since 1960, when the annual cost was around $2.9 billion. This was before the enactment of Medicaid and Medicare in 1965. In 1970, it cost $17.8 billion; in 1980, $195 billion; and in 1993, $280 billion. This represents a 9655% increase over thirty years.

State and local government health expenditures rose from $3.7 billion in 1960 to $9.9 billion in 1970, to $33.3 billion in 1980, to $90.7 billion in 1990, and to $107.3 billion in 1993. This represents a 2900% increase.

Between 1960 and 1990, expenditures benefiting older adults increased from 15 to 30% of the federal budget. Over one-fourth of federal outlays is for Medicare. The federal government spent approximately $217 on each Medicare enrollee in 1967. Between 1975 and 1985 this figure rose from $585 to over $2000. By 1995, it was up to $4818, with a projected cost of $10,677 per enrollee by the year 2005, a 4920% increase. (Adjusted for changes in the Consumer Price Index, it is a 770% increase.)

The cost of health care for this population, using Medicare as an indicator, has gone from $7.3 billion in 1970 to $105 billion in 1980, to $696.9 billion in 1990. This represents over a 9500% increase.

Medicare enrollments grew from 19.5 million in 1967 to 25 million in 1975, 31.1 million in 1985, and 36.2 million in 1995. By 2005, it is estimated there will be 42.1 million enrollees.

Private sector spending has also grown at a rapid pace. Nursing home care cost America $4.9 billion in 1970. By 1993, this was up to $69.6 billion, in increase of 1420%.

During the same period, hospital-services costs rose 1066%, and physician-services costs 1159%. In 1993, the government paid roughly 63% of the nursing home bills, while private citizens paid over 33%. More than twice the amount of nursing home costs was spent on home- and community-based care.

These megatrends and mega-costs indicate that America in general and Hawaii in particular has a significant challenge ahead. This challenge is complicated by a political culture that rejects any increases in public expenditures.

In the 1970s at the Congressional level, the Pepper Commission focused an enormous amount of attention on the subject of aging, but little was done. When the health care reform movement swept the nation in the late 1980s and early 1990s, long-term care was not part of the agenda.

Likewise, in Hawaii there was a concerted effort to develop a statewide financing scheme for both community-based and institution based care. This too was set aside in the enthusiasm over universal access in the form of the State Health Insurance Program (SHIP). SHIP was not an easy scheme to design or implement, but it was depicted as a relatively smaller drain on the budget, only about $10 million a year. Its client base was limited to about 20,000 residents who fell into an insurance gap.

One must pose the following questions: Why has our political and governmental system failed to adequately address the long-term care issue? Are there elements of our system that work against complex and potentially costly programs? If we look closely at this failure, might we be led to a series of reforms that would create a system that is better able to cope with issues such as long-term care?

The health care system itself is among the most complex. Policy makers seldom have the time to become well acquainted with its dynamics, and there is too little time to educate generalist legislators, let alone engage them in a sober deliberation of the merits of this or that reform. Policy-making structures (departments, agencies, legislative committees) are often unable to cross jurisdictional lines to cope with systems that cannot be easily fit into a simple organizational chart. Data required to integrate disparate parts of the health system are not available and would be very difficult to develop. In times of economic distress, such as Hawaii is currently experiencing, limited funding tends to reduce collaboration.

Our basic challenge is to design

1. a political system better able to address complex issues like long-term care,
2. a policy-making management system (both public and private) appropriate for longterm care issues and clients, and
3. a bureaucratic structure flexible enough to transcend agency boundaries.

OUTSIDE OF THE BOX

Long-term care issues, particularly those that deal with naturally occurring communities and community-based and client-based services, require a rethinking as to how to organize for the future. Large, second wave bureaucracies, as described in 1980 by Alvin Toffler in The Third Wave, simply will not work.

Exploration of alternative delivery systems and organizational structures is not new. Recent efforts in Hawaii include University of Hawaii professor Dr. Eldon Wegner's investigation of the new German long-term care insurance plan, and a pre-proposal concept paper from the Executive Office on Aging that combines concerns such as personal financing, self-determination, and empowerment of consumers.

The German system incorporated benefits not usually associated with the realm of health insurance, including personal services for ADL-type tasks, such as transferring, bathing, toileting, and eating; household help services for shopping, cooking, laundry, and housecleaning; and payments for emergency alarm systems, home renovations, and wheelchairs. The need for these services creates a tension between conventional organizational and insurance delivery systems and the type of agency required to provide them successfully.

Even those in academic medicine pondered the nature of the new approaches: Can medicine's institutions reorganize to deal with the elderly's health-related needs that have not traditionally been the province of medicine? As a society, we need to take into account the nature of community and the individual as we contemplate how to manage when 20% of the population is over age 65 ... Perhaps more important is what we think a community is. In the past, community was at root a matter of geography. Communities were people who lived together. Today we often consider a community to be those who are like ourselves, in ethnicity, ideas, pastimes. (Editorial, *Academic Medicine*, 1997)

In November 1998, a group of university and community leaders began meeting to design a new elder-wellness delivery system. They identified a number of key assumptions to guide their efforts. These included:

1. Like the rest of the nation, Hawaii will experience an elderly population explosion. Over 34% of the population are baby boomers, who by 2011 will number 380,000 persons, more than three times the current older adult population.

In addition, there are over 20,000 nonelderly disabled who currently require services similar to those the elderly require.

2. A significant number of elderly or disabled persons are relatively healthy, have adequate housing, and enjoy some disposable income. However, they are isolated, uncertain as to what services they need, and anxious about what would happen in the event of an illness that might compromise their physical or financial independence.

3. This relatively healthy cohort of seniors and disabled individuals cannot afford expensive assisted living arrangements, and most do not qualify for government assistance.

4. Affordable social services delivered through a nonmedical model for large numbers are generally not available for a substantial portion of the gap group, nor are consumerdeveloped and consumer-driven activities and services.

5. Intergenerational workforce models (such as high school students, college students, and older adults) offer several opportunities to develop skills, provide quality care, and create commu-organizational model in which a computer network links existing resources with clients and facilitates the creation of gap services where none exist today.

The Wisteria Project operates outside the box on a number of levels. First, it disdains the larger sources of government funding (Medicaid and Medicare) in order to preclude those programs from dictating the scope and nature of the project.

Second, it seeks to combine similar but not yet collaborative efforts, such as the school-to-work program, the college-based Service Learning Program, Americorps Volunteers, church volunteers, and a workforce using high school students, college students, and people now on welfare.

Third, it thoroughly rejects the usual bureaucratic structure in favor of a cluster of equal partnerships among participating agencies and leaders.

Fourth, it seeks to engage its clients as co-designers in their own benefit packages, and consciously avoids terminology with pejorative implications, such as insurance, health care, or patients.

And fifth, it intends to use communication technology to the fullest to overcome spatial and individual barriers to services.

The Wisteria approach seeks to maximize potential collaborative energies and resources in ways that most agencies find not only difficult, but also incomprehensible. Consider its stated objectives:

- To link and complement the efforts of the dedicated people and programs already active in community-based health and social services for the elderly and disabled, especially churches, natural geographic communities, and nonprofit organizations.
- To create a financially sound complementary service system for subscribers in the senior-citizen gap group that is designed to enhance and maintain their physical and financial independence.
- To develop a continuous training pipeline that incorporates experiential and project-based learning, especially through the University of Hawaii's service learning programs and the Department of Education's school-to-work initiative.
- To support well-paying jobs in community-based services, especially for motivated and qualified people on welfare, college students, and high school students.
- To pursue the above goals in a manner that increases our knowledge of natural communities, elderly and disabled consumers, and appropriate and effective delivery systems.

The Wisteria Project's participants recognize that in today's institutional climate the issue is not why government cannot come to grips with the megatrends discussed above, but rather how a collection or a network of mostly nonprofit entities can create a process and a type of organization that can achieve success in a Third Wave economy based on information.

Even for the enlightened few, the Wisteria experiment will be a challenge. It is difficult to reconcile traditional academic curiosity and the infatuation with information with the need for a stable, ongoing, self-sustaining enterprise. If the organizers of Wisteria succeed, they will have created a new form of organizational life that is often dreamed of, but seldom attained.

WISTERIA INSIDE THE BUREAUCRACY?

A much more difficult challenge is to adapt the nonprofit organizational partnerships that are at the core of Wisteria to the internal workings of a large governmental department. Several incremental steps could facilitate this adaptation:

- "Volunteer" internal staff could be assigned to work as extension agents in nonprofit organizations as part of their regular work assignments. This would be, in essence, a form of subsidy for the nonprofits, and it would reorient the civil servants to the nonprofit world.
- Collective bargaining agreements would need to be negotiated with explicit allowance for off-site work, with appropriate compensation for travel, etc.
- Legal guidelines would need to be drawn up to ensure that the relationships would indeed be consistent with public duties and policies. For example, a public health nurse could be working either at a state facility or at a nonprofit community health center. The job description and duties would be the same; only the physical setting would be different. However, by co-locating with the nonprofit, the nurse would represent a new partnership with little or no bureaucratic supervision from the internal hierarchy.
- Flexible "partnership funds" would need to be carved out of the budget to allow for the development of an advisory committee (kitchen cabinet) made up of both internal and external participants who would collectively allocate these funds to accomplish public purposes. This is not too different from the allocation of purchase of service funds or grants-in-aid, but it would be a more extensive and formalized version of these systems.

- Administrative reallocation of funds could be allocated to support interdepartmental projects. A small council of agency representatives would need to convene with the basic informal agreement and authority to commit and restrict funds to projects that crossed jurisdictional lines and that contributed more effectively to the mission.
- The volunteer provisions of Chapter 90 of the Hawaii Revised Statutes would need to be used more aggressively to allow external agencies to loan experts to a department while continuing to pay them, thereby contributing to the breakdown of the distinctions between public and private workers and agencies.
- Data collection and analysis (and the necessary hardware) would need to be contracted to the private sector. One of the most difficult elements of coordination is the incompatible and proprietary attitude toward computers and information systems. It is better to share state-of-the-art services with the private sector and thus ensure that incompatibility of technology is not a barrier.
- "Town and gown" kitchen cabinets (made up of private sector and university people) would need to be established for each department head, division head, and branch chief. Bridging town and gown has always been difficult, and the more the university people interact with line agency people, the better both worlds will come to understand each other and appreciate common goals and resources. But this advisory arrangement cannot be an end in itself. It must evolve toward a kind of friendly audit and policy commentary for the line agencies. Otherwise, it will just be another meeting among many other meetings, and the leaders will assign nonpolicy underlings to sit in for them.
- Each department should develop a school-to-work or service learning activity in each section and program. This would infuse the personnel with the pride of teaching, while also infusing the agencies with the energy and "why can't we do it this way?" perspectives of learners. Community health centers that participate in such programs find that they are enriched

and invigorated by the presence of the young people they are mentoring. It also leads to more analysis and reflection on the missions and jobs of agencies.

- A three-year organizational evaluation would need to be designed to match the most current and pressing needs with the proper structures and personnel. For this to be useful, the Legislature must grant generic reorganization authority to the executive branch. • The authority of the state Department of Human Resources Development to overrule departmental judgment in job descriptions and minimum qualifications must be abolished. It is too difficult and too protracted a process just to hire someone who is qualified. • A standard yearly bonus should be provided for civil servants who volunteer for community service projects in work-related areas (generally reviewed and approved by the department). This would further encourage community-based perspectives and a sense of urgency, which the external people often feel more acutely than the internal people.

Executive leaders who encourage the above policies and programs will move public agencies and workers toward a greater link with the private sector and the consumers/clients of their services. They will also blur hierarchies and organizational charts in an effort to tap individual talents and knowledge that are often inaccessible in the bureaucratic world.

The bureaucratic organization of the future, if it is to be capable of forming partnerships that respond to challenges that cut across traditional agency lines, will need to become less of an entity and more of a process. Yes, partnerships can be planned and formally established, but more importantly, they can evolve and mature. The multiplicity of human services required by a huge aging population will demand both flexibility and capacity. These two attributes have, in the industrialoriented Second Wave society, been at odds with each other. In the information- oriented Third Wave society, capacity will depend on mobility and evolution.

Without innovation within state agencies, it is difficult to see how even a better-informed, more enlightened Legislature can cope with the pace of change that time and technology are demanding. You can't fix the box from inside. You've got to get outside.

LESSONS

1. Legislative bodies have a difficult time coping with technology and other complex issues. In fact, all of government is challenged by the growth of technology. Generalists are asked to make decisions without the time or technical knowledge required to ensure sound policies.
2. The tidal wave of baby-boomers about to become senior citizen and the need for expanded long-term care services are pressing issues that both federal and state lawmakers have been unable and unwilling to address. The number of seniors and the skyrocketing costs of their care threaten to overwhelm government at all levels. The failure to enact the recommendations of the Pepper Commission at the federal level or the Executive Office on Aging's long-term care financing plan in Hawaii are evidence that both the executive and legislative branches of government need reform.
3. There are efforts to design systems that overcome the current limitations of bureaucracy, but they require greater innovation and flexibility.
4. There are strategies designed to blur the membranes between public and private institutions without threatening the job security of public workers.

9 | THE POLITICS OF HEALTH IN HAWAII

All sorts of bodily diseases are produced by half used minds.

— George Bernard Shaw

Everything to be said about Hawaii and health care must be put in the context of an ongoing, tragic failure: Hawaii's Native Hawaiians have among the worst health statistics in our state. Not only does the host culture suffer from higher disease rates, but markers for future disease, known as risk factors, are also high. Native Hawaiians have the highest incidence of hypertension and obesity. Surveys indicate they drink and drive more often than other groups, and engage in acute drinking at higher rates. Just under 20% of Hawaii's residents are smokers, while over 27% of Native Hawaiians regularly light up. On August 17, 1999, the Honolulu Advertiser ran the front-page headline, "Hawaiian health record 'a disgrace." Hawaii's senior U.S. Senator, Daniel K. Inouye, was pictured at yet another public hearing on the subject. Discouraging data on Native Hawaiian health has become one of those clichés that is mentioned so often that the population has become numb. The average person may feel that something should be done, but all of us in government must admit that whatever has been done has not been effective.

I began my political career not focused on health but as a self-proclaimed environmentalist. I knew our environmental laws and regulations and how they worked or failed to work. In the 1970s, it was both fashionable and appropriate to resist the developers and to support the citizen advocates and scientists who were devoted to preserving Hawaii's beauty and ecological balance. For the first two years of my legislative life, 1985 and 1986, I served on the House environmental committees, and wanted to be an influential player in the implementation of a future water code for the state. Unfortunately, my ability to make an immediate impact was diminished by the fact that I had joined a group of eleven other representatives in a failed coup attempt to overthrow the powerful Speaker of the House, Henry Peters.

Among those who entered legislative "Siberia" in our opposition to Henry were Danny Kihano Oater Speaker of the House), Mazie Hirono (later lieutenant governor), Russell Blair (later a judge), Ray Graulty (later a state senator, an insurance commissioner, and recently a judge), Donna Kim Oater a City Council member, now in the Senate), Rod Tam (later a state senator), Romy Cachola (a House member, now on the City Council), and David Hagino. I was in fine company. It was a good way to start a legislative career because it taught me to think about the big picture, and how the Legislature could be a more effective, democratic, and ethical institution.

During the summer of my second year, 1986, a veteran lawmaker from Kauai, Richard Kawakami, decided Henry's conflict of interest as a new trustee for the Bishop Estate was an opportunity for his kind of leadership. He began gathering supporters in the House, including those of us who had opposed Henry two years before. When he finally won a narrow majority of democrats, Richard proceeded to reorganize the leadership of the committees.

Kawakami wanted someone to chair the Committee on Health and to tackle the rising costs of health care for the public and the state. I am not sure whose idea it was to offer me the chair of the committee, but I do remember it took some persuading. I wanted to be a leader in the environment, a realm in which I felt knowledgeable and comfortable.

It was an ideal time to make the switch, and I will always be grateful to Kawakami for giving me the opportunity. Health opened up an entirely new segment of the community, those who provided health services. I found the laws that governed them and the politics that drove them to be an exciting and challenging environment.

This is one of those examples of change and opportunity that could never be planned or orchestrated. I did not seek it. I did not even imagine it. I certainly lacked the credentials to be a logical candidate for the position.

Advocacy for the environment requires the ability to relate to the natural environment, finding passion not with people but with ecosystems. You go for hikes in the rain forest, visit an isolated beach threatened by plans for a hotel, contemplate saving an endangered species, or ride on a boat cleaning up an oil spill in Pearl Harbor. It is no accident that so many leaders of Hawaii's environmental community came from the mainland, with images of urban pollution and ruined wilderness areas dancing in their heads. They have seen how bad it can get, and they fight hard to prevent such degradation in paradise.

Advocacy for health, on the other hand, requires involvement with individual and community-wide health problems that cannot be separated from the very personal stories and lives of people who meet you face-to-face. You are escorted through a mental hospital with patients locked behind doors. You meet with the terminally ill, the disabled, and the victims of abuse. You bend down to speak in the ear of the frail elderly woman in a wheelchair. You visit awkwardly with teenage mothers holding their infants. You attend a meeting at a Hawaiian homestead community center, the only haole (Caucasian) in the room. Public life is given a human face. This particular shift in focus forced me to expand my knowledge, my personal contacts, my sensitivity, and the way in which I saw the world.

Health was becoming a very hot issue in 1987. A new Native Hawaiian governor, John Waihee, chose as his health director an energetic and creative physician from Maui, Dr. Jack Lewin. Jack was full of new ideas, and we seemed to hit it off immediately. He was not embedded in the usual special interests of health care: the medical association, the hospitals, the insurance companies, or the pharmaceutical firms. Before coming to Hawaii, Jack Lewin got his feet wet trying to bring desperately needed primary care to Native Americans.

In 1987, there were new, controversial issues, not the least of which was how to deal with the human immunodeficiency virus (HIV) and AIDS. AIDS forced the health care world, as well as the political world, to confront its prejudices and stereotypes. Because HIV spread initially through the gay community in the United States, issues of social justice, equal treatment, confidentially, affordability of new drugs, and public funding for outreach to unpopular groups became heated public health issues. Of all the conferences I was privileged to attend, none was as exciting and informative as the International AIDS Conferences in Washington, D.C., and Montreal.

There was also a renewed commitment to challenge the tobacco companies, as Surgeon General Koop elevated this to a national debate. There was the deinstitutionalization of the mentally ill and the developmentally disabled. There was alcohol and drug abuse, especially among the young. There was an outrageous rate of tooth decay, and we proposed to fluoridate the drinking water. Almost overnight, a sleepy legislative committee became the focal point of controversial issues and intense media coverage. In the background, growing as a national movement was a sense that the entire health care system needed reform. The primary advocate for this view was a young and articulate governor from Arkansas, Bill Clinton.

In the past, those who chaired the House Committee on Health tended to be comfortable as advocates for the health care establishment. Hospitals, physicians, and insurance companies contributed generously to their campaigns. They tended not to rock the boat. Perhaps in their defense, there was not yet a clear, alternative agenda to pursue, even if they had wanted to be less than cozy with the establishment.

Nationally, the health care establishment was developing a tarnished reputation. Between 1980 and 1992, the proportion of the population not covered by some form of health insurance increased by 22%. Out-of-pocket expenses rose by 42%, while funding for health administrators quadrupled. Physicians made nearly seven times the average wage in 1992, and the profits of the top twenty pharmaceutical companies had recorded yearly increases of 15% for the previous ten years. During the 1980s, the health insurance industry's political action committees contributed $60 million to key members of Congress.

The controversies that most Hawaii legislators remembered before Waihee and Lewin were turf fights between different health professions. Ophthalmologists resisted efforts by optometrists to gain more independence and authority in their practice. Physicians resisted efforts by advanced practice nurses to gain the right to prescribe medications. These are not pleasant disputes for generalist legislators to resolve. Arguments tend to become highly technical in two ways. First, the dangers to the patient of unqualified professional treatment are complex and require a sound knowledge of biology and medications. Second, the evidence that optometrists or nurses have performed well in other states where they have been given broader legal authority is often highly dependent on statistical analysis. This, too, is an area generalist politicians are often unable to fully comprehend.

It is not surprising that without a strong point of view one way or the other, legislators will tend to take the side of the most powerful status quo interest groups. These interests are certainly better financed, and anxious to reward those who will uphold their prominent position in both the pecking order and the reimbursement game.

There is an excellent book by Paul Starr titled The Transformation of American Medicine. Starr traces the history of the medical profession and how it came to dominate the delivery of health care. It is a fascinating tale, including how members of the American Medical Association (AMA) opposed mandatory insurance during the 1950s, 1960s, and 1970s, and then came to be its most highly paid beneficiaries. In a stroke of political public-relations genius, during the anticommunist McCarthy era of the 1950s, the AMA came up with the phrase "socialized medicine" to stigmatize efforts to provide widespread insurance coverage. You can still find use of this term today as conservative groups attack plans to extend basic health insurance coverage to those millions of Americans without it. The interplay between the physician community and the insurance companies has continued to this day as a persistent source of tension.

Perhaps the most dominant journal of the health care establishment is Health Affairs. This journal, which began its inaugural issue with an article by Ronald Reagan's budget guru David Stockman, has provided a great deal of coverage of the 6500 hospitals, 600,000 physicians, 54,000 pharmacies, and countless insurance companies who have dominated the delivery of health care in America. Through the 1990s, there were very few articles on the nursing profession or any other group other than physicians. Health Affairs, as the voice of the establishment, was also not printing many articles about alternative care, primary care for the poor, community-based clinics, environmental health, or public health efforts to prevent disease.

When Jack Lewin became director of health for the state of Hawaii, his view was that the health care establishment was unwilling or unable to deliver care to the marginalized groups in society, such as Native Hawaiians, and that the care enjoyed by the middle class tended to be short on prevention and high on treating illness. Lewin's vision was to shift the efforts of the state from providing illness care to promoting wellness and universal access to basic health care. This was in a state that, by all accounts, had a higher percentage of insurance coverage for our population than any other in the United States.

Along came Jim Shon as chair of the Health Committee with little knowledge and little political baggage involving the politics of health care, perfectly willing to challenge that establishment on as many fronts as possible. At another time, in another place, I might have been forced to just tinker with the system as my predecessors had. I was lucky. My ignorance of the powerful forces involved in the health care industry, along with a national movement for reform and a lively, iconoclastic, peripatetic health director, made it possible to pursue a stimulating agenda.

Looking back, I'm sure many of our initiatives could have been more successful with a more incremental or diplomatic approach. On the other hand, some of our successes can be directly attributed to a willingness to go for broke.

One advantage I enjoyed was that the voters of my district were a mixture of old-time Democrats, conservative Republicans, and independents. I felt they would appreciate someone who did not beat around the bush in shaking up the establishment. On a purely political level, my perception was probably unjustified, but the fact is that I was convinced that a middle-of-the-road, wishy-washy performance was the pathway to defeat. I had many close reelection campaigns, and to this day I'm not sure if my willingness to challenge powerful interests was a positive or a negative in the minds of voters.

It may be that these issues were simply not of great importance to my constituents, most of whom did have health insurance - and those who didn't were the least likely to vote. The campaign money of the health care establishment flowed toward my opponents who, for the most part, did not run on an alternative health care platform. They used the hospital and physician contributions to produce brochures to tell voters how I was soft on crime, or a big liberal spender, or whatever the hot-button issue of the year was.

The politics of health is not a passionate issue for the majority of voters in Hawaii. Health insurance is taken for granted. The rights of people with HN are not on their minds. They are unaware of funding for the mentally ill, unless they have a family member who needs those services. The homeless are often invisible. Native Hawaiian health issues have not been of great concern to non-Hawaiian voters, and Hawaiians themselves tend to vote in lower percentages than the general population in Hawaii.

It is extraordinary how the Clinton proposals for national health reform were able to penetrate the political consciousness of so many Americans. A careful analysis of how the opponents were able to frame the issue as one of big, nosy government versus personal freedom is instructive. Once it was no longer a hope that health insurance would become cheaper for the average American, and once the voters grew tired of hearing about those 41 million uninsured, the electorate began to drift back toward the anti-government philosophy promoted by Ronald Reagan. Republican spin doctors effectively framed the issue: To be for national health care reform was to be for big government. That perspective meant that the nuts and bolts of universal access, improved services, and a reorientation toward wellness and prevention would be lost in the battle over the role and size of government.

In Hawaii, because of the large percentage of residents who were covered by employer-based health insurance, the efforts to change the system came to depend on appealing to people's consciences and mobilizing the nonprofit organizations that so often were able to see at firsthand the failings of the current system. As in many states, Hawaii's governmental budget people were quick to notice the growing demand on the state to provide its share of Medicaid funds for the poor. Small businesses, with a greater burden to pay health premiums, also yearned for reform, but their preference was to eliminate mandated health insurance altogether.

The struggle to include preventive services, such as well-baby checkups, as part of everyone's regular insurance package is an interesting example of the politics of health in our state. While Hawaii's dominant health maintenance organization, Kaiser Permanente, had such services, the majority of residents (about 60%) were insured by the Hawaii Medical Services Association (HMSA), which is the local Blue Cross/Blue Shield insurance plan in Hawaii. HMSA plans allowed people to choose almost any physician in the state, but required the patient to pay 20% of the cost out of pocket. Each service, including referrals for access to expensive technology, had its own set cost and reimbursement, known as "fee for service." The more patients who walked through the door, the more the doctor would earn. The more X-rays, C-section births, or MRIs ordered, the more patients were charged and providers were paid. The economic bias in fee-forservice insurance is to over-treat. In 1987, HMSA did not reimburse physicians for well-baby check-ups as part of the benefit package. I thought that was not only unreasonable, but also unwise. Why not make sure the infants were healthy rather than spend more later to treat more serious illness?

At the time, HMSA decided it would oppose all efforts by the legislature to require new mandated benefits. They took the same position with mammograms, mental health treatment, and in-vitro fertilization. HMSA represented a highly respected segment of the business community that felt these preventive services would tap a hidden demand and increase the overall cost of health care. In the past, the views of HMSA prevailed at the state Capitol. During the WaiheeLewin years, however, they were on the losing side. A combination of public health advocates in the Legislature, a new proactive health director, and the national movement toward health reform made it increasingly difficult for HMSA to derail new, mandated, preventive services.

An important political struggle to control the impacts of tobacco in Hawaii illustrates the attitudes of many segments of our island community toward public health. Tobacco smoke had been identified as Class A carcinogen. This meant it was just as likely to cause cancer as other dangerous substances, such as asbestos. Even secondhand smoke was implicated during this period. The serious implications of this scientific information made it impossible to ignore the regulation of smoking as a priority for the Legislature.

Tobacco politics also provided one of those rare occasions where liberal Democrats and conservative Republicans were in agreement. Those born-again Christians who had been elected in the 1980s were anxious to restrict any behavior they considered sinful. Those driven by the science of public health were anxious to prevent disease. The only other similar issue that brought these two groups together was opposition to organized gambling.

In spite of the hard evidence and the leadership of outspoken Surgeon General C. Everett Koop, the business community was slow to accept controls. Restaurants were convinced they would lose customers, as were many in the visitor industry, who noted that Asian visitors tended to be smokers. Corporation executives who smoked cared little for schemes to restrict their habits inside the workplace. Even the unions were slow to recognize that their workers were essentially captives of secondhand, cancer-causing pollution, and many of the union leaders were smokers themselves.

I recall one year sitting at a very large table at the headquarters of the Hawaii Government Employee Association, Hawaii's largest public union, which represents nearly all the white-collar government workers in the state. I was there to be interviewed for a possible endorsement in the next election. HGEA had usually supported my candidacy because I was generally sympathetic to their workers and to union issues. My father had been a member of a trade union all his life, and I appreciated the advocacy of unions for the working people of Hawaii.

During the interview, conducted by a committee of some thirty union representatives, at least one-fourth of those at the table were smoking. I was upset that in the previous session they had not supported my proposals to restrict smoking in the workplace. It was obvious that they were not sympathetic. Perhaps I was feeling a little overconfident, but I remember chiding them for their insensitive behavior and policies. They were contributing to the ill health of their own membership, and seemed unconcerned about it. Their minds told them I was right, but the nicotine in their systems overruled their responsibilities to HGEA members.

A few legislators pounded away at the tobacco industry year after year. I remember Representative Joan Hayes as one of the earlier advocates for tobacco control, as were Senator Mary Jane McMurdo, Senator Bert Kobayashi, Senator Andy Levin, and Representatives David Hagino and Fred Hemmings, to name a few. We were up against perhaps the most accomplished and powerful lobbyist in our state, Red Morris, who represented the tobacco firms. When we proposed restricting the free distribution of cigarettes, a ploy to get younger citizens to take up the habit, we realized we had hit a raw nerve in tobacco land. An army of tobacco attorneys in their expensive suits descended on the state Capitol in an effort to intimidate legislators. They were able to derail the offending bill, but they were unable to prevent tobacco from becoming a controversial issue.

At one point, the tobacco lobbyists decided to sponsor a performance of the Bolshoi Ballet. 0 wondered if it was a coincidence that a large number of the Russian dancers were smokers!) They installed their agents in an expensive hotel and sent complimentary tickets to most of the Legislature. (A few of us who did not receive this bribe felt honored to be so identified as beyond their influence.) A good many opponents of smoking rationalized their acceptance of the tickets. "It will not influence my vote," they insisted. This issue blew up in their faces when a front-page newspaper article quoted me and a few others as disappointed that any legislator would accept anything from those lobbyists. My colleagues who got caught were not happy about the public embarrassment, especially since it was generated by a fellow legislator. The incident is indicative of the public's ambivalent attitude toward forcing changes in personal habits and restrictions on personal freedom. Big Tobacco was not yet the big villain it has now become.

Those were the days before sensational court settlements and jury awards. Today, if you mention tobacco, nine out of ten government officials in Hawaii will begin to salivate over the yearly payments ranging from $38 million in the year 2000 to several consecutive years of $50 million deposited into state coffers. By the year 2025, Hawaii will collect over $1.1 billion.

Public health initiatives designed to require us to use seat belts, or refrain from drinking alcohol when pregnant, or wear helmets while riding motorcycles must directly confront the American mythology of personal freedom. Sex, wealth, personal control, rebellion, masculinity, and liberation have all been key marketing themes associated with unhealthy behavior. Cigarette companies have even tried to associate the women's liberation movement with smoking. Virginia Slims is a prominent advertiser at Hawaii's malls, depicting fashionably dressed, attractive young women with cigarettes. They sponsor women's sporting events, as do companies selling alcohol.

There is also a strong liberal tradition that resists these impositions on personal freedom. For years, the motorcycle helmet law was stopped cold by a liberal Kauai Democrat who chaired the Senate Transportation Committee. The debate over helmet laws was part of a growing internal struggle for the philosophical soul of the Democratic Party. We could show how many permanently damaged head-injury victims were supported by the state, and calculate the millions saved in a universally helmeted society. The citizens who came forward with their tragic stories of loved ones permanently damaged provided heart-wrenching testimony in support of new laws. On the other side, opponents argued that the evidence was inconclusive and that helmets might actually be more dangerous as a cause of neck injuries. They could mobilize larger numbers of freedom-loving bikers with leather jackets and tattoos. As one often counted among the most socially liberal, I was sometimes torn between the citizen's traditional right to choose and the government's traditional health and safety responsibilities.

Within the public health community there are philosophical contradictions. People should be made to wear seatbelts and prevented from smoking, yet the state should respect the privacy of those testing positive for the AIDS virus. Your personal life is no business of a government bureaucrat, yet insurance companies could raise your rates if you were a known smoker. Even employers were seen to have a legitimate interest in high-risk behavior of employees outside of work. Testing for chemical dependency, whether it obviously affects behavior or not, has become almost routine.

In a recent book on public health, Marketing Public Health: Strategies to Promote Social Change, Michael Siegel and Lynne Doner advocate turning the freedom arguments around to work in favor of social controls:

- Freedom: By not smoking, you can remain free of the power of nicotine.
- Independence: Be independent of the tobacco corporations.
- Control: Be in control of your own image, don't let tobacco define you.
- Identity: Don't be manipulated into behaviors by advertising. Be your own person.
- Rebellion: Rebel against these corporate giants trying to addict you.

A similar litany can be developed for advocating safe sex or eating healthy foods. The point here is that many public health measures, while they may make perfect sense and save government and society millions of dollars and lives, are not willingly embraced by American culture. Our efforts to move Hawaii toward health promotion and disease prevention put us in direct conflict not only with corporate interests, but also with many citizens. Not all voters were happy about my role in making their personal habits illegal.

One advantage we had in the 1980s was that the state of Hawaii had a substantial budget surplus. This meant that we did not have to rely solely on the passage of restrictive laws. We could create publicly funded programs. A good example was the peer education program for high school students. The legal basis for the program, enacted in 1992, was brief:

Hawaii Revised Statutes, Section 321- 241.5: The department of health, in cooperation with the department of education, may establish a statewide teenage health program designed to enhance self-esteem, facilitate communication between students and their parents, incorporate ho'o'pono'pono techniques in group

185

discussions, expand peer counseling efforts, and provide more counseling opportunities. In implementing this program, the department shall strive to respect and include the diverse needs and values of parents and teens served by the program.

In the spring of 1998, a series of newspaper articles praised the Peer Education Program (PEP), which now operates in about twenty-six high schools and involves over 800 students. PEP began as an attempt to transform the peer group from a source of temptation to a source of support and problem solving. It was based on the notion that selfesteem is a crucial ingredient for healthy teenage lives. It was conceived in part by the hard work and insight of others who pioneered a number of similar programs at private schools.

Part of the credit goes to a dedicated health educator, JoAnn Tsark, who took the time to explain to me the importance of selfesteem and the power of the peer group in influencing behavior.

It is the program of which I am most proud. I wrote the fairly brief enabling language, which, incidentally, is the first time the Hawaiian term ho'o'pono'pono (a Native Hawaiian mediation and reconciliation process) was used in Hawaii's state law. It was initially funded not by the Department of Education, but by the Department of Health. This was by design, for if the PEP program were simply just another class, it probably would not gain the kind of trust and acceptance required to have a positive impact on teenagers. Based on the feedback from PEP faculty leaders and students who have participated in the program, there is no doubt that it has saved lives. Not too many programs can say that.

One lesson we can learn from the Peer Education Program is that everything worthwhile in our community is really a partnership of many contributors. Without the intelligence and dedication of people who work with teens every day - not something many people would volunteer for these days - programs like PEP would never have a chance. It is part of the idealism and the inherent goodness of public service.

Another lesson we can learn is that just the right support at the right time and in the right place can transform frustration into satisfaction. The Department of Education and the Department of Health were not able to collaborate to create PEP It took a legislative intervention to overcome their disparate cultures and missions. The outside intervener is an absolute necessity in our age of complex institutions, and the Legislature is positioned to play this role if it wants to.

Perhaps the most powerful issue that drove the politics of health was AIDS. In the late 1980s, Hawaii and the nation were confronted with an uncomfortable conflict: Public sensibilities over sexuality demanded that we shield our youth from explicit sexual material. At the same time, a growing number of young people (both gay and straight) were sexually active and at risk for venereal disease, hepatitis B, and HIV. Hawaii's nonprofit AIDS education and service organization, the Life Foundation, was able to secure a small amount of state funds in the mid-1980s for health education. They produced a brochure that was meant for outreach workers and their clients on the streets and that was, frankly, rather shocking in its explicit advice on how to protect oneself. The initial response of the political and legislative system was so hysterical that when I think back on it, I still am overcome with tear-filled laughter.

A number of legislators saw the materials and objected to the use of state funds to print such sexually explicit materials. Their means of protest was a comedy of errors. In an effort to expose and castigate the authors, they actually reproduced the offensive content in a House resolution. Instead of a few dozen copies of a brochure circulating among street kids, literally thousands of copies were printed and distributed to the Capitol community. And anyone walking into the print shop could obtain, free of charge, explicit directions relating to sexual acts!

This was my first exposure to the issues relating to AIDS, and I thought little about it until I became Health chair in 1987, a time when HIV prevention had become an important part of the public health agenda. That year, I helped draft an omnibus AIDS funding bill, one of the first in the nation to deliver a significant amount of funds to private nonprofits in the fight against this disease. Omnibus funding bills in mental health and other areas soon followed. To his credit, Finance chair Joe Souki supported our bill.

During this period, we supported confidentiality as a cornerstone in gaining trust and compliance in the community. There was near hysteria among some to strike out at gays and lesbians for their part in the initial spread of the disease. I had the advantage of attending numerous of conferences and enjoying the support of an international community dedicated to a sane approach to this public health threat. Many of my colleagues deserve even more credit, for without these advantages they stood up to harsh conservative forces and supported our bills.

Unlike the more recent clashes over same-sex marriage, HIV and AIDS policy in Hawaii stands out as a beacon of reason and good sense. The volatility over the early transmission of HIV through the gay community was held in check by the extraordinary efforts of public health advocates and professionals, who recognized that the pursuit of public health could be done compatibly with the defense of individual civil liberties. A huge coalition, put together by true community leaders, such as public and civil liberties advocate Pam Lichty, was able to push through legislative approval of the first state-sanctioned needle exchange program, convincing even the law enforcement community that simply locking people up could be counterproductive. (News articles in the spring of 2002 are still crediting this program with Hawaii's significant reduction in reported new cases of HIV)

The lesson of HIV and the needle exchange program for our democracy is that you really can buck the tide by diligent and persistent organization. Coalitions can be built, pressure can be applied, and minds can be changed. It is a lesson of hope. Democracy is capable of harnessing knowledge and reason, even at a time when scapegoats are being sought. A second lesson of the HIV policy experience in Hawaii is that there is no substitute for having sympathetic legislative gatekeepers. As Health chair, it was my role to endorse and fight for their cause. I could have, with little risk, bottled-up all those bills in my committee. There was at the time a growing conservative religious movement seen as a potential political threat to those who might "flirt with the devil" on social issues such as abortion or gay rights. They made it clear who they would go after in the next election.

The legislative system is designed to support committee chairs who serve as gatekeepers for controversial proposals. The power of the needle exchange coalition was only consummated when the key committee chairs gave it a green light. Thus, the third lesson is that gatekeepers by themselves cannot succeed, nor can coalitions achieve legislative success without the support of sympathetic and well-placed elected officials. This was a dance between community-based advocates and elected officials that did work. This was a case where you really could not tell who was leading and who was following.

THE INSURANCE SYSTEM AND MANAGED CARE

In April 1997, Richard Meiers, the president and CEO of the Healthcare Association of Hawaii, an affiliation of hospitals and longterm care institutions, estimated that as many as 131,000 Hawaii residents might be without health insurance - representing 12% of the population and including at least 8% of the children. He noted that it was difficult to say just how many were not covered on paper, or what exactly was happening to them in terms of illness Meiers's remarks were made at the same time the Legislature was engaged in a spirited debate over the wisdom of granting health benefit to same-gender couples. Leaders in the House were insisting that the cost of providing these health benefits would be too great a burden on both government and private business.

What was known was that community health centers were seeing larger percentage of uninsured patients, averaging 25% of their client visits from July to September 1996. The majority of patients visiting some of these centers were Native Hawaiians. Included among the most needy were the homeless, more than half of whom were gainfully employed. Stereotypes did not always accurately depict reality. Twice I volunteered to spend nights sleeping at homeless shelters. I met fulltime employees of the utility companies, adult correction officers, and even a nurse. A 1996 report from the City and County of Honolulu noted that the death rate per 1000 was 5.9 for the general population, 7.4 for the sheltered homeless, and as high as 45 for the unsheltered homeless. To state this another way, the median age for death for the entire population was 77.6 years, but for the unsheltered population in Hawaii, it was as low as 42.3

years. In urban Honolulu, you will find an ethnic mix among the homeless, but travel out to the Waianae coast of Oahu and you will find that a preponderance of those living in tents on the beach are Native Hawaiians.

A self-conscious political scientist will immediately recognize what Deborah Stone calls a story of decline: "In the beginning, things were pretty good. But they got worse. In fact, right now, they are nearly intolerable. Something must be done." In Hawaii, the story has a slightly different twist: Things were on the road to reform and improvement, but the task was not completed. We have lost momentum. We no longer embrace the same goals. We are in decline, and something must be done or the situation will indeed become intolerable.

THE WAY WE ALMOST WERE

What a difference between 1997 and 1987! In 1987, Hawaii dreamed of a "seamless" system, as Health Director Dr. Jack Lewin called it. We already had the most insurance coverage of any state through our Prepaid Health Care Act of 1974. (Some said 98% of our citizens were covered!) Ours was the only employer mandate for health insurance in the nation, thanks to a special Congressional waiver from the 1974 Employee Retirement Income Security Act (ERISA) statute, which prohibited all the other states from enacting an employer mandate for health. With the initiation of the State Health Insurance Program (SHIP) in 1989 to cover the remaining gap group, Jack Lewin sought to position Hawaii as a model for national legislation.

Former Massachusetts governor and unsuccessful presidential candidate Mike Dukakis came to the University of Hawaii for six months to draft a proposed health plan based on Canada's singlepayer model. The Legislature increased the mandated benefit package for health insurance by including well-baby checkups, mental health and substance abuse treatment, and mammograms.

The first comprehensive state-funding bill to provide support for nonprofit groups working on HIV and AIDS was enacted. Hawaii was striving to become the Health State.

Enter the Clintons and their dramatic and ambitious plans to transform a trillion-dollar national industry. Hawaii's health leaders were called upon again and again to explain our system, and to tell why the employer mandate had not shut down the economy. Indeed, Enter the Clintons and their dramatic and ambitious plans to transform a trillion-dollar national industry. Hawaii's health leaders were called upon again and again to explain our system, and to tell why the employer mandate had not shut down the economy. Indeed,

Spurred by increasing Medicaid costs, many states also began experimental reform programs in moves toward both cost containment and universal health insurance coverage. The Milbank Memorial Fund convened a series of conferences designed to identify the lessons learned at the state level for other states seeking health care reform, and to ensure that national initiatives would not interfere with homegrown legislation.

Based on their collective experience, government leaders from a number of states reached general consensus that all should work to:

1. Devise ways to achieve universal access to health care for the currently uninsured and uninsurable.
2. Decide on the method of paying for universal access.
3. Take steps to control costs by:
   a. Reforming the health insurance industry.
   b. Moving toward community rating.
   c. Cutting administrative costs by integrating state agencies that deal with health care and developing common billing requirements across all payers, public and private.
   d. Regulating high-cost technology.
   e. Changing the behaviors of providers and patients
   f. Increasing the ratio of primary care physicians to specialists.
   g. Undertaking and applying research on the outcomes of particular treatments in order to use resources more efficiently.
   h. Encouraging preventive health services and managed care.
   i. nstituting practice guidelines for physicians.
   j. Reforming the tort system.

Hawaii was one of those states envied by others because of our employer based health insurance mandate and reputation for innovation in health reform.

In spite of the attempted canonization of the SHIP program as the last successful increment on the road to universal coverage, a careful examination of the late 1980s and early 1990s demonstrates the difficulty Hawaii found in attempting to match its stated goals for health care reform with conventional insurance mechanisms. The sad fact was that the politics of health in Hawaii had built into the system a number of gaps that allow a fairly large number of people to live their lives without adequate health care.

WORKER AND COVERAGE GAPS

Because all forms of insurance seek to control and predict costs, there are always limits to benefits, and frequently complex regulations for eligibility copayments, deductibles, and termination. Hawaii's 1974 Prepaid Health Care Act is no different. Gaps in coverage include:

- Anyone who works less than 20 hours a week is not covered.
- Coverage for family members and dependents is optional.
- Large employers can self-insure.
- Mandated benefit packages do not include many services in high demand in Hawaii, such as acupuncture, naturopathy, chiropractic, and so on, which are often paid for out-of-pocket.
- Many preventive services were not part of the original benefit package, including well-baby check-ups, mammography, and mental health and substance abuse treatment.
- Government itself was completely exempt.

In a striking example of self-interest overwhelming idealism, at the same time the state of Hawaii was promoting itself as the first state with virtual universal coverage, Governor John Waihee vetoed a bill that would have provided health insurance for hundreds of so-called state emergency hires. These are individuals who often were long-time state employees but were technically fired every thirty days in order to disqualify them from health insurance. Waihee's veto stunned even Health Director Lewin, who, in a half-hearted effort to defend his boss, publicly stated, "It's not as pathetic as it seems!"

It is not surprising that a state government would seek to achieve universal coverage through insurance, since over 90% of the population already enjoyed health insurance in some form. At the same time, another state responsibility, controlling expenditures, led policy makers to incorporate into its insurance plans the same mechanisms commonly adopted by the private-sector insurance managers.

AGE GAPS

In the 1980s, Hawaii's State Executive Office on Aging developed an expensive statewide insurance proposal for long-term care. A vigorous debate on its philosophy and specifics kept it from being implemented. We knew that Hawaii's population was rapidly aging and that the longevity of our seniors would eventually become a problem. We knew that the federal Medicare program for seniors would not cover long-term care, and that not all seniors would qualify for Medicaid. The proposed solution would have created an intergenerational responsibility, like Social Security, to fund long-term care. But just as the Pepper Commission's recommendations were set aside at the national level, when Jack Lewin and Governor Waihee embraced universal health insurance coverage through the SHIP program, longterm care was again told to wait in line.

It is important to reiterate that "universal" did not apply to all ages or all members of society, for many of them could not pay. Instead, it was an attempt to broaden and reduce the cost for those who were already working full time and in the system.

Much of the rhetorical justification for SHIP emphasized closing the gap on the uninsured and paying hospitals and others for what had been uncompensated care. SHIP, however, was never designed to actually deliver care, but to deliver an insurance product. SHIP's limited enrollment periods, limited benefits, and sliding scale for premiums were designed to reduce financial risks and to gain participation by the private insurance market.

In an effort to ensure that SHIP would only cost the state $10 million per year, emphasis was placed on enrolling those who could afford the full premiums, rather than the homeless or other high-risk individuals. When Governor Waihee vetoed the above-mentioned emergency hire bill, it was commonly believed that this was partly to ensure the participation of those emergency hires in SHIP, thus increasing the enrollment while minimizing the financial burden. Few emergency hires, however, found SHIP attractive.

EFFICIENCY GAPS

At the onset of SHIP, many of Hawaii's gap groups were clients of nonprofit community health centers. These centers commonly saw a large number of uninsured patients; this was in part paid for by direct subsidies from the state. In the shift to SHIP, administrative burdens associated with eligibility determination and billing were imposed. The original promise of a fixed $10 million cost was soon exceeded as more uninsured than the state was willing to admit existed began to sign up. The actual cost of the program grew to $14 million, which served only 20,000 SHIP enrollees.

An instructive comparison of costs showed that the KalihiPalama Health Center's 1992 budget ran to about $1.4 million, which serves several thousand patients per year. As an alternative to the SHIP insurance program, the state could have chosen to fully fund the operational services of ten such community health centers. This would have delivered real health care, not just paper coverage, to far more clients. Flexibility to use premiums for direct subsidies to the health centers was built into the law, but policy makers were reluctant to depart from the pure insurance model. Very little money made its way as cash payments for services.

GEOGRAPHICAL GAPS

The National Health Service Corps defines a medically underserved population as those people who must travel at least 30 miles for health care, and a medically underserved area as one where there is fewer than one physician per 3000 residents. In 1992, several years after the SHIP program was in operation, the physician-to-population ratio for the Puna district on the Big Island was 1 physician for every 23,203 residents. Rural Kahaluu on Oahu's windward coast had a ratio of 1 physician for every 15,736 residents.

SAFETY NET GAPS

Hawaii's SHIP program proved to be a transition to a more ambitious and more radical experiment in managed care for the gap groups and the needy, namely, QUEST. In the face of a shaky economy, a drop-in state revenues, cutbacks in federal funds, and a growing number of residents qualifying for the Medicaid program, Hawaii sought and received a special waiver to combine several populations into a new managed care program.

QUEST, which stands for "Quality care, ensuring Universal access, encouraging Efficient utilization, Stabilizing costs, and Transforming the way health care is provided" (what a mouthful!), was solely the product of the Department of Human Services, whose traditional role was more of a financial manager and eligibility screen for state and federal assistance to the poor. This department was not in the business of providing health care, as was the Department of Health.

Due to the financial woes of the state, QUEST quickly began to backtrack on its fantasy of eliminating the gap group once and for all. Its eligibility rules were a moving target, and finally, with its enrollment ballooning from 110,000 up to 160,000, a cap was imposed and 30,000 people were simply removed from the program.

In January 1996, QUEST enrollment reached its peak at 160,438. By January 1997, this had been pared down to 132,861. The removal of 27,577 individuals represented an abrupt 17% reduction. An alternative, QUEST-Net, was developed in anticipation that at least 10,000 would enroll. This approach failed miserably because only 3000 chose this alternative, which could cost a family $180 a month.

In July 1996, the Hawaii State Primary Care Association, a coalition of the community health centers who care for the poorest among Hawaii's residents, wrote of QUEST:

> The many recent changes in the QUEST program have so far succeeded in reducing enrollment numbers but at a considerable cost to both the people who continue to be eligible and to those who can no longer maintain QUEST coverage. The program seems to have abandoned even the pretense of universal coverage. These changes

spell real trouble for low170 income residents without employersponsored insurance for themselves and their dependents for the safety net providers.

In January 1997, the association published an analysis of the uninsured seen at the health centers and found a significant increase of the uninsured of 16.5%, or an estimated 21% of all clients being without insurance. This is not surprising since QUEST premiums for a person earning only $500 a month could run to $160 a month!

Because legislators had joined the QUEST bandwagon, it became nearly impossible to modify the program significantly, or, if it was found wanting, to eliminate it. It is often the case that innovations can capture the imagination of lawmakers, compromising their objectivity. No matter how many horror stories were brought forth from the health centers, the Legislature chose to give the administration more time to smooth out the rough edges.

The changes in the QUEST health insurance program could be seen in combination with other developments that further compromised the safety net, specifically,

1. the refusal of the state to pay extra reimbursement to health centers for accepting higher-cost, higher-risk clients (this despite a federal mandate to do so);
2. the constantly changing eligibility rules for QUEST, which are particularly hard for smaller providers to administer;
3. the federal withdrawal of benefits for legal immigrants;
4. the federal limits on welfare benefits;
5. the loss of SSI benefits for those enrolled in QUEST;
6. deep cuts in public health prevention programs at the state level;
7. the shortfall in Aloha United Way and other foundation funding for the nonprofit organizations that deliver care;

8. cuts in the food stamp program; and
9. the increase in unemployment in Hawaii associated with the sluggish economy.

Reductions in staff to oversee programs like QUEST, both at the state and federal level, have made it difficult to keep track of the medically transient uninsured population. Consequently, the most current and accurate numbers on QUEST enrollments are often not obtained from the QUEST office, but from the Hawaii State Primary Care Association (HSPCA), which, in 1997, had taken upon itself the task to survey all the health insurance plans. (It was able to do this with a staff of two.)

According to HSPCA, there had been a wide range of uninsured clients showing up at the health centers. In 1997, for example:

- The Bay Pahoa Family Health Center on Hawaii was seeing 9000 patients per year, with 27% uninsured.
- The Community Clinic of Maui was seeing 8000, with 44% uninsured. • The Kalihi-Palama Health Center was seeing 13,000, with 53% uninsured.
- The Kokua Kalihi Valley Health Center was seeing 4200, with 19% uninsured.
- The Waianae Coast Comprehensive Health Center was seeing 20,500, with 12% uninsured.
- The Waikiki Health Center was seeing 3400, with 58% uninsured.
- The Waimanalo Health Center was seeing 3000, with 12% uninsured.

The bias of the state of Hawaii in choosing an insurance model is symbolic of the bias of health care reform. Often the gap between the needs and behavior of marginalized groups and a middle-class delivery system is a prescription for frustration and unmet expectations.

As we have seen, the most ambitious state-level health insurance system in the United States suffers from worker and family gaps under the Prepaid Health Care Act, exclusionary gaps under government coverage, age gaps with the absence of long-term care insurance financing, rural gaps in the ratio of health professionals to the population, and efficiency gaps when compared to the real cost of delivering primary care through nonprofits.

THE MIDDLE-CLASS BIAS OF INSURANCE

In the design of these programs, the concept of universal and affordable health care was replaced by the concept of universal access. As political scientist Deborah Stone might well point out, the pictures we paint in our mind's eye for care are quite different from the concepts surrounding access. Care is concrete; access is potential. Care is actually received; access must be proactively pursued. The politician's stereotypical patient receiving universal access was not a child, nor an immigrant, nor a part-time employee, nor a minority woman of color, nor a person with a rare disease. The model patient for access was a well-educated, active consumer with disposable income and with no unusual health problems. In other words, they were voters.

The middle-class, democratic rhetoric of equality also has worked against marginalized populations. During the national debate over the Clinton health plan, analysts and political activists alike spoke out against a two-tiered health care system, which treated the poor differently. If the corporate CEO did not go to a community health clinic, why should the poor? What this bias misses, however, is that the marginalized populations might need a different delivery system, one that was particularly sensitive to their economic, cultural, and social circumstances. The preferred middle-class and upper-class systems used insurance, and thus access to insurance became the politically correct norm.

THE NATIONAL RETREAT FROM UNIVERSAL CARE

Retreat from State Reforms

It would be unfair to consider public policy decisions in Hawaii outside of national trends. In a review of state initiatives in health care reform, P. S. Paula-Shaheen concluded that most of the reforms were pragmatic and incremental, often dependent on a particular combination of leadership, state politics, and hard-to-define "windows of opportunity," during which reforms were possible. In most cases, however, the retreat from the grander visions of universal care examined at the Milbank Memorial Fund conferences has proceeded apace in most of those states, and many of the initial leaders of reform have left the scene.

The enthusiasm for health care reform began with mounting stat Medicaid deficits. From 1988 to 1992, national Medicaid expenditure increased an average of 22.4% per year, growing from $53.5 billion I 1988 to $119.9 billion in 1992. Enrollees went from 22 million to nearly 30 million. States sought to be in sync with national reforms, and most entertained false hopes that somewhere, either through employer mandates or government revenues, there would be more cash in the system to pursue universal care. When even the previous levels of federal subsidies began to shrink, interest in governmental solutions evaporated.

The hot topics in Hawaii and in other states became Medicaid managed care waivers, auto insurance, and workers' compensation reform. Both auto insurance and workers' compensation contain major health insurance components, but neither is being reformed from the point of view of the overall health care system. Health care costs are items of discussion only because they are areas of potential savings, and thus possible areas to cut. While the idea of so-called 24-hour care, a single system for all health delivery, has been tossed about, its complexity has removed it from serious consideration. When the Hawaii Legislature cut the reimbursement for chiropractors under workers' compensation, many in that profession left the state. The politically active Chiropractors Association in Hawaii closed its offices as there were too few members to support the organization.

RETREAT FROM EMPLOYER-BASED INSURANCE

While Hawaii was losing its fervor for the universal employer mandates in the 1990s, employers nationally were cutting back on health benefits that they had voluntarily adopted. A 1996 study by the Lewin Group, prepared for the American Hospital Association, found that the percentage of workers and their dependents who had employer-based coverage declined from a high of 77.7% in 1990 to 73.9% by 1995. The study found a number of employer trends affecting health coverage, namely:

- Use of more part-time workers.
- Outsourcing of functions to smaller firms less likely to provide coverage.
- Discontinuance of retiree programs.
- Increased employee cost sharing (premiums and deductibles).
- Discontinued coverage for some specialized services.
- Increased premiums for family coverage.

The combined effects of these trends were an increase in the numbers of uninsured and a decrease in access to health care services. On February 25, 1997, the New York Times reported that 24.8% of New York City residents under 65 had no health insurance, and most of them held full-time jobs. In New York State, the uninsured grew from 13.9% in 1990 to 17.2% in 1997.

Karen Davis of Health Services Research reported on the "steep decline in children with private, employment-based insurance from 66 percent in 1998 to 59 percent in 1994." She also noted that the uninsured are much less likely to obtain preventive care: 52% of uninsured women did not obtain a pap smear in the previous year, compared with 36% of insured women, and 69% of women ages 40-64 did not get a mammogram, compared with 38% of insured women.

If there is a lesson for policy makers it is that there are windows of opportunity to make change, and those windows can close. One should never assume that today's trend will always become tomorrow's reality.

RISE OF THE HCFA CULTURE

Hawaii's experimentation with managed care for its Medicaid population was part of a national trend of waivers granted by the Health Care Financing Administration (HCFA), the federal agency that administers both Medicaid and Medicare. This shift of the health care reform action from state departments of public health to their Medicaid programs could be seen as significant when viewed from the point of view of agency attitudes and policies. The culture of HCFA and its state counterparts has a strong "are you really eligible?" flavor to it. Thus, lip service regarding universal access all over the United States was forced to compete with administrative traditions that were far more interested in fiscal accountability.

The cultural shift was intensified as many public health programs were cut, not only at the federal level, but also at the state level. I Hawaii, the Health Department's Family Health Services branch sustained massive cuts. Family planning was nearly eliminated. These health promotion and disease prevention services were not incorporate into managed care insurance plans.

Because it is easier to count dollars saved than illnesses prevented there is a natural bias in favor of the former. Public health programs are always scrambling to generate quantifiable data to offset the compelling numbers of the budget analysts. (In 1999, the University of Hawaii administration undertook a concerted effort to eliminate the School of Public Health. To determine the "facts" regarding its true costs, the University president appointed a five-member task force, none of whom was directly involved in public health. However, there was a bank economist and a hospital board member.)

THE PROMISE AND THE LIMITS OF MANAGED CARE

The first and perhaps most amazing aspect of the managed care mania that has swept the nation is the wide range of definitions and connotations implied in the term. Deborah Stone points out how managed care can be described as promoting the autonomy of health providers because, within a certain capitated (fixed) budget, they can decide how much care and how much profit will be available. On the other hand, it could be seen as a shift in decision making from physician and hospital authority to insurance-company control.

Sometimes managed care is used merely to denote health insurance that is supported by fixed premiums, like any other insurance. A variation on this theme is the capitated (limited or fixed) insurance premium without a significant copayment or deductible. By eliminating most out-of-pocket costs for the patient, the managed care insurance plan collects an inflexible but totally predictable amount of revenue from each enrollee.

An additional implication in many definitions is the use of a gatekeeper primary care giver, usually but not always a physician, who controls referrals to specialist providers within the plan. Most managed care plans have a more limited number of professionals who are hired to serve a specific group of enrollees. Thus, the flexibility in the amount of income received by these physicians as well as the number of services provided in traditional health insurance indemnity plans has been purged from the system. This permits a clearer picture of the relationship between physician decisions and the profits of the managed care plan. Finally, managed care often implies an impartial utilization review of physician decisions, even to the extent that disincentives are incorporated to discourage treatments that deviate from the norm in the direction of costing the managed care plan more.

Legislative understanding of this complex world is difficult. Effective legislative oversight is almost impossible, particularly for part-time, generalist politicians. There are always new technical terms, acronyms, and agencies popping up that challenge even the most diligent official. The new world of managed care requires knowledge of insurance, copayments, deductibles, and provider incentives. All of these may have either a positive or negative impact on the delivery of timely, appropriate services to the public.

In 1994, Hawaii's deputy director of health, Geri Marullo, questioned the research that sought to link managed care with successful cost control and improved outcomes. She wrote: "To suggest that managed-care programs reduce overall health costs or increase the quality of care, especially for poor women and children, is purely an intuitive statement in most of the literature and discussions of this controversial issue. Of more than 200 articles surveyed, not one suggests a significant correlation between increased quality of care for women and children ..."

The health care market's infatuation with managed care led Fitzhugh Mullan, M.D., of Health Affairs to comment," ... the poor are still with us, or, to put it differently, whatever the marketplace is doing about cost and quality, it is doing nothing (good) about the medically indigent."

THE EVAPORATION OF USEFUL POLICY DATA

In 1997, as one group of students and professors in the University of Hawaii's School of Public Health were planning a conference called "Managed Care in Hawaii: A Reality Check," others were pondering a growing curiosity over what had happened to the 30,000 former QUEST members who were abruptly removed from the rolls in mid1996. The following questions were formulated in the hope that the participants in the managed care conference might offer some answers:

1. How can we know exactly how many were removed? Is this a moving target?

2. What exactly has happened to tllese people in terms of health insurance? Can we assume they are uninsured?

3. The Hawaii State Primary Care Association did a study of the uninsured in June of 1996. Is it likely the snapshot of the uninsured seen at their health centers is an accurate one? What other data would be needed to complete the picture?

4. Is it possible to gather data on the former QUEST clients in terms of their age? Ethnicity? Other demographic characteristics?

5. Is there any way to know if they are continuing to receive care but paying out of pocket?

6. How do financial planners for hospitals and clinics project the amount of uncompensated care they expect to deliver? Do they have internal data that helps but would not be easily shared for proprietary reasons under managed care? Do they have data they could share? Do insurance companies use different data?

7. Under managed care, would useful data become less available? More proprietary? Collected differently?

8. How long a "tail" is required for the typical QUEST population before changes in utilization, payment, deferral of treatment, and so on show up? Are there any rules of thumb that health planners use (e.g., it takes a year before emergency rooms see an increase, etc.)?

Unfortunately, most of the panelists and experts at the conference admitted that these questions could not be readily answered. In the fee for- service world, which is rapidly disappearing, all kinds of public data were collected on specific diagnoses and charges. The particular case mix could be analyzed, and weighted fee schedules developed, for those serving the high-risk patients. In the managed care world, capitated reimbursements are no longer based on the number of health care services actually delivered, but rather on the number who have enrolled in a plan, whether or not they actually receive services. While these and other questions might be answered within a private managed care organization, such an organization might not feel that it is in its best interests to share that information.

Consider the existing data gaps a managed care world inherits. First, in Hawaii, is the Prepaid Health Care Act, which is administered by a skeleton crew that collects very little data. They don't cover parttime employees. They don't cover the larger companies. Prepaid staff cannot tell us exactly how many people are currently covered. There is no data on trends. Is prepaid growing or shrinking? How do September 1999 enrollments compare with September 1998 if the economy has changed? What counts as a significant deviation in average number of hours worked? What months are we likely to see migration from prepaid to QUEST? Without accurate information and analysis on the employer mandated health insurance segment of the work force, data on QUEST provides an insufficient data to determine the numbers of uninsured.

In addition, prepaid cannot track behavior among specific employers who shift from full-time to part-time employees to avoid paying health benefits. Are the employer's contributions (well over 80%) driving the workforce out of prepaid? Prepaid is also unable to track the movement of employees among types of plans, especially to and from managed care.

It is important to note that the state of Hawaii does not regulate health insurance in the same way it regulates auto insurance or workers' compensation. If the Department of Labor's office administering our Prepaid Health Care Act doesn't do it, who will? In an era of government downsizing, it is unlikely that new regulatory offices will be created.

When we begin to ask the same questions of the QUEST program, it is clear the commitment to collect good data is weak. A legislative auditor's report noted the following deficiencies several years after the program became operational:

- The computer data system was still not in.
- Research staff positions were vacant.
- Utilization patterns were unknown.
- Two divisions of the same department keep duplicate case files.

QUEST project costs and enrollments were consistently inaccurate. There was no explanation as to why some QUEST plans seem to have stabilized while others continue to decline. The actual content of benefits, especially bilingual or outreach services, were unknown. With inadequate staff to monitor performance, it was hard to go beyond the crude numbers of enrollments. The staffing patterns within plans and delivery systems, especially community health centers, were unknown.

The transfer of responsibilities from the federal government to the states in the form of large block grants represented a form of managed care in terms of data. With little accountability or oversight, Kala Ladenheim of the Institute for Health Policy, Outcomes, and Human Values commented," ... special efforts are needed to reach immigrants. In addition to economic and legal or institutional barriers, health care may be inaccessible to immigrants because of problems with language or cultural barriers. Welfare reform is an exercise in federal hand washing that abrogates federal constitutional responsibility for the consequences of immigration policy for lower levels of government."

The pursuit of universal health care for all Americans was, and is, a worthy goal. For a nation with at least 41 million of its citizens without health insurance, it was logical that expansion of insurance would be a high priority. Some may have believed that insurance was the best mechanism to achieve universal care because it provided financing. Providers (doctors, hospitals, etc.) could embrace such a solution because it offered the prospects of reimbursements for what had often been uncompensated care.

Not only has insurance failed to achieve either universal care or universal paper coverage, but also its inherent management characteristics and economic dependence on government subsidies make it a clumsy and ill-equipped tool to extend care to marginalized populations.

Hawaii's experience as the most complete health insurance system in the nation should be instructive. In spite of energy and leadership at a time of government surpluses, Hawaii was unable to overcome the limits of insurance in its attempt to create the Universal Health State. Its current flirtation with Medicaid managed care appears to be an extension of the same approach, and is already experiencing the same frustrations. With at least 12% of the Islands' population without health insurance - a number that is growing every day - alternative approaches were in order.

The politics of health care in Hawaii illustrate the complexity of legislative life. A generalist is thrown into controversies with voluminous contradictory data, manipulated by huge corporate interests determined to get their political way. To become even superficially informed takes a lot of effort and time. The challenge for any legislative body is to assemble enough intelligent and interested members to cope with issues like health care and ensure that decisions are based on reason and good data.

LESSONS

1. Change and opportunity often arrive unannounced. Few politicians can predict the path of their careers or what doors may open unexpectedly.
2. Legislative assignments link a politician to a particular segment of society with its own distinct network of issues, advocates, and dimensions. The world of education is quite distinct from the world of business development, environmental protection, or health. Competence or knowledge in one subject area does not automatically transfer to another. Consequently, legislators may grow isolated and uninformed about other segments of society.
3. Legislators dislike turf fights between professional groups.

4. When health insurance is taken for granted by a majority of the electorate, the politics of health may not generate a great deal of interest or passion.

5. Public health issues that require restrictions on personal behavior are seldom embraced by all segments of society. Strange alliances can develop as conservatives and liberals adopt similar positions for very different reasons.

6. Insurance is an imperfect tool for delivering services to the poor or marginalized segments of the population.

7. In spite of Hawaii's positive reputation for health insurance coverage, there are significant gaps in our system.

8. Hawaii's health care system cannot be separated from national health care financing and reform.

SOME USEFUL WEB LINKS

For state and national data:

http://www.state.hi.us/health/shpda/shl02012.htm

For health trends in Hawaii:

http://www.hhic.org/healthtrends/index.asp

10 | SEX AND RELIGION AT THE CAPITOL

. . . .

A state cannot so deem a class of persons a stranger to its laws.

— U.S. Supreme Court justice Anthony Kennedy

In addition to the players, the organization, and the structure of government, there is one wild card that can at times sweep away all other factors: the power and passion of a single issue to seize the minds and hearts of a community and not let go until it is resolved. This is a tale of such an issue and how it came to overshadow the business and politics of at least two legislative sessions and two state elections.

What do a child abuser, a murderer imprisoned for life without parole, a promiscuous philanderer, a divorcee, a drug abuser, and just about any young man and woman in love all have in common? They all have the right to apply for a special piece of paper from Hawaii's Department of Health.

That paper carries with it certain legal and financial rights and responsibilities, such as the sharing of retirement and health benefits, inheritance rights, and estate and transfer tax benefits, to name a few. It might also convey the right to visit a spouse in the hospital, the right to apply for immigration and residency, and even the right to care for a child. What kind of document is so universally handed out to both law-abiding and law-breaking residents? It's a marriage license.

Let's be clear about what it is not. Two people do not become married simply by receiving it. They still have to find someone recognized by the state of Hawaii as having the authority to perform a marriage. Usually it is an ordained minister, for religion has long had state recognition. But it could also be a judge or a boat captain or an Elvis impersonator in Las Vegas. All of these people could have the legal power, in the eyes of the state of Hawaii, to perform a ceremony or a rite, which is considered to be financially, legally, and sometimes spiritually binding.

If anyone ever tells you that words have no power in themselves, they are wrong. The word "marriage" is one of the most potent, emotionally charged terms on the political planet. Those who cherish a religious faith may well feel that marriage is a sacred union, sanctified by God, and only incidentally noticed by the state. Other citizens look upon marriage as a legal commitment, with little or no religious significance, one of many alternatives in this society of diverse lifestyles.

The role of the state in issuing legal marriage documents is relatively new. Two hundred years ago American pioneers did not require licenses to wed, and they are not thought less of by today's moralists. Historians trace the role of state-issued marriage documents to the need to settle disputes between legitimate and illegitimate heirs. Since women did not count in the eyes of the state, the fundamental issue was the distribution of property among men. Churches might well record weddings, and the records might well be lost in a. fire. A similar situation arose with records of birth, where years later, only the baptismal documentation could be found. My parents did not have birth certificates. My dad has only a census report indicating there was a new baby (him) in the household. My mom had a document written in Slovak from a Pennsylvania mountaintop mining camp, issued by a church that no longer exists.

It is the twentieth century that has embraced legal documentation of all kinds with a passion unknown in prior eras. But I'm sure that theologians of all stripes would agree that the sanctity of any marriage never depended upon whether or not a civil authority required a license.

Religion, with its social values, is not something to be hidden away in a closet with a sense of shame or embarrassment. In spite of all the misguided applications of it, the wars, the discrimination, the use of it to divide brothers and sisters, religion can soften the nastier sides of human nature. A life of virtue, honesty, humility, kindness, charity, purity, love ... we all need more of that.

You can find plenty of religious-based arguments on both ends of the political spectrum. Liberals found the basis to fight slavery in religion. Black ministers led the civil rights movement in the 1960s. Sincere conscientious objectors developed the concept of the just and the unjust war. Secular capital punishment foes do not reject alliances with spiritual opponents. Many conservatives today oppose abortion, promote prayer in schools, and reject anything other than traditional marriage. Religion will play a role in our decisions over cloning, genetic testing, and the right to die.

The same-sex marriage issue in Hawaii goes far beyond the application of religious values to social policy. It is part of an ongoing struggle to define the difference between a particular set of spiritual beliefs and the fundamental principles of a democratic government that was established to serve the needs of its entire people, regardless of their beliefs and lifestyles. It is also a debate over how best to achieve social harmony: Should government impose a "superior" majority view on all, or should it uphold a standard of tolerance, even for those we may not understand or even like?

The 1996 legislative session in Hawaii brought two incredibly personal and volatile issues, sex and religion, together in one proposal: a constitutional amendment to ban the issuance of marriage licenses for same-gender couples. It proved to be a potent political issue, contributing to the defeat of state legislators Rey Graulty, Eve Anderson, Jackie Young, Devon Nekoba, Len Pepper, Annelle Amaral, and yours truly.

On the final night of the 1996 legislative meetings and conference committees, lobbyists, advocates, and nearly the entire House of Representatives crowded into the Senate galleries to witness the long awaited attempt of Senator Milton Holt and his allies to require that the constitutional amendment defining marriage be removed from the Senate Judiciary Committee (chaired by Senator Rey Graulty) and brought to the Senate floor for a vote.

It was high drama because of its importance, but rather tame in terms of its rhetoric. After a few perfunctory remarks for and against, Holt was able to muster the nine votes needed to bring it to the floor. He lost the most important tally, however, since the count was ten to fifteen against the passage of the bill itself. The twenty-five-member Senate was split along existing factional lines, suggesting that the votes had more to do with power than with sex.

It was clear Senator Holt did not have the votes, but that the same-sex marriage issue had taken its toll in time and attention that could have been better spent on other highly controversial and complex problems. Those who wished to prohibit the issuance of marriage licenses to same-sex couples had created such a turmoil that other issues, such as the reform of no-fault auto insurance and the revision of the legislative pension system, were not resolved when time ran out on the negotiations.

Immediately following the vote, the Senate chamber became a sea of crawling House and Senate members seeking to sign conference committee reports before the stroke of midnight turned yet more legislative proposals into pumpkins. House and Senate leaders shouted stridently into one of the microphones - "Representative Lee, Representative Lee ... Senator Chumbley, Senator Chumbley" - an obvious edge of panic in their voices as the clock ticked away and the deadline approached to deck all bills for final passage the following Monday.

It was not a pretty sight, but somehow it seemed a fitting end to a contentious, chaotic, and ugly legislative session. Special-interest groups and single-issue advocates dominated. I sat near the wall on the edge of the Senate chamber and shared whispered postmortems with colleagues, most of whom were glad it was finally over. Somehow the thought of returning the following week to vote on the many bills that were scheduled for final reading was unappealing, unimportant, and anticlimatic.

A disclaimer is in order. As a participant who took a position on one side of a controversial issue, I obviously have my own view. But as a student of history and politics, as one who dearly loves democracy in spite of its flaws, I feel the need to explain what happened, to offer insights, to invite people to place themselves in unfamiliar shoes.

The same-sex marriage controversy of 1996 was played out at a time in Hawaii's history when power had become increasingly concentrated in a very few legislative hands. This trend had been exaggerated to some extent because of Hawaii's budget crisis and the natural tendency to focus more and more attention on financial issues. Senator Holt's attempt to pull the bill to the Senate floor was the result of a stalemate in the conference committee. In fact, the same fate befell other major bills, such as those calling for no-fault insurance reform and the revision of the pension system. Versions of all these bills were passed by both the House and the Senate, but a small number of key players in charge of them in conference led to their demise. Senator Milton Holt was involved in all three, and, in my view, was glad to see them fail.

While the average number of conference committee assignments for House members was about 21 in 1996, the chair of the Finance Committee, Calvin Say, was on 132, usually serving as conference chair. The Judiciary chair, Terrance Tom, had 120 such assignments, and the Consumer Protection chair, Ron Menor, had 89. Thus, three or four individuals were given primary responsibility to work out agreements on a high percentage of all the bills that made it to the final gate, and their grip on the most complex and controversial bills was even tighter. The same was true of their Senate counterparts. This set the stage for brinkmanship, abetted by the lack of sufficient time. The desire to control all major events by key players, including House Speaker Joe Souki, who likes to play an active role, could be seen as a formula for failure.

Perhaps the issue Hawaii residents cared about most was reform of the no-fault auto insurance system, specifically in a way to guarantee premium cuts. Governor Ben Cayetano vetoed the 1995 bill because of its obvious insurance industry bias. An attempt to override that veto did not improve the relationship among Senator Holt, House Speaker Souki, and the governor. The 1996 no-fault debate found the conference committee trying to reconcile an almost pure no-fault Senate bill, which was strongly supported by the insurance industry, with an almost pure tort-system House bill strongly supported by plaintiff attorneys and consumer groups. Senator Holt, the principal Senate advocate for a same-sex constitutional ban, was also preoccupied with negotiating the no-fault bill. Time is unforgiving at the end of a legislative session. Whether or not the same-sex issue contributed to the demise of no-fault, only a handful of officials will ever know, but it left the entire community, including most legislators, anxiously and helplessly awaiting the outcome of decisions made by too few individuals with too little time.

The emotional roller coaster of 1996 produced many vivid memories. One was a well-timed visit from mainland conservative religious activists opposed to any antidiscrimination laws that might protect homosexuals. Their agenda, whether it be on abortion or other social issues, was to imprint the laws of the land with their views of a fundamentalist Christian government, thereby creating a modern-day theocracy.

Upon the arrival of nationally known moralist Randall Terry (known for his antigay preaching) and his mainland entourage, many Hawaii legislators found themselves confronted in their offices by angry, fervent, insistent advocates of a constitutional amendment to ban same-sex marriages. (ferry was seen as radical even by Hawaii's conservative coalition, Hawaii's Future Today, which asked him not to interfere.)

In my office, I was met by a white-haired priest from the mainland accompanied by a dozen followers, some from my district. One fellow, who was a staffer for City Councilman Henry Felix, later spent his mornings and evenings standing right next to me and holding up signs urging commuters from my district to "Say No to Jim Shon, Say No to Same-Sex Marriage." (He later, while serving as minister for a wedding business in a home located in a residential neighborhood, got his boss in trouble with the city for zoning violations.)

The mainland priest quoted from the Old Testament and insisted that we would suffer as a society if we didn't obey the Bible on this issue. I found it interesting that all his quotes were from the Old Testament. I reminded him of New Testament sentiments such as "Let he who is without sin cast the first stone" or, reinforcing the tolerance in Hawaii that is part of our spirit of aloha, "Blessed be the peacemaker."

No sooner was "peacemaker" off my lips than the priest raised his fist in the air and shouted, "NO! NO!"

My visitors were, as it turns out, not quite sure how they felt about majority rule, for while they insisted I would be arrogant if I did not follow the latest poll that supporting their position, they were glad to pat me on the back for standing with them against the introduction of legalized gambling in Hawaii, a position I held for years, even when a majority of the voters in my district favored gambling. Somehow the contradiction did not register.

On the rare occasions when we have a poll sampling public opinion on an issue, legislators must decide if their personal views of what is best for society should prevail over those revealed by the polls. If I felt strongly about something (opposition to capital punishment or gambling), I had the obligation to inform my constituents. It was then up to them to decide whether they felt comfortable in supporting me in the next election.

The coalition lobbying for the amendment to ban same-sex marriages took the name Hawaii's Future Today. Their principals included leaders in the Mormon and Catholic Churches of Hawaii. This group set as its legislative agenda preventing the legalization of prostitution, gambling, and same-sex marriages. On the subject of gambling, an early 1996 proposal would have placed a number of gambling issues on the general election ballot. Hawaii's Future Today strongly opposed such a referendum. Yet in the May 9, 1996, issue of the Honolulu Advertiser, they paid for a three-quarter-page ad in favor of a constitutional ban on same-gender unions, chastising senators who "not only voted against this bill but against your right to decide this issue at the ballot box." Public opinion polls and the placement of issues on the ballot had become expedient tools to be used according to one's best guess of the likely outcome.

Contradictions and rational arguments appeared to have little weight in this debate. What really counted was a strange chop suey of pure emotion, religious fervor, and crass political manipulation. There was great sincerity and great hypocrisy operating side by side, with a good many of my colleagues caught in the political middle, asking, "How can we get out of this without too much damage?"

Perhaps the most bizarre aspect of the same-sex controversy was how little of it focused on the legal matter that started it all: the issuance of a state marriage license. In conversations with colleagues, I found very few who believed that this issue would have been as big or distracting as it was in the 1996 session if three individuals had less interest in it, or less influence over it: House Speaker Joe Souki, House Judiciary chair Terrance Tom, and Senator Milton Holt. I do not mean to say it would not have provided a spirited debate, but only that the issue would not have continued to rise from the ashes again and again, usually with questionable undemocratic tactics, without these three players. Those who cheered them on unwittingly gave credence to the suspicion that as long as people get what they want, they really don't care how they get it.

The internal politics of the Legislature provided additional incentives to use the same-gender marriage issue for other purposes. In the House, some analysts felt that conservatives Joe Souki and Terry Tom would be able to inoculate their closest followers from the electoral wrath of the Religious Right by championing the antihomosexual agenda. Under this scenario, an additional benefit would be that the more progressive or rebellious members of the House Democratic caucus would be forced on principle to vote against the ban, thus exposing themselves to electoral defeat. It was these liberal independents (of which I counted myself a member) who openly disagreed with a number of leadership initiatives, such as legalized gambling. Of course, this is overly simplistic since independence comes in many ideological and religious forms. Some liberals consistently supported Speaker Souki, and some moderates and conservatives on social issues yearned for change. Whether intended or not, the same-sex marriage issue could play out to the advantage of those who welcomed the thought of those liberals having their political wrists slapped for lack of loyalty. Where electoral expediency is concerned, some politicians assume that the electorate can be swayed by emotional appeals against small and not-too-popular minorities, such as gays and lesbians.

A curious twist to speculation over alliances can be seen in the opposite political effects of legalized gambling and same-sex marriage. The gambling debate actually united the most conservative members of the House, such as the former Republican Representative Gene Ward, with the most liberal, such as myself. Whether it be the moral degradation of gambling or the negative social impacts, the conservative wing of the Republican Party in the House worked hand in glove with the liberal wing of the Democratic Party on this issue. The same-sex marriage issue, however, divided this alliance along more traditional lines. Because Hawaii's Future Today chose to concentrate on the latter, a broader dialogue on social issues did not develop.

A final point in favor of the argument that the same-sex marriage issue was used for political purposes is that Souki repeatedly promised members of his own leadership team that they could "safely" continue to vote with the leadership and for his proposals, knowing that the Speaker guaranteed the bills would eventually die. A true believer might not make such promises.

The politics of the Senate made members of the House look like procedural purists by comparison. Senator Milton Holt, plagued by well publicized personal problems, faced a tough reelection battle in 1996, as well as an internal continuing fight over control of the Senate. As the main legislative representative of the enormously powerful and wealthy Bishop Estate (holding over $10 billion in assets), Milton was expected to be strongly urged by his employer to continue his political career and seek reelection. His likely opponent was House Human Services chair Suzie Chun Oakland, a liberal Snow-White of a figure taking on the Big Bad Wolf. At least that is how the media played the contest.

I remember sitting in the back of the conference room two nights before adjournment, observing the ritualistic exchange of "apple and oranges" same-sex marriage proposals by the House and Senate conferees. Milton Holt was sitting behind me against the wall. Everyone knew it was only a matter of time before he would lead the charge to pull the constitutional amendment out of committee to the Senate floor for a vote. Rumor said he had the votes to do it. The cameras were rolling. Directly behind the House members was a door to the hallway, in line with everyone's gaze. Enter Suzie Chun-Oakland carrying her infant son, the personification of "family values." Perhaps I only imagined Milton's gasp and grumble behind me. I dared not actually turn around to see his expression. I am certain a reasonable person might interpret her entrance as the opening salvo in a hotly contested election. (She did run, and she did win.)

How cynical we have become, interpreting every act in the context of a photo opportunity for political advantage. It was certainly one of the unseemly effects of the same-sex marriage confrontation. It corrupted our perspectives on many levels.

Informal conversations analyzed the relationship of the same-sex marriage issue to the Holt/Chun-Oakland race in the following way: Milton would use the Religious Right over same-sex, the Bishop Estate money and Hawaiian connection, and the powerful insurance lobby (State Farm Insurance especially) on the no-fault bill to protect him from Snow White. She would emphasize wholesome family values. The Honolulu Weekly pointed out that the same public relations firm, McNeil Wilson, handled the Bishop Estate, the Mormon Church, and State Farm Insurance, which was the driving force behind Milton Holt's pro-insurance no-fault bill.

Suzie Chun-Oakland was on the opposite side of Milton on all these issues. Few of my colleagues questioned the sincerity of her positions. On the other hand, many found it hard to believe that Milton Holt had just been struck by religious lightning. While this may be unfair, not one legislator with whom I spoke during that session felt that Holt was doing anything other than playing politics. It is interesting that the entire 1996 legislative drama was played out with a Capitol consensus presuming this was, in fact, the case.

That the political stakes were high was confirmed by the mutilation of the process in order to repeatedly resurrect the same-sex marriage bills. Representative Terry Tom held interim hearings, hinting that his previous position against a constitutional ban might be softening. The bill was heard and simply put on indefinite hold during decision making. This was the first violation of the spirit, if not the letter, of the rules. Chairs were not supposed to kill a bill without a formal vote. You either moved to pass it or to hold it, and then the committee voted. A bill could be deferred to a specific date for a final decision, but it could not be held in committee as an indirect way of killing it.

Some interpreted Tom's deferral to an indefinite, theoretical future decision-making date as a face-saving device. Few objected at the time since a collective political sigh of relief went throughout the House. This was a mistake, for later we were to discover that it allowed Speaker Souki to bring out the bill with little warning, giving opponents no opportunity to persuade colleagues to resist.

This is, in fact, what happened on the last day House bills were scheduled for debate to cross over to the Senate.

It was just before this crossover that crusader Randall Terry arrived in Hawaii with his noisy gang, walking door to door at the Capitol, hoping to intimidate those who did not already share his views. Although there was some stiffening of resolve as a backlash to their tactics, most legislators were caught off balance and made less certain about the political wisdom of resisting the antigay juggernaut.

In spite of promising to House floor leader Annelle Amarel that the bill was dead, the very next morning, Souki decided to interrupt the House floor session, waive the 48-hour public-hearing notice, and call the Judiciary Committee back into session to force a vote on yet another constitutional amendment, this one defining marriage as exclusively a union of opposite sexes. Predictably, the constitutional proposal passed with only fourteen House votes in opposition. (This added irony to the defeat of House members on this issue since their removal did nothing to change the outcome in 1997.

> Mr. Speaker, I am a Christian and a Southern Baptist at that - one of the most conservative. I am a public servant as well, serving in a pluralistic democracy. You and I, Mr. Speaker, as well as our colleagues, have been given the privilege to create conditions so that all of our citizens can live with dignity, and with a reasonable degree of freedom. I do not have to agree with everyone who does what he or she does with that freedom but, at the same time, by guaranteeing that freedom, I guarantee my own. I protect my right to be a Christian by preserving your right to be a believer of another denomination or faith, even if, in my eyes, your behavior is considered sinful.

> Former New York Governor Mario Cuomo, himself a Catholic who reconciled his faith with his duty as a politician, explained it this way to his constituents: "We should appeal to the best in our people, not the worst. Persuade, not coerce, lead people to truth, by love, and still, all the while, respect and enjoy our unique pluralistic democracy, and we can do it, even as politicians."

Our state constitution, like our federal Constitution, serves as the unifying and symbolic evocation of our island community. Our federal Constitution, in fact, has endured relatively unchanged over the course of our nation's history, and this sparse and lean document, with its words of unchallenged wisdom . . . has nevertheless managed to govern the hearts and minds of our people, even with the march of time and changing circumstances.

With regard to our state constitution, Mr. Speaker, we should also be careful whenever there are proposals to amend this document. This is also a document that upholds the ideal that individuals should be free from government imposition, inquisition, and intervention, free to enjoy life as they see fit, so long as they do not do injury to others. This ideal is underscored in Article I, Sections 2, 3, and 5 of our constitution, which simply state that all citizens of the state of Hawaii are entitled to equal protection under the law.

Mr. Speaker, the business of government is to protect each and every citizen's rights, even if their behavior is viewed with distaste and disdain by the majority. Governments and politicians should devote themselves to the health and welfare of their constituents, to defending the borders against threats to its survival and security, and to matters regarding the economy and commerce. They are not to concern themselves with ensuring that the citizenry abide by doctrinal purity or salvation, or that they should lead moral or virtuous lives. That is the stuff of religion, and should be viewed as the responsibility of our religious leaders, Christian and nonChristian alike.

It is a wonder that while we debate this measure, I see that parties on opposite sides of this issue pray to the same God, read from the same Bible, and purport to follow his teachings. It is a wonder that as I made my way to the Capitol this morning, I saw, as I see almost every day, the wish played on bumper stickers to "live aloha." If this measure were to be signed into law, I wonder whether the mention of Hawaii as the Aloha State would come with an asterisk, an amendment, if you will, that would say aloha is not extended to those who do not abide by the letter and the spirit of this particular constitutional provision.

President John F. Kennedy once said: "If we cannot end our differences, at least we can help make the world safe for diversity." Here in Hawaii, we celebrate diversity, and, at the same time, we honor the ideal that all men are created equal. The danger is that this proposed amendment would declare that some people are more equal than others. This leads to my greater concern over whether this measure is the proverbial camel's nose entering the tent. If it is allowed to enter, then what is to come next? More precisely, Mr. Speaker, who, and what kind of behavior will be targeted next?

We argue constantly over whether we should be in the business of legislating morality. This amendment strikes a moral tone, with proponents declaring that marriage between a man and a woman is crucial for procreation, and hence, the survival of the human race. They say we should worry about the sensibilities of our children because anything other than traditional marriage would violate our children's view of the proper roles of men and women in polite society; and there is the opinion that says if we do otherwise, this state will help to drag down a country that is already fast becoming morally bereft and without a Christian foundation.

I will counter that the country has survived even a war within its own borders, not to mention all other kinds of challenges, both manmade and natural, from within and without, with its institutions and values intact. I might also add that the arguments that America is subjecting itself to moral decay had their genesis even as our forefathers were deliberating over the United States Constitution. If you review that document, Mr. Speaker, there is no mention of God, or Christianity, for that matter. In fact, religion is mentioned once, in Article VI, which declares that "no religious test shall be required as a qualification to any public office or trust under the United States." As that document moved towards ratification, there were those who denounced the obvious attempt by the drafter to separate church from state in matters relating to the governance of the nation. The antifederalist Charles Turner declared that "without the presence of Christian piety and morals, the best Republican Constitution can never save us from slavery and ruin." More than two hundred years later, the nation, and the Constitution, are still the inspiration and the envy of others the world over.

I will close, Mr. Speaker, with a reference to a man who, in no small measure, was responsible for the drafting of the so-called Godless Federal Constitution, a constitution that served as the inspiration of our very own state document. There is a memorial to this man, which was dedicated on the bicentennial of his birth in 1943. If you, or any member of this legislative body, were to have the opportunity to visit this memorial, there is a passage at the base of the memorial's rotunda that is worthy of pause and reflection. It is a passage lifted out of a letter the honoree had sent to a friend, a distinguished physician in Philadelphia by the name of Benjamin Rush. That passage is one that I have taken to heart with respect to this bill, and it reads: "I have sworn upon the altar of God eternal hostility against every form of tyranny over the mind of man."

Those, of course, are the words of Thomas Jefferson, written when he was in the midst of his presidential campaign in the year 1800. This year, we are in the midst of yet another contest for the right to lead the American people, and there is a candidate that preaches the politics of exclusion. Here in Hawaii, there is, in this measure before us, in both the letter and spirit of its language, an all too transparent attempt to exclude those who are different because of their behavior - because they choose to be with someone of their own sex. While I disapprove of this behavior, I cannot bring myself to impose my beliefs on others - and I simply cannot condone this particular amendment to the state constitution and deny to those who cannot abide by this provision the same rights that marriage accorded to my wife and me.

As a student of both history and democracy, Nestor Garcia reminded me of some of the reasons I chose to enter public life. At the same time, he evoked my bitter disappointment that such articulate debate seldom moved my colleagues to change their views.

My "courage" award went to Devon Nekoba, who spoke for Americans of Japanese ancestry by reminding the House that discrimination comes in many forms, and that to turn our backs on one group was to turn our backs on all minorities. Devon knew that his remarks might well be used against him in the election. They were, and he lost.

> What is right is not always popular and what is popular is not always right. I have to thank the minority leader for last week coming up to me, pointing to this pin that I have on my label, and saying, "Remember the 442, remember the 100th battalion" [legendary, highly decorated World War II U.S. Army units made up of Americans of] Japanese ancestry].
>
> ...I wear this pin on my jacket to remind me that the 442 and 100 fought so that I could be here today doing just what I am doing right now. And they fought for a country and fought against persecution that kept their loved ones imprisoned while they defended the very country that put them there. And the reason they were there is that a majority of the people felt the same fear and loathing towards them that they feel now towards the gay community ... and the government went with the majority. Can you honestly say now that only listening to the majority is the true test of how we should make our decisions? I can't. Will we be able to say twenty years from now that what is popular now was right? Finally, I ask everyone here, when it comes down to protecting the rights of the minority from the majority, the question truly is "If not us, who? And if not now, when?"

I came away from that day reminded that serious debate was one of the reasons I entered politics in the first place, to be part of a dramatic dialogue on the most pressing and poignant issues of the day. Many of my colleagues were genuinely inspiring. I was honored and humbled to have the opportunity to participate. Perhaps one of the genuine benefits of the same-sex marriage conflict was to challenge elected officials to look into their hearts and minds and to ask, "Why am I here? What do I stand for? What is the role of government? What are rights? What is the role of tolerance? Can I make a difference? "Too bad so few of our citizens never had the chance to hear it.

An important context to the debate on this particular amendment was the emergence of a formidable group of liberal church leaders who opposed it. Twenty-six ministers representing the United Church of Christ (the modern incarnation of the original New England missionaries to Hawaii), Unitarians, Lutherans, Presbyterians, Episcopalians, Buddhists, and others signed a joint statement affirming "Hawaii's traditions of tolerance, diversity, acceptance of different religions, cultures, and lifestyles and commitment to equality. "They represented the historical religious establishment in Hawaii, yet their voices were weaker due to the superior organization and financing of the Mormons, Catholics, and others who sought the ban. The liberal ministers did little to change votes, however, and we received plenty of phone calls from self-proclaimed born-again or fundamentalist individuals who literally screamed over the line that those folks were not real Christians.

Later, the fourteen members of the House who voted against the constitutional ban received letters similar to this one sent to me:

Dear Representative Shon,

On behalf of the 26 members of our clergy coalition, I want to thank you again for your courageous stand against the constitutional amendment.

We realize the enormous pressure that was put upon you by those favoring discrimination against gays and lesbians. All along the way, we greatly appreciated your reasoned approach and careful consideration to all viewpoints.

Our most basic civil rights were advanced by political leaders such as yourself throughout our national and local history. Your conduct epitomizes the values most treasured in Hawaii. Your voice for fairness is respected especially by those who cannot speak for themselves.

Sincerely yours,

Reverend Yoshiaki Fujitani

The Senate was not to be outdone in its effort to curry favor with Randall Terry and the "real" Christians. Following its passage by the House, the amendment was quickly referred to the Senate Judiciary Committee, led by Senator Rey Graulty, who preferred we leave the constitution alone and enact instead a domestic partnership law. The amendment appeared to be dead, and a slim margin of Judiciary Committee members held firm behind Graulty. This was in spite of volunteers going house to house in some districts, or others picketing the fundraiser events of Senators Levin, Chumbley, and Matsunaga.

Senator Holt, who did not have jurisdiction over same-sex marriage issues in his Consumer Protection Committee, found a bill with a convenient title - "Relating to Licenses" - and stuck into it anti-same-sex marriage language. A howl of outrage rose from his Senate colleagues, and this new bill was immediately referred by Senate president Mizuguchi to Graulty's Judiciary Committee, where Hawaii's Future Today and others could continue to target a handful of stubborn senators who believed the issue should be left to the courts.

The limits of legislative rules were tested. Another unfortunate result was that advocates of a ban on same-sex marriages were found making public statements to the media characterizing these rule violations as "acts of courage" or "brilliant strategic moves." They had lost their perspective on the process of government. Winning became everything in public statements. This was a disappointing turn of events. Here were prominent forces in Hawaii's religious community ready to declare that the procedural ends do justify the means.

A big loser in all this was the poor. Throughout the 1996 session, we had also debated what to do with the costly General Assistance

Program, which provided stipends of about $414 a month to certain disabled persons who did not qualify for Social Security. It was clear from the beginning that they were not a high priority. Funding proposals were debated right up to the very end, even after the budget debate had been closed. If there was any issue that all churches could have united behind, you would think it might be providing a safety net for the most vulnerable.

Unfortunately, the power of the same-sex marriage issue over the emotions and the minds of Hawaii's Future Today led them to neglect the General Assistance Program. Several of us called our contacts in the Catholic diocese and begged the bishop to visit Speaker Souki (a Catholic) to make a plea for the poor, just as he had visited the Speaker on the same-sex marriage issue. When Souki moved to resurrect the legalized gambling proposal late in the session, an issue the various churches recognized would impose a heavy moral and social impact on poorer families, those same leaders rejected a plea to become more involved. The bishop's point man on these matters declared on TV, "We will not be distracted." (As a Catholic, I found it especially troubling that our church, which is a leader in providing social services and education in Hawaii, would shortchange the poor on the issue of general assistance.) In the end, general assistance subsidies were cut in half, too little over $200 a month. Since many of the recipients used their GA checks to pay the rent, nearly everyone predicted we would see more homeless people in Hawaii.

You may call me a bleeding-heart liberal, but I found it hard to ignore the relationship between the compelling preoccupation with preventing same-sex unions and the lack of attention to our moral obligation to take care of those who cannot fend for themselves, including the disabled. The same-sex marriage issue will probably fester in the courts, but the disabled were out on the streets in months. (Later that year, a member of the Catholic diocese's policy-making committee admitted that perhaps more attention should have been given to the poor.)

I have one final thought about the ideas and arguments on all sides of the same-gender marriage issue. A legitimate case can be made that we should let the courts decide. It can be also argued that the courts went beyond the intent of the state constitution. People can sincerely fear economic and other reprisals against a state that moves too fast in an uncertain direction. They can always take the position that a change needs more time to gain public acceptance. Others may feel that to deny any minority full rights is intolerable for even one day. Legislators articulated all these perspectives. The reactions on both sides were sometimes exaggerated. It was not a controversy most officials welcomed. like many conflicts in a democratic society, it was thrust upon us all by unforeseen circumstances, in a time not of our choosing.

Author Erich Fromm defined mature love in a way that makes sense when applied to government in general, and to a complex issue in particular. To love, according to Fromm, you must be knowledgeable about the object of your affection. You must really care about that person's welfare and respond to that person's needs. Finally, to avoid arrogance or paternalism, you must respect the person you love. I would argue that if we had, as a whole community, used these guidelines, perhaps we would not have followed the same path. Perhaps we would have been kinder in our debates and strategies.

There are some obvious lessons for politicians that may not have been anticipated by the concerned and angry public who punished those who were vulnerable in the 1996 elections. One might be: Watch the polls, put your fingers to the wind, don't stick your neck out, and go with the flow. An anonymous poem was sent to legislators during the 1996 session, which pretty well embodied this lesson:

Just read our lips! The people cried,

You need to understand

That we don't want weird unions as

The law across our land.

For marriage means ONE MAN & WIFE,

No other pair will do.

Don't try to change this Godly law

To please the few who sue.

If you don't get the message, then

I'll say without a doubt

That in the next election I'll

Be sure to VOTE YOU OUT!

Just after the election, when I was cleaning out my office, I had an interesting discussion with a fairly new colleague. She confided that if people like myself and others were defeated after taking an unpopular stand, she and others would think twice about being independent. Another lesson, this for the whole community, might be that consistency or logic or adherence to democratic openness or a process are very fragile elements of our community consciousness. Volatile and emotional issues can sweep them all away, turning the best of intentions into hypocrisy.

When the dust settles, hopefully our commitment to reason, fairness, tolerance, and equal protection under the law will be restored. The dust will not settle soon, however. In 1998, a constitutional amendment was placed on the ballot that allows the Legislature to enact laws restricting marriage to same-gender couples. The measure passed with some 70% approval. Valiant efforts by civil liberty groups were overwhelmed in a tidal wave of religious and general rejection of same-sex marriage. The amendment seemed to reduce voters' appetite to strike out at defenders of same-sex marriage rights, as they had in 1996. While the mood of the electorate was clearly restless, this explosive issue was not a major factor in individual races in 1998.

As all candidates were asked how they intended to vote, I was personally disappointed how many liberals chose to protect their hides and declare they would vote in favor of the amendment. They were frightened by the defeat of incumbents two years earlier, and decided that survival was more important than falling on one's sword for a losing cause.

There is one more political impact of the vigorous debate over the 1998 amendment. While only 30% voted against it, I believe these were mostly traditional Democrats who were reminded by the American Civil Liberties Union and by others why they were Democrats in the first place. This reminder must have benefited

Democrat Ben Cayetano in his narrow victory over Linda Lingle. Ben should thank former Representative Jackie Young and the hundreds of other civil libertarians for his victory in November 1998.

LESSONS

1. Issues relating to sex and religion can distort the usual dynamics of legislative life. They also tend to create great inconsistencies among the public in their attitudes toward reflecting public opinion when it is on their side, or standing up for principle when it is not.
2. When such issues cannot be avoided, their political power and volatility among the electorate should be recognized. The minds of voters may well focus on these are the single reason to vote for or against a candidate.
3. Unscrupulous legislators will be tempted to use such issues to political advantage, forcing sincere advocates on the other side to take politically damaging positions unnecessarily. Candidates who care little one way or the other are likely to be tempted to stiffen their moral indignation during a campaign.
4. Placing explosive issues on the ballot is one way of insulating individual legislators from electoral risk.

11 | MAKING LAWS: A CITIZEN'S PRIMER

You cannot imagine the beauty of an intricate, mazy law process, embodying the doubts and subtleties of generations of men.

–Arthur Helps

Even for those who regularly dabble in legislative activity, the nuts and bolts of making laws remains a mystery. Lots of books can give you that cute chart showing a piece of paper (a bill) being passed from one fat cartoon lawmaker to another. These are moral equivalents of organizational flow charts, and they leave most people puzzled and unsatisfied. Citizens want to know what really goes on. Unfortunately, I can't tell you. I can only describe my experience as one of many blindfolded scientists feeling one part of a very large elephant. ("It's like a tree," said the one feeling one leg. "It's like a snake," said the one feeling the trunk. "It's like a huge leaf," said the one feeling an ear.) Having provided this humble disclaimer, I can now tell you what really does go on.

THE KEY PLAYERS

Elected Officials

There is a handbook printed by the House Majority Staff Office and the Senate Majority Staff Office titled A Citizen Guide to Participation in the Legislative Process. Information can also be found on the legislative web pages. There is a general citizens guide:

http://www.capitol.hawaii.gov/sitel/info/guide/time. asp?press1=info&press2=time

You can look up the status of a bill, its amendments and the content of the committee report:

http://www.capitol.hawaii.gov/sitel/docs/docs.asp?pressl=docs

If you want a diagram of the Capitol building, a seating chart of the House or Senate, a legislative timetable, and everyone's committee assignment:

http://www.capitol.hawaii.gov/sitel/info/time/time.asp?pressl=info&press2=time

But it won't attempt to politically or functionally decode Hawaii' legislative process. It seeks to describe fictional hierarchies and relationships. The formal structure of the House or Senate is helpful. You must know it to enjoy a satisfying experience as a participant in the democratic process. But it is not enough. It will not give you, for example, the following power ranking of players in the House of Representatives:

1. Speaker
2. Chair, Finance Committee
3. Clerk, House Finance (The Finance staff often overrule the recommendations of other elected chairs! The knowledge, attitudes, and personal agendas of staff in general for any major committee can be crucial for the life or death of a proposal.)
4. Chair, Judiciary Committee
5. Chair, Consumer Protection and Commerce
6. Majority leader of the House
7. Chair, Water and Land Use Committee
8. Chair, Legislative Management Committee (all the resolutions and studies go through this committee)
9. Vice speaker of the House
10. Chair, Labor and Public Employment Committee
11. Chair, Health Committee
12. Chair, Human Services and Housing Committee
13. Chair, Energy and Environmental Protection Committee
14. Chair, Tourism Committee

15. Chair, Transportation Committee
16. Chair, Economic Development and Business Concerns Committee
17. Chair, Hawaiian Affairs Committee (when it is separate)
18. Chair, Education Committee
19. Chair, Higher Education Committee
20. Chair, Public Safety and Military Affairs Committee
21. Chair, Agriculture Committee
22. Chair, Culture and the Arts Committee
23. Majority floor leader
24. Minority leader
25. Meaningless titles: majority whip leader, assistant majority floor leaders, etc.

This power list is by no means a reflection on the importance of any subject matter. It is an attempt to rank positions as they control or influence the actual passage of laws. It is not a bipartisan list, for Hawaii's House and Senate still have too few Republican minority members to be a controlling voting block. It does not measure political influence outside of the Capitol. The minority leader, for example, will often be quoted in the media, and is called upon to make one of the important speeches on opening day. However, when push comes to shove, his or her opinions are often ignored. In other words, the minority leader is not a decision maker in the same way the chair of a committee determines which bill is heard or approved.

The Speaker of the House is:

1. the leader of a political faction (which he may have created),
2. the primary administrator for onehalf of the Legislature and the Capitol building, and
3. the primary gatekeeper for all bills introduced, referred, scheduled for floor votes, and dealt with in negotiations with the Senate. In addition,
4. he (we haven't had a "she" in Hawaii yet) appoints the chair of each committee and its membership. The Speaker is also

likely to be involved in any complex or controversial bills that involve the governor.

He is also - and this is very important - a kind of father figure to young or insecure House members. There are many anxieties along the political road to a successful career. A speaker who serves as a protector can be a great comfort. It's a jungle out there. On Oahu, elected neighborhood board members who are legislative wannabes abound, as do members of the other party who want your seat. You need to point to passed bills and improvement appropriations to your district. You do not need to have the Speaker out there whispering in the ears of the big contributors that your opponent is worthy of support.

Next in importance is not the vice speaker, nor the majority leader nor the majority floor leader. Their importance is limited by the good humor and tolerance of the Speaker, although the majority leader does preside over the majority caucus and thus plays a role in managing controversy.

The next most important person, who may at times wield more actual power than the Speaker, is the chair of the Finance Committee. Every cent spent, every tax collected, as well as a good number of pure policy bills, goes through this person. The chair, the chief of staff (clerk) of the committee, and the substantial staff hired for each session wield more power than most elected representatives when it comes to spending tax dollars. Often the Finance Committee members find themselves as mere rubber stamps.

For virtually every committee, you must consider not only what kinds of bills it can promote, but also what kinds of bills it has the power to stop. Only 10% of all the legislation introduced every session emerges for the governor's signature. Next to the Finance Committee, the Judiciary and Consumer Protection Committees received the most bill referrals. When I was Health chair, I would always be frustrated that important bills could be bottled up in these committees, even though the chairs' knowledge and interest in health matters might be marginal. As close confidants of the Speaker, chairs of these committees could be counted on to filter out proposals not favored by the inner circle.

The first echelon of the House hierarchy, in my personal opinion, was and still comprises eight members: Speaker, chair of the House Finance Committee, clerk of the House Finance Committee, chair of the Judiciary Committee, chair of the Consumer Protection and Commerce Committee, majority leader, chair of the Water and Land Use Committee, and the chair of the Legislative Management Committee.

These eight were the most powerful during my terms of office, mainly because so much significant legislation was likely to fall under their jurisdiction, either via a primary committee or via the second committee to review a bill. The majority leader might or might not be a trusted confidant of the inner circle. If included in the Speaker's kitchen cabinet, the majority leader would be called upon to ensure that the majority package bills (those publicly supported by the majority caucus at the beginning of session) would at least have a public hearing in key committees. The majority leader would usually sit as chair of the caucus, presiding over daily and special meetings and serving as the speakers right-hand man on policy. Yet, the majority leader was powerless to force a committee chair to hear a bill, or amend it, or decide to pass or kill it. Often, once the sessions were in full swing, all functional power disappeared from the majority leader's sphere of influence.

Because land and water are so central to power in Hawaii, we must rank the chair of Water and Land Use high on our power chart. In the implementation of the state's water code, the operations of the Department of Land and Natural Resources, the purchase of land, and the preservation of sensitive ecosystems and species, this committee can be enormously important. Not every session will generate hot and heavy agendas in Water and Land Use, but most will. Environmentalists and developers take a keen interest in who chairs the committee and who sits as a member. A business or development orientation in this committee can do enormous damage to the environment.

While the committee on Legislative Management might appear to be a lightweight assignment, in recent years all officially requested departmental studies needed to pass through this committee. For those House members whose pet bills had died earlier in the session, getting a substantive resolution passed would be the second-best accomplishment. The chair of this committee would always sit as a loyal and trusted member of the Finance Committee, and could be found in the Speaker's kitchen cabinet.

I have not included the vice speaker among the first eight most powerful positions because the functional duties are so sparse as to render the position primarily one of status. There was a time when the most important duty of this position was to assign parking stalls. During leadership struggles, status-conscious members might be thrown such a bone to buy their vote. Vice speakers typically sit idly throughout the session, unconnected to the substance of significant legislation. If a vice speaker is part of the Speaker's inner circle, he or she might have influence. For this reason, the vice speaker is not listed last. In 1999, the vice speaker was Marcus Oshiro, a bright and energetic legislator with a high-quality staff who seemed to be able to inject himself into substantive legislative business. However, we have had vice speakers whose only meaningful activity might be presiding over the House when the speaker was ill, or when the agenda was too superficial or boring to be worthy of the Speaker's attention.

The next level of legislative power through committees can become enormously important only because of specific bills or issues, like workers' compensation (Labor), health promotion or disease prevention (Health), the building of a convention center (Tourism), or funding for the poor (Human Services). When downsizing government or substantially adjusting labor-management relations through civil service reform, the Labor Committee can be key. When there was money to create needed programs, Health was more important than it is now. At present, the Health Committee, along with Human Services, must sadly preside over painful cutbacks for programs serving clients with little margin of flexibility. Energy and Environmental Protection in recent years has mostly been able to prevent the gutting of pretty good environmental laws passed in previous years. There was a time when the development of alternative energy and recycling were hot topics, but not in recent years. The second echelon consists of four members: chair of the Labor and Public Employment Committee, chair of the Health Committee, chair of the Human Services Committee, and chair of the Energy and Environmental Protection Committee.

The next and last level of importance is based not on the subject matter, but rather on recent practices: chair of the Tourism Committee, chair of the Transportation Committee, chair of the Economic Development Committee, chair of the Hawaiian Affairs Committee, chair of the Education Committee, chair of the Higher Education Committee, chair of the Public Safety and Military Affairs Committee, chair of the Agriculture Committee, and chair of the Culture and the Arts Committee.

It is rare for the Education Committee, for example, to significantly change the educational system. The Board of Education is supposed to make policy. The Finance Committee has the final say on all appropriations. The Education Committee, while occasionally able to promote modest reforms, such as school community-based management or greater relative autonomy for individual schools, usually spends its time as an advocate for a larger education budget. The same goes for Higher Education, which, because of the university autonomy movement, has even less influence. We could not even force the system to build a better library before it built a new sports arena. In the University of Hawaii crisis of 1999, when an accreditation committee severely criticized the administration, and when the Health State's only research university contemplated closing both its medical school and its school of public health, it was this notion of university autonomy that further reduced the important of the Committee on Higher Education.

Agriculture has always been important in the Islands, but the Agriculture Committee seldom does more than pass appropriation bills for research and extension service - usually the same ones every year. A different speaker with a different orientation could make this committee more important.

The Tourism Committee had its heyday during the debate over the new convention center. What actually happened, however, was that the Speaker set the agenda, and the chair, Romy Cachola, had to swallow hard and play along like a good soldier. Tourism is basically a cheerleader for more promotional funds.

Transportation presides over myriad special funds, the contents and operations of which are jealously hidden from casual legislative eyes. The airports and highways are all embedded in an arcane budgetary maze designed to keep probing or embarrassing inquiries to a minimum. These funds are also highly constrained by federal regulations. Major transportation issues, such as mass transit on Oahu, have been mostly dealt with at the county level. The biggest issue I can recall was the bailout of Hawaiian Airlines.

The Hawaiian Affairs Committee has yet to come into its own, and has already found that the Hawaiian community does not welcome initiatives by non-Hawaiian legislators. Without consensus in the Hawaiian community, significant proposals by the Legislature may be resented. There is always a temptation to label the author of an unpopular proposal as anti-Hawaiian. Native Hawaiian legislators with an ounce of smarts think twice before injecting themselves into the center of these policy debates. In 1999, the Hawaii Affairs Committee was folded into the Judiciary Committee. No one wanted it. With the state-funded Office of Hawaiian Affairs, whose elected board is made up of Native Hawaiians and whose funding sources are substantial, legislative action is a sideshow.

Depending on the issue, you can periodically readjust the ranking within the third echelon. When building a new prison is an issue, the chair of Public Safety becomes more important. But soon the limelight will move on to others. Many do not covet the committee. There was a time when the budget surplus allowed the state to be more proactive in the support of the arts, but not recently. Being appointed chair of this committee is what you might call a legislative crumb. It is better than nothing, but not much.

In the Senate, you will find a similar arrangement, but because its members tend to be more experienced and independent, the power of the Senate president may actually be less than that of the House Speaker. If the president of the Senate is holding onto a narrow margin in the factional wars, he will need to tread lightly on all toes. Generally, the smaller the legislative group, the more democratically it will be forced to operate. This does not mean that members cannot be iced out, but rather that there is nowhere to hide in a smaller group. Collegiality is more central to the organizational culture of the Senate than it would be to a larger body, such as the House.

Another difference in the Senate is that there are fewer committees, with more responsibilities and fewer members. Unlike the House, Hawaii Senate committees are not grouped into convenient brackets for purposes of eliminating scheduling conflicts. Therefore, you are more likely to attend a Senate committee hearing with only the chair at the table. For decision-making and official votes, the other members will be called.

Having seemingly diminished the importance of a good half of the committees, I hasten to add that for particular segments of our society, their respective committees are truly the most important. A whole cluster of interested parties, clients, and constituencies surround the chair of each committee and its members. In every legislative session, there will probably be one or more legislative bills of significance to someone in each committee. Simply being a passive "yes" to a whole list of bills can be a welcome service to a particular community. And having shepherded its pet bill through one committee easily, that community can then concentrate its efforts on convincing the Finance or Judiciary or Commerce Committee to approve it.

In spite of this basic structure of Hawaii's Legislature, the most important elements - the individuals who operate within this framework - can transcend its constraints. Representative Romy Cachola (who was chair of Tourism for at least fifteen years) could become a creative architect for hurricane insurance, a communitybased program to house the homeless, and an innovative international nursing program. Representative David Hagino, who held numerous posts, could become the conscience of the House on myriad social policy issues. Representative Tom Okamura could hold a shattered House together in the aftermath of Speaker Richard Kawakami's untimely death in 1987. Former Senator T C. Yim could become "Mr. Alternative Energy" as well as a key member of a liberal faction that opposed the death penalty. Henry Peters, after being deposed as Speaker, could become an effective opponent of mandatory leasehold conversion (sale to lessees) of condos, and an articulate spokesperson for the Bishop Estate. Representative

Dennis Arakaki could become an important international and local liaison with the Okinawan community. Dennis and Senator Suzie Chun-Oakland could become persistent advocates for the elderly and the poor. Former legislator Mary Jane McMurdo could become the voice of the residents of Waikiki in the face of larger economic steamrollers.

INDIVIDUAL LOBBYISTS

A lobbyist is someone who tries to influence the legislative process through direct contact with legislators. Direct contact includes appearing before committees to testify on specific bills, visiting legislators in their offices, and otherwise interacting with them. It is technically possible to be a lobbyist by generating written documents only, but this is rare. There are citizen lobbyists, and there are professional lobbyists.

A lobbyist is only as powerful as legislators allow him or her to be You can become powerful by representing powerful interests, and by being indispensable, or at least very helpful, to the most powerful legislators in the hierarchy. In recent times, the most influential lobbyist in Hawaii has been arguably Red Morris. Red walks in the door and you never know if he has come to talk about tobacco, the Nature Conservancy, the optometrists, the liquor industry, or a variety of other clients he represents. He is the fair-haired champion of the establishment and big-money interests. He has had the friendship and confidence of the Speaker, the chair of Finance, and many others. He influences the flow of large sums of money to campaigns by advising his many clients on their political interests. Red's involvement in issues, clients, and elections gives him the widest possible power base.

Other lobbyists tend to be more narrowly self-defined. The environmental movement must rely on information and persuasion, as it cannot command large amounts of money for contributions or for sophisticated packaging of its point of view. Active members of environmental groups tend not to have large amounts of disposable income. Large and wealthy corporations naturally have their own well-paid lobbyists, as do banks, credit unions, labor unions, hotels - you name it. To be really successful as a lobbyist, you need to establish yourself as a credible source of information, even if that information is unfavorable to your client. Reliable information is everything in the bubbling cauldron of a legislative session. Another important attribute of the successful lobbyist is the willingness to compromise and to treat everyone with civility and respect. Yelling and screaming only goes so far. You must not cry wolf too often, or claim disaster when facing only inconvenience.

A good lobbyist will find out what is in the minds of key decision makers, how they think in general, and what they think in particular about this or that issue. A good lobbyist will appreciate the political and legislative constraints of a committee chair. A healthy, long-term relationship is the most effective approach, rather than a single dramatic victory. Both elected officials and lobbyists operate in a traditional system that structures how ideas become laws. A client organization should count its blessings if its lobbyist can help it avoid overreacting or offending legislators in ways that only spell doom for its cause. He or she understands the psychology of the legislative community, the importance saving face, and the tolerance level individual legislators have for open defiance or disagreements. A good lobbyist will know when to advise the client to go public, and when to keep one's mouth shut.

ORGANIZED INTEREST GROUPS

Hawaii is still a relatively intimate community. Most of the organizations engaged in state-level lobbying in Hawaii employ individuals who are personally known by members of the Capitol community. Call it aloha or call it small-town culture, there is a civility to the push and pull of lobbying in Hawaii that has, by all accounts, been lost in Washington and larger state capitols.

When the health maintenance organizations (HMOs) and their corporate partners lobbied the Texas Legislature in 1995 to kill a bill designed to regulate HMOs, they employed sophisticated research and marketing firms to package their message. One prominent polling organization was the Virginia-based American Viewpoint, which had helped Newt Gingrich in his 1994 reelection campaign. Among their recommendations was the adoption of key buzzwords, such as "government involvement... higher costs... bad for business...

rich doctors versus consumers and employees... matters that should be decided in the marketplace, not the legislature."

Opponents of the HMO regulation bill set up phony organizations to give the illusion of grassroots support. They found ways to first call a small businessperson with a frightening message, then directly patch them to the personal office of an offending legislator to vent their anger instantly and directly.

These hardball tactics, adopted as take-no-prisoners militarystyle campaigns, are less common in our state, but increasingly they do occur. Focus groups supported by special interests tell the PR firms which phrases and tactics are most likely to move voters to support their cause. Fear and distortion are the common currency in attempts to vilify and demonize the opposition. To say that big-time organizational lobbying is often dishonest would be an understatement. Just as lastminute negative campaigns against a candidate will sometimes use fabricated horror stories, the conduct of organizational lobbying is often unethical and unscrupulous.

In a telling comment on the Texas HMO regulation battle, one observer noted tl1at those with the best imagery and attacks often won over those who relied on the facts. This is certainly reminiscent of struggles I've observed where, for example, nurses were able to cite chapter and verse of how the authority to prescribe certain drugs has not been a problem in other states, while the Hawaii Medical Association kept repeating over and over again that the practice was irresponsible and unsafe. Physicians walked door to door in my district with horror stories they just made up, while the public hearings pitted rational nurses versus emotional lobbyists for the doctors. In the Texas case, it was the doctors who relied on the facts.

Hawaii has seen some of this harsh lobbying over automobile insurance reform, where the plaintiffs' attorneys clashed with the insurance companies. To the extent that such campaigns can be reduced to sound bites on TV or compelling imagery, the role of factual information and rational discussion is diminished. The high-profile and well-financed campaign over the constitutional amendment to restrict same-sex marriages in Hawaii had a similar dynamic. The Save Our Constitution coalition, working against the amendment, appealed to voters' sense of history, civil rights, and legal protections. This approach was not nearly as effective as Save Traditional Marriage's image of two men on a wedding cake. When it comes to saving things, marriage is much more personal and emotional than an abstract constitution.

The civility of lobbying in Hawaii can be expected to drift toward the mainland approach. As we become a more formal, less intimate society, the importance of hardball lobbying will grow. Citizens who want to influence legislation will find that organizational strategy is almost as important as personal contacts.

HOW A BILL REALLY BECOMES A LAW

Step One: The Idea

Every legislative bill begins with an idea. Every idea is based on the assumption that some action is necessary, desirable, or at least politically expedient. Sometimes the situation begging for change may be simply to preserve a status quo, such as saving a financially troubled sugar plantation. In other situations, the new idea may involve the Legislature in an area, such as regulating health insurance, that previously was without a statewide law. There is a continuum of changes, perhaps illustrated by the following oversimplified progression:

1. Prevent a state law, program, or policy from lapsing or "sun setting. (Many laws are passed with a built-in dropdead clause forcing policy makers to revisit and re-justify the statute. Thus, I 1998, the Legislature renewed the solar energy tax credit.)
2. Prevent a previously stable or desirable situation from deteriorating due a change in the economic or political environment. (We discovered that there has been an increase in Peeping Tom offenses, so we passed a law to single out this crime and increase penalties.)
3. Prevent the recurrence of an undesirable event. (In 1998, the Legislature acted to negate an outside contract between the library system and a private book-purchasing firm. Sometimes this is seen as inappropriate meddling in order to

appear responsive to a particular situation. At other times, an event points out a weakness in our regulatory structure. An oil spill in Pearl Harbor resulted in the creation of a special office to coordinate efforts to prevent such spills.)

4. Criminalize objectionable, but previously technically legal, behavior. (Those who take endangered species can now be fined and sent to prison. Lap dancing is now prohibited.)

5. Create a completely new program based on new insights into old problems. (The creation of the Peer Education Program was based on an understanding of the power of the peer group and the importance of self-esteem in molding or influencing teenage behavior.)

6. Reorganize, restructure, or transfer existing programs. (The running of elections was removed from the jurisdiction of the lieutenant governor. The Department of Health has been reorganized a number of times, adding deputies as appropriate. Hawaii's Aquaculture Development Program has been batted from one agency to another, reflecting its overlap with land based agriculture, coastal-based mariculture, restoration of Hawaiian fishponds, and economic development.)

7. Change who makes a final decision; for example, requiring that the governor be responsible (and accountable) rather than his or her department head. Or change the decisionmaking process itself; for example, requiring a two-thirds vote to approve a land use reclassification. Other bills may assign a new duty to an existing board or commission, or actually create a new commission. The fine-tuning of democratic forms to improve the processes of government, policy making, and public input is one of the most important and persistent tasks of legislative bodies. Occasionally, this triggers a power struggle, as when the Legislature insists that only it can make a decision that was previously the responsibility of the administration. Needless to say, the governor rarely approves proposals of this nature.

8. Prepare all funding bills, adding, subtracting, or restructuring publicly funded programs. (Sometimes the creation of a special or revolving fund to isolate a program from day-today budgetary rules is desired. This strategy is often used to

earmark a source of revenue. Environmental response actions are funded in this way.)

9. Clarify a law that attorneys say is too ambiguous to be enforced or that invites legal action. The more controversial and contentious laws are, especially if they deal with rights or privileges covered by state or federal constitutional law, the more likely they are to need almost perpetual tinkering. Often this is done in direct response to a judicial decision. The proposal to modify the First Amendment to allow prohibition of flag burning would be one example, as would laws dealing with gay rights.)

10. Draft constitutional amendments, which includes determening the exact language to be placed on the ballot for citizen approval or rejection.

Step Two: The Translation of the Idea into Legislative Language

All legislative bodies rely on a small army of bill drafters, who may be personal staff, majority or minority party research offices, representatives of bipartisan research groups, or lobbyists and advocates of many stripes. There is a special vocabulary and language to the law, an agreed upon syntax, and styles that may or may not be necessary for a clear and effectively drafted bill.

There is the title, such as "A Bill Relating to a State Lottery" or "A Bill Making an Appropriation for the Brown Tree Snake Control Program." Once a bill has been given an official title and formally introduced, you are stuck with that title. This is why so many titles are very broad: "Relating to the Department of Health" or just "Relating to Health." The broader the title, the more leeway there is to amend or add to the bill. Bills are referred to as "vehicles;" meaning that you can load lots of compatible ideas onto each one. The state constitution specifies that bills should contain one main idea, but this is usually a very flexible concept.

Every bill is divided into sections, which typically conform to a sequence such as:

1. Findings and purpose. For example, "The Legislature finds that conflicts of interest undermine the public's confidence in

government .... The purpose of this act is to reduce conflicts of interest by ..."

2. Contains a specific amendment to an existing section of the Hawaii Revised Statues (HRS).
3. Might add a completely new section or chapter to the HRS.
4. Might add an appropriation section. For example, "There is appropriated out of the general funds of the state of Hawaii for fiscal years 1999-2000 the sum of $1,000,000, or so much thereof as is necessary, to support the Aloha Health Corps. The funds shall be expended by the Department of Health."
5. Might be a clause indicating that if any part of the bill is found unconstitutional, the rest of it should continue to be in effect.
6. Might indicate the date on which the law takes effect. For example, "This law shall take effect upon approval" or "This law shall take effect on July 1, 1998."

Obviously, complex bills might have dozens or even hundreds of sections. Others might be so short as to fit on half a page. There are also so-called short-form bills, introduced purely to provide a broadtitled context in case a great idea is left without an obvious vehicle.

The two most important words to look for in any bill are "may" and "shall." "The department shall regulate health insurance premiums." If you change "shall" to "may," you have just eliminated the likelihood of it ever happening. Influential lobbyists are always looking for opportunities to make an advantageous switch in long bills that most members will never read.

Step Three: Introduction of the Bill

After each election, the Legislature begins a two-year cycle, and each cycle is numbered, like the U.S. Congress practice. The Fourteenth Legislature ran from 1987 through 1988; the Fifteenth ran from 1989 through 1990, and so on.

All bills that are introduced in the first year of a two-year cycle are technically still alive for the entire two years. They are given an exclusive number. In the first year, you will find bills numbered up to about 2400 in both the House and the Senate. Bills introduced in the second year will be given higher numbers (H.B. 2401, S.B. 2700, etc.), but they can be considered alive only for that legislative year. After a new election, you start from scratch.

Bills can be introduced only by a member of the Legislature, and in Hawaii, a personal signature is required. Legislators may cointroduce a bill, indicated by a line drawn under their names, or they may just cosign by adding their signature. Sometimes, to remove the introducer from the source, you might find "by request" written under the signature. (I don't necessarily believe in this, but I was asked to place this idea into the hopper for consideration.) Every year, everyone in the Capitol community has to spend time learning the signatures of new legislators. Often their scrawls are so obscure as to make any attempts to read them futile. A few actually make an effort to write their names legibly.

Those who officially introduce a bill, that is, sign with their names underlined, will be given credit or blame if the bill passes the House or Senate, and especially if it becomes law. It matters not that the entire content of the bill has taken a 180-degree turn for the worse; you are still stuck with the historical credit. By custom in Hawaii and most other states, the governor's administrative package of bills (official proposals that come up through the various executive departments as well as other initiatives the governor wants to push) is introduced by the Speaker of the House and the president of the Senate. This is why you see their signatures on so many. It is not because they are filled with ideas.

Politics and people being what they are, outside advocates must think carefully before asking a specific legislator to introduce their bill. In Hawaii, Republicans and irritatingly independent Democrats are not wise choices. Their bills seem to fail to appear on hearing notices, or, if they are heard, are not reported out of committees. The public often believes that just because a plethora of signatures appears on the signature page that their bill is likely to pass. Dream on. It only means that the content is not obviously objectionable and that the primary introduce has not burned all his or her bridges. It does not indicate, in and of itself, that signers agree with the bill, will fight for it, or even will vote for it. They are just being courteous. On rare occasions people will indicate their strong support, but you can't tell by just looking at the signature page. Legislators who gain the reputation for introducing controversial proposals will have their bills read carefully before colleagues affix their reputations to them. Colleagues who trust your judgment are more likely to sign as a matter of friendship or courtesy.

The public could well view this as manipulative, insincere, or hypocritical. Yet if you step back, the purpose of introducing a bill is just that, to place it in the official pile of proposals beginning a long and perilous journey through the legislative maze. Dozens of policy makers and citizens must examine and ponder the wisdom of each. It must compete for attention and time with thousands of other proposals. A bill must be lucky, and it must be well drafted. There is no shortcut to knowing the future fate of a bill. Success is a process, not a single event. If you think of the most disgusting legislative bill imaginable, you will be glad that introductions are seldom long-term blank checks of approval.

Step Four: The Filtering Process - February through April

Bills introduced

House: 2400   Senate: 2400

Bills not scheduled for hearing

House: 750   Senate: 750

Bills heard but killed in committee

House: 200   Senate: 200

Bills still alive after first committee

House: 1500   Senate: 1500

Bills killed by second committee (i.e., Finance, Judiciary, etc.)

House: 750   Senate: 750

Bills sent to the floor at first crossover

House sends 750 to Senate   Senate sends 750 to House

Bills from other body held in committees

House kills 450 Senate bills   Senate kills 450 House bills

Bills sent back to authoring body on second crossover

House returns 300 Senate bills   Senate returns 300 House bills

Bills sent back to authoring body on second crossover

House loses 100 bills   Senate loses 100 bills

Total number of bills passed and sent to the governor

400

Governor vetoes

30

New laws

370

Of the original 4800 bills introduced, only 7 or 8 percent survive!

One can also think of a legislative session as a series of doors. Imagine that you are walking a piece of paper (a bill) through a long corridor with many offices. Each door has a title, and each office represents a committee or a step in the process. They appear in the following sequence.

FIRST DOOR: HOUSE CLERK

The House clerk gives your bill its own unique number, H.B. 22, and attaches it to an official heavy, colored-paper jacket.

SECOND DOOR: SPEAKER OF THE HOUSE OR PRESIDENT OF THE SENATE

The Speaker decides to which committees the bill must be sent, or "referred." All of the committees have an abbreviation. In the legislative language, a slash means that two committees get the bill at the same time, the first being the lead. If they hold a public hearing on it, they will do it jointly, hence this is called a "joint referral" An example might be HLT /HUS, meaning referred jointly to the committees on Health and on Human Services. A comma between committee abbreviations means that the bill goes first to one and then, after being voted out, to the other. Thus, HLT/HUS, FIN means that your bill will first be referred jointly to the committees on Health and on Human Services, and it will next go to the Committee on Finance. Other examples might be:

- OMR,JUD: First to Ocean Marine Resources, then to Judiciary
- AG/OMR: Jointly to Agriculture and OMR, but not to a subsequent committee.
- TSM/ECD/WL,]UD: first a triple referral to Tourism, Economic, Development, and Water and Land Use, and then on to Judiciary.

Obviously, it is useful to memorize the abbreviation and notation system. In 1998, there were nineteen standing (permanent) committees in the House and ten in the Senate.

THIRD DOOR: FIRST COMMITTEE(S)

After getting a referral from the speaker, it's on to the first committee(s). Often these are called the subject matter committees, because they concentrate on a particular subject (health, tourism, culture, education, etc.) rather than a particular function of government (such as finance or judiciary).

Back to our metaphor. You must stop and enter at each office along the corridor. As you open each door, there is person at a desk who collects your piece of paper. She's the committee clerk (Be nice to her or she may conveniently lose your bill) You cannot go any further until that piece of paper is approved by the occupants of that office, which means the committee chair and ultimately the committee members, who meet in that office to consider your bill. You can't skip over any office.

FOURTH DOOR: FIRST LATERAL- HOUSE OR SENATE CLERK

This door opens to a room with a desk for the House or Senate clerk, who wants to see every bill that is still moving. This is called the first lateral, which means that all bills must pass out of the committees listed before the comma on the referral sheet. In our first example - HLT /HUS, FIN - the Health and Human Services Committees need to hold a public hearing and a decision-making meeting (which could be on the same day) to vote out that bill to the Finance Committee by 6 p.m. on the day of the first lateral. This deadline usually comes early in February of a session that begins the third Wednesday in January and ends in April. Obviously, there is not a lot of time to take a serious look at 2400 bills in the first month of the session, and this adds to the pressure to choose only those bills that are of highest priority.

If the committee clerk doesn't write the official committee report in time or the attorneys don't review it or any other administrative glitch prevents the House clerk from officially receiving the bill in its official jacket by 6 p.m., the bill has missed the deadline and is considered still stuck in the first committee. It will stay there, technically, until the next legislative session in a two-year cycle.

The process leading up to the first lateral may filter out ("hold") up to 40% of those bills introduced. Out of the original 2400 House bills, 750 may be duplicates or considered "stupid" (in the words of a former committee clerk who has followed the process for years). There are many duplicate bills, since legislators often have the same idea or want to take credit for introducing bills on the same issues. After the initial public hearings, perhaps another 200 bills that were heard will also be held back in committee. Thus, out of 2400 introduced in the House, perhaps 1500 will continue to move at the first lateral. Another 1500 Senate bills will follow the same pattern.

FIFTH DOOR: HOUSE OR SENATE CAUCUS

Just before the first lateral, House and Senate majority and minority members will meet separately over the weekend in a closed-door caucus to review the bills that will be considered by the entire body on the floor the next legislative day. (In fact, there is a caucus meeting to cover every bill or resolution before a floor vote is taken. On days when the number of bills requiring action is small, tills will be done during a recess of the floor session, in the special caucus room just off of each chamber.)

Before major deadlines, the House majority caucus will usually meet in the third-floor conference room with the majority leader presiding. Members will arrive in casual clothes, often bringing their own binders with all the bills. A one-inch thick pile of bill summaries will be passed out. Food, especially snacks, will be abundant. Former

Representative Karen Horita used to supply popcorn and chips. Someone else will provide instant coffee, juice, and cookies. The marathon sessions, beginning usually around 10 a.m. and lasting sometimes until midnight, will be broken up with orders for food, which will be brought into the conference room. The outsider may yearn to be present at such august meetings, but the insider soon learns that there is little romance or drama, and that such meetings must be endured as one of many duties.

For each bill, the chair of the committee proposing its passage will be called upon to describe the contents, amendments, rationale, and so on for the other members. When the chair is not available, the vice chair or some member of the committee will be asked to do the honors. For the most part, this will be a "grind through the list" occasion. Representatives who may not be members of a particular committee will thus have the opportunity to decide for themselves whether to vote for or against each bill when it comes up on the floor.

Legislative attorneys have reminded each body that it is unconstitutional to make a decision in a closed meeting. Therefore, no votes are taken during a caucus. For controversial bills, however, spirited debates or even arguments are not uncommon. Sometimes these discussions break down along factional lines. On other occasions, they revolve around a particular point of view or ideology: Should we help Kauai Electric when its mainland-based parent company had a record year of profits? Should we cut the budget of the Office of Hawaiian Affairs? Should we reduce the workers' compensation benefits for injured workers? Should we increase the fines for pollution? Should we require that all health insurance policies cover mental health benefits?

For a time, the caucus was open to the public. This reduced it to a series of bland descriptions of each bill. Debate and controversy were avoided and suppressed, except when a few members chose to play to the crowd or the media, and the caucus took on the flavor of a preliminary floor debate. Openness is healthy, but in this situation, the tradeoff was a lack of spirited, candid discussion and debate.

I remember the emotional and extended debates during closed caucuses between former Speaker Henry Peters, who had become a Bishop Estate trustee, and those of us who were sympathetic to condominium owners who wanted to purchase the land they leased from Bishop Estate for a fair market price. I remember having to defend at length the proposal to allow nurses to prescribe certain drugs without physician oversight, and many other memorable debates. The caucus helps prepare individual legislators for the action on the floor, and it helps shape the arguments they will use in their public speeches. It also gives a preliminary indication to the leadership (Speaker, vice speaker, majority leader, etc.) of which bills might be in trouble. It is the leaders' job, by tradition, to help pass all bills reported out of a committee.

Back to the filtering process. While a Health Committee might receive 200 bills through the Speaker's referral, the last committees, usually Finance or Judiciary or Consumer Protection, will be reviewing many times that number. Since there is not enough time or money to honor all the appropriation bills, Finance and the other major second committees will probably hold back another 750 bills, about half of those sent to them.

SIXTH DOOR: FIRST CROSSOVER- FLOOR VOTES

The next door in our legislative corridor is labeled "first crossover" and leads to a very large room with a desk for each legislator. First crossover refers to the time when the House committees send bills to the floor for a vote by the entire body, and the bills it thus approves are formally transmitted to the Senate, and vice versa. About 1500 bills (750 from each body) make this journey.

When one or more House members decide they will vote against a bill, there is usually an informal, person-by-person lobbying effort to gather more green slips. In the House, where roll call votes used to be rare, you record a "no" vote by handing in a special green slip to the majority floor leader just before the vote is taken. Factional colleagues will often look to one or two leaders on an issue to advise them on which bills to oppose. There will be some representatives who need to vote against a bill for political survival. Others, as an act of loyalty to the leadership team, will never vote "no."

If the number of green slips approaches twenty or more (twentysix votes are needed to pass), the chair of the committee that has passed the bill out will be informed, and given the option of recommitting the bill to committee to avoid an open and embarrassing public rebuke. A floor session may well be punctuated with a number of recesses to allow members to lobby one another, gather those green slips, and encourage the chair to recommit a bill, effectively killing it for the remainder of that year's session. It is very rare for a bill to die in public on the floor.

The actual motion on the floor uses archaic terms like "consent calendar," which means that in a voice vote all are regarded as "yes" except those who have turned in green slips. The green slips are read aloud by the majority floor leader: "Will the clerk please record a 'no' vote for the following representatives: Hagino, Hiraki, and Thielen."

An additional method of recording the vote is through a roll call vote, where each member's name is read, and he or she verbally calls out "aye" or "nay." Roll call votes are time consuming, and thus tend to be limited to two circumstances. The first is when an opposition group feels it is close to killing a bill and may move one or two votes in their direction by putting everyone on the spot. The second is when an opposition group, usually the minority party, knows the bill will pass anyway, but wants to force members to go on the record. Presumably this will have ramifications in the next election.

By the rules of the House, it takes seventeen members to call for a roll call vote if the speaker does not want to grant it by request. While the public may be puzzled by a reluctance of legislators to have their votes publicly recorded for each bill, in an institutional culture that often seeks a collective rather than individual product, protection of members from political vulnerability is a legislative tradition.

We can thus break down the path of each bill into at least twelve steps before the House and the Senate exchange their respective bills. For each legislative body, all bills must

1. be formally introduced;
2. receive a referral by the Speaker of the House or president of the Senate;
3. be scheduled for a public hearing;
4. be formally voted out of committee;

5. be attached to a committee report by an inflexible day and time for the first lateral;
6. be considered by party members in a caucus;
7. be approved by a floor vote and moved to the last committee;
8. be scheduled in the last committee;
9. be voted out of that committee;
10. be attached to another committee report filed with the clerk of the House or Senate in a timely fashion;
11. be again considered in caucus; and
12. be approved by a floor vote for first crossover before transmission to the House or Senate.

DOORS SEVEN THROUGH TWELVE

The process begins all over again with the Senate looking closely at House bills and the House looking closely at Senate bills. If two bills cross that are essentially the same, the first one approved (by the clock) and sent to the other body is usually the bill that survives. The bill that was approved last is, by general agreement, held up and not acted upon, unless the Speaker and Senate president come to a special agreement to allow it to be used later in the session.

There is a second lateral (holding back perhaps 450 bills on each side) and then a second crossover, which sends approximately 300 bills back to their originating body. Thus, the first year of a two-year legislative cycle may begin with 4800 new proposals and by April only 600 have survived.

If a bill is well written and manages to pass through both bodies with no amendments, it will go directly to the governor for his signature of approval or veto. If one body has amended the bill and the other body does not object, it will move to "agree to the Senate [or House] amendments," after which it too will be forwarded to the governor.

Most of the time as a matter of principle, the respective legislative bodies disagree with the House (or Senate) amendments. In this case, it is up to the Speaker and president to appoint a conference committee for each bill where there is a disagreement. In the House, the first subject committee chair is usually appointed the lead chair of the conference committee. The chairs of the other committees that considered the bill will be named as co-chairs. Other members of these special committees are drawn from the standing committees that originally approved the bill. Usually, all co-chairs must agree to schedule and convene the conference committee with their Senate counterparts and to approve any final compromise. In order for this to happen, you need the cooperation of your Senate counterparts, or the bill dies. Often, unfortunately, there is a lot of one-upmanship and brinkmanship that goes on between conference committee chairs dealing with controversial bills. A positive and collaborative relationship between House and Senate conference chairs can improve the quality of legislation. A contentious relationship can do the opposite.

Again, it is helpful to think of passing a bill from office to office, step by step. Usually, at each stopover something is added to the code at the top of the bill. Perhaps it began as H.B. (House bill) 22. Next it will become H.B. 22 H.D. 1 (House draft 1). It will also at this time receive a committee report, and that report will have its own separate number: S.C.R. (standing committee report) 344. This is important to know because when you go to the print shop and want a copy of the latest version, it is best to give the SCR number rather than the bill number. Just asking for H.B. 22 will probably get you a copy of the original bill, but not the amended version with a committee report attached. House committee reports are yellow; the Senate's are pink. These reports can be very useful because they often explain the original purpose of both the bill and its amendments. Those who testified for and against will often be listed.

Next your bill will emerge from Finance as H.B. 22 H.D. 2 (House draft 2). In the Senate, it will become H.B. 22 H.D. 2 S.D. 1 (House draft 2, Senate draft 1), if amended. Perhaps the second Senate committee will also amend the bill, resulting in H.B. 22 H.D. 2 S.D. 2. Then on to conference committee, where it becomes H.B. 22 H.D. 2 S.D. 2 C.D. 1 (conference draft 1). At each stage, a new committee report will be attached. Conference committee reports are green.

As in the U.S. Congress, all bills must receive three readings, meaning that they must receive a majority of votes of all members on the floor three times. Usually, all bills are given a blanket approval on first reading when they are introduced. Next, they might be brought to the floor between committees, at the first lateral. In some cases, the second reading might occur just before the third. The bill must lay on each legislator's desk for at least 48 hours before each body passes the bill on third reading. After the conference committee, an additional passage by each house is called final reading.

Following the process can be challenging. In the second year of a two-year cycle, all bills that were held in various committees are technically still alive. This means that the public and the Legislature need to keep a wary eye not only on the new batch of some 2400 bills introduced at the beginning of the second year, but also on all those others, some 2000, that might just pop out of a committee at any time. Thus, any one of nearly 7000 bills could theoretically be scheduled for another hearing and moved along in the process. Every time a committee holds a bill back in the first year, there is always the possibility that that proposal could be used as a vehicle in the second year. Occasionally, when there is just not enough time, a chair will declare that the bill will not receive a public hearing but will instead be put off until so called interim hearings can be scheduled during summer and fall.

There are two ways to look at this. On the one hand, it is just another example of an arrogant, arcane, and elitist system making it hard for the general public to follow. On the other hand, it is a sophisticated process that permits flexibility and numerous procedural opportunities to enact the best possible legislation. I could make the case for both points of view. If you simplify the process, it will be easier to follow. However, oversimplification can make it much more difficult to respond to a complex and ever-changing society.

DEBATES

When do legislators debate bills? The first occasion is during the committee hearings when observers may hear arguments or debates during questioning of those who came to testify. Many of these people are experts representing executive agencies or well-heeled special interests. Second, when a committee meets to pass or hold the bill, you might again hear the reasons for individual votes, and perhaps some open debate. Third, there may be a debate in the respective Republican or Democratic caucuses prior to the vote on the floor. However, because these latter meetings are closed, only members and key staff will be present.

Formal debate usually takes place prior to voting on the floor in the second, third, and final readings. Everything said on the floor is recorded and later transcribed and printed in a six-inch-thick book documenting all official actions of the House or Senate. Each body has its own publication. They are a gold mine for students of history and the democratic process. They are also seldom read either by legislators or by the media. Candidates looking for ammunition, however, may well sift through the official statements and voting records of incumbents.

In the 1980s the media regularly covered floor debates, particularly for anticipated controversial issues. Nearly every day three or more cameras would be set up to record the proceedings. In addition to the daily newspaper reporters, television news departments often assigned more than one person to the Capitol during the session. A camera seemed to be nearly always available for spur-of-the-moment interviews.

In 2002, many TV stations assign only one reporter to cover both House and Senate. They are lucky if they can secure a free camera for interviews. Coverage of the floor debates almost never makes it to the nightly news reports. Consequently, the open and formal debates on the floor of the House or the Senate are witnessed only by those with special interests, such as state agency people or lobbyists. The value and role of debates has thus diminished to play a minor role in Hawaii's political life.

Legislators who are articulate or persuasive have few opportunities to move public opinion. As news departments shrink, reporters become what I would call big-issue groupies. Only the most important and controversial bills and actions rise to a level deemed worthy of public consumption. For those who stay at home during the day, one can occasionally view a selected committee hearing or debate from the previous week on the public access channel. Needless to say, the ratings for these broadcasts are not sensational.

If out of sight is out of mind, the public's isolation from the formal articulation of reasons and positions through debate has further increased the perception that nothing gets done, or that legislators are only interested in partisan fights. In a strange way, Hawaii is reverting back to a time when committee meetings and decision making was done in secret. Thirty years ago, the public was kept out. Today, the public is left out.

At the beginning of the 2001 legislative session, Republican House members made the front pages for several days in their attempt to bring a few controversial bills to the floor of the House for a vote. The Democrats easily voted them down, but foolishly also limited debate, creating a public issue that gave the majority a black eye. They need not have bothered. No one was watching anyway.

LESSONS

1. The institutional traditions of a legislature determine the relative importance of its positions, especially its committee chairs. But in all American legislatures, the Speaker of the House and the chair of Finance are among the most powerful.
2. Leadership may be found in individual legislators regardless of the particular positions they may hold.
3. The more bills that are funneled through a particular committee, the more powerful it becomes. The most influential legislators are those who have their fingers in the greatest number of legislative pies.
4. In a complex society with a history of representative lawmaking, there are thousands of legitimate issues. They form a continuum of trivial to earth-shaking problems that legislators must address. The public may feel that the legislature does "nothing." However, regardless of one's political ideology, it is important to recognize that effective government requires annual tinkering, amending, initiating, and reevaluation.

5. The formal process of lawmaking is not very complex or difficult to understand. It is the wide variety of social issues, people, and proposals passing through the Legislature that makes for confusion and challenge. The limits of a part-time, relatively short legislative session further muddy the water. The internal timelines work against part-time community participants and favor paid, full-time lobbyists.

6. Organizational lobbyists are changing the character of the Capitol from one of civility to one of hardball, take-noprisoners tactics.

7. The gatekeepers of this process, the committee staff, can be among the most important actors in moving legislation along.

8. The lack of media coverage has greatly diminished the traditional function of formal debate, and made public scrutiny of the legislative process technically possible, but operationally beyond reach.

9. Compared to other organizations, the Hawaii State Legislature could be considered quite an efficient operation. Where else can you find seventy-six independent employers (legislators) hiring hundreds of surprisingly competent short-term employees (session staff) in less than one month, training them in operational procedures, reorganizing their administrative leadership nearly every two years, and proposing, evaluating, and processing literally thousands of distinct ideas into a form suitable for inclusion in the law? People may not like the product or enjoy watching the process, but no other public or private institution goes through such a tour de force every January through April.

12 | OUTRAGEOUS AND UNCONSTITUTIONAL LEGISLATIVE REFORMS

··

If you want to make enemies, try to change something. You know why it is: to do things today exactly the way you did them yesterday saves thinking.

—Woodrow Wilson

If we like a man's dream, we call him a reformer~· if we don't like his dream, we call him a crank.

—William Dean Howells

A MORE THOUGHTFUL DEMOCRATIC FUTURE

The democratic and political changes required to meet our basic challenges involve electoral, internal legislative, and direct democracy reforms. Clearly, for citizens and their elected officials, there is the need for more deliberation, thoughtfulness, and community dialogue. Single issues, hot-button electoral strategies, and secrecy must be minimized. Legislators need time to learn, time to weigh pros and cons, and time to engage in thoughtful dialogue. Hawaii needs both increased internal democracy in our legislative bodies and increased direct democracy to engage our citizens more meaningfully in the political process that molds public policy.

The following is a list of prescriptions for change designed to achieve these goals. The reader is invited not so much to accept each proposal, but rather to focus on its purpose and the problem it seeks to solve. Remember, the primary purpose of these suggestions is not to kick out the crooks, or kick out the machine, or deliver "power to the people," worthy as such goals may be. The purpose is to create more critical and informed discussion about the pressing issues of the day.

LEGISLATIVE REPRESENTATION THROUGH MULTI-MEMBER DISTRICTS

Multi-member districts (where two or more are elected from the same geographical area), are worthy of consideration. Single-member districts, while appealing to a simpler sense of democratic purity, actually drag the electoral system toward a more and more spiteful, winner take- all contest. In addition, minorities of all stripes are at a disadvantage, for if only one person can win, everyone else loses. In a multimember arrangement, women, smaller ethnic minorities, young voters, and geographical sub districts would all have the potential to gain just enough second or third votes to share representation. An additional benefit is that each resident of such a district has more than one office and office holder to petition for change. If the highest vote getter won't respond, perhaps the next highest will. Perhaps all will compete to serve the public better, fearing that they will lose their standing by comparison to their fellow district colleagues. Multimember districts add a more civil and broader-based flavor to the electoral system, and these are important attributes for deliberation and public input.

BICAMERAL SYSTEMS

There is occasionally an interest in developing a so-called unicameral legislature, with just one group to elect, pay, and keep track of. However, the dynamics of bicameral policy-making diminish the ability of one or two powerful committee chairs to dominate the agenda. Checks and balances are more than a tit-for-tat strategy. They encourage more public input because they provide more opportunities for that input. In a bicameral system, the impacts of corruption or abuse of power are limited by the existence of another legislative body with its own committees and individuals. In a unicameral system, where there are no checks or balances, there is also more opportunity for mischief. Most country or city councils are unicameral. The Board of Education is unicameral. These institutions do not impress the public as superior.

COMPENSATION

There is no more insidious corrupting influence than the undercompensation of elected officials. It may be true that when many young people first nm for office they are without burdensome debts or mortgage payments. They may be single and not yet face the awesome costs associated with raising children. In Hawaii, preschool costs run in excess of $3000 a year. Payments on an average home or condo might well run over $2000 per month. If you are caring for an aging relative, add another $3000 a month for support services.

An elected official in his or her mid-thirties is essentially giving up me best earning years of life, meanwhile forfeiting most opportunities to develop seniority and experience in a field or profession. If it were not for spouses who have more lucrative and stable work, few legislators could afford the luxury of working as a part-time lawmaker. Nor are they like to find an employer who will allow them to take from onethird to one-half of a work year off for politics.

There at least three ways in which the joys of service at a part-time.

Salary level can be overwhelmed by the need to seek additional compensation

1. accepting employment from a large firm, and thus incurring an obligation to favor such firms in legislative decisions;

2. by paddling one's post-electoral nest by furthering the interests of a future employer: or

3. by ensuring that one's post-legislative employment at a higher salary in a state agency will boost one's pension to make up for years of mediocre earnings. None of these is desirable. We want our public officials to be as ethical and independent as possible. We want them to judge legislative proposals in terms of their impact on the whole community, and not just on themselves personally.

It is sad to say that too many legislators have reached beyond the ethical and legal boundaries to improve their economic well-being.

Some have been indicted. Some have gone to prison. They do not represent the norm, but they are symptomatic of a problem.

To avoid these conflicts, I propose that all members of the Legislature receive an annual salary of not less than that of a department deputy. But such a benefit should come with a tradeoff: no sitting elected official could receive any outside income for services rendered during the term of their service. The only exception might be if they held a teaching position in the University of Hawaii or the Department of Education; they could continue to serve at a prorated salary while the Legislature was not in session.

This exception for educational service is to encourage officials who have the qualifications, skills, and disposition to contribute in a different realm, to connect with the public on a more grassroots level, and to engage in a profession that requires thoughtful reflection on society and perhaps on legislative work.

To remove the public disdain for some of the retirement system perks while still speaking to the need for adequate security, I would also propose that all legislators who have served two four-year terms be eligible for individual health benefits only after their fiftieth birthday, and be eligible for retirement benefits based on their years of service only after their sixtieth birthday.

EXPANDED LEGISLATIVE BODIES

Critics of government are going to hate this suggestion. Let's assume that we desire more participation and more intimacy in our system. To increase representation while at the same time enjoying relatively smaller neighborhood districts with the multi-member approach discussed above, I would propose a 102-member State House and a 51- member State Senate. Under this system there would be two members per existing House or Senate district. This would obviously cost more, but not as much as one might think. The addition of fiftyone additional employees in a multi-billion-dollar annual budget would be worth the benefit. All efforts to better connect the public to their government have a price. In politics, tradeoffs are always involved. I doubt if today's society would ever approve such a scheme, but I am convinced we would all benefit if it did.

LONGER TERMS, WITH REASONABLE LIMITS

To encourage a longer-term perspective, without the requirement of beginning a campaign the day after each election, I would suggest that the House members be elected for four-year terms, rather than the current two years. Incumbents would be limited to three consecutive terms, but no lifetime restrictions would be imposed.

The 51-member Senate would have two from each existing Senate district. Like members of the House, they would also be elected every four years and be limited to three consecutive terms. Traditionally the Senate has longer terms, but the larger districts, combined with increased influence and power in a legislative body half the size, should be sufficient incentives to create a desire to become a senator rather than remain a representative. Thus, without forcing the early retirement (other than electoral) of someone who is just becoming knowledgeable enough to make an intelligent impact on the system, this approach suggests that twelve years in either elected body should suffice. There should be no prohibition on moving from one body to the other for those who choose to make public service a career. At the same time, the most senior members would be retired periodically to make room for those moving up. These reforms also acknowledge that there will always be some citizens who wish to pursue a longer political career, since other career paths will necessarily be off-limits during their tenure.

RECALL ELECTIONS

Recall elections make sense only when there are longer terms, but they should not be so easily imposed as to essentially reduce the fouryear term to a two-year-plus-recall arrangement. To strike a balance, I suggest that the following process be required: Upon receipt of a petition by no less than one-third of the number of registered voters in a particular district who voted in the previous election, a representative or senator may be required to stand for reelection after two years. This process should not be used more than once for the same elected official in any ten-year period.

THE NOMINATION PROCESS

In Hawaii, it has always been extraordinarily easy to get on the ballot. This may be good for newcomers, but in general it fails both to inform the electorate and to engage the candidate in any meaningful public dialogue. I have seen newly elected legislators who had no particular agenda or philosophy and who had not taken the time to become informed on major issues of importance to the community. To create a more deliberative electorate and a more thoughtful set of candidates, I would propose the following nomination process.

Each person who wants to be on the ballot would be required to participate in the following:

- Record a 15-30 minute Olelo (public access cable) tape answering five questions to be formulated by the League of Women Voters shortly before each election.
- Attend at least two Senate district town meetings where all prospective candidates are present to answer questions and discuss their ideas.
- Provide in writing the answers to five questions selected each year by a nonpartisan group for publication by a nonpartisan editorial paper printed and sent to all residents of the state at public expense.
- Collect fifty (rather than the current twenty-five) signatures of registered voters in the district he or she proposes to represent, and accomplish all this no later than June 1 of the election year.

Those familiar with Hawaii's election laws will notice that such a system would establish a list of candidates a month and a half earlier in the year. This is intentional, for last-minute entry can only limit the ability of the public and the other candidates to create meaningful comparisons. It provides more time for the candidate to attend community meetings, and to find out what their future constituents may be thinking.

CAMPAIGNS

Political campaigns and the expenditure of funds need attention as well. Under our current constitution, we cannot limit the amount of money a candidate spends, although we can limit how much an individual contributes. In addition to the wisdom of providing significant public funding for candidates, I suggest a slightly different, complementary approach: Enact a uniform campaign schedule law, and disseminate nonpartisan information on candidates and their positions at public expense.

Under this (perhaps unconstitutional) scheme, candidates would be prohibited from spending their campaign funds between June 1 and September 1. This would encourage earlier entry into the races, and create an American version of the limited electioneering periods found in other nations. In summary:

- No public campaign funds could be expended in a campaign year between June 1 and September 1.
- Between June 1 and September 1, all primary contests would hold a minimum of one town meeting each month within their districts to facilitate public discussion with candidates.
- Between June 1 and September 1, the state would pay for a newspaper supplement allowing one half page (tabloid) for each candidate's platform.
- Between June 1 and September 1, the state would pay for one half hour of Olelo time for each candidate in a contested race.
- Public financing would be available based on the number of inaccessible households in a district (i.e., locked condominiums) to offset the increased cost of postage.
- The complete voting records of all incumbents would be posted on an official website developed and maintained by the Office of Elections.

INTERNAL LEGISLATIVE REFORMS

For most citizens of Hawaii, the inner workings of the Legislature remain a mystery, generally contributing to a growing contempt and distrust of the system. The media refuse to shed much light on this crucial facet of democratic government, except when it can be interpreted either as petty squabbling or as abuse of power. However, even when the internal system operates as intended, it discriminates against the open, thoughtful, and knowledgeable deliberations that issues like long-term care demand.

THE LEGISLATIVE SESSION AND TIMETABLE

The following proposed reforms could well be incorporated today, except that the overall length of the session and a few of the other timetable items might require adjustments to the state constitution. The reforms are designed to increase internal and external access to information, proposals, and drafts of bills. The initial so-called subjectmatter committees are given more responsibility for refining the initial bills, whereas under the current system much of the real decision making is done by the largest and most powerful committees, those dealing with judicial or consumer protection issues and the budget. There is a hefty attempt in these proposals to mobilize the current technological innovations in distance communication to open up the process, even to those on the neighbor islands. Specifically, I propose:

- Bills could be administratively introduced by any legislator any time after December 1 of each year. They would be assigned a permanent number within one week upon receipt by the clerk of the House or Senate. These bills would be officially introduced when the session officially begins, and they would retain the same administrative number. In this way the public would be able to properly identify any bill by number well before the session begins.
- All bills would receive a committee referral no later than two working days following its receipt by the clerk of either house after the opening of the session. This would allow more time to schedule and publicize hearings.
- There would be a mandatory recess from the third Wednesday in February until the first working day on or after March 1. This would allow more time to study all bills.

- No bill could receive a public hearing before March 1 of each year. This would encourage all committees to engage in information briefings and allow time for the public to review all bills.
- Before any hearing, each committee would be required to post a proposed hearing agenda to cover the period until the next deadline for movement. All those concerned would be permitted to comment on which bills would be heard.
- Upon the written petition of one-third of a standing committee, a bill would have to be heard. This would provide a safety valve for a chair killing a popular bill.
- No bill could be heard before posting on the official legislative webpage, with full text, for at least one week. This would encourage the introduction of bills as early as possible.
- All bills could be introduced up to and including the third Wednesday in February, but no later. This would ensure that all bills would be accessible to the public fifteen days before official hearings begin, and it would give those wanting to testify time to post their texts on the web.
- The first lateral would not occur until after April 1. The first crossover would not occur before April 15. This timetable would front load the deliberations to an earlier part of the session and reduce the number of late amendments and manipulations. The initial subject-matter committees would be expected to do a better job, with the big picture being the mission of subsequent committee reviews.
- Upon the written petition of one-fourth of the respective members of either house, a bill would have to be brought to the floor in its most recent form for consideration.
- All state budget bills would be initiated in the House in the following manner:

    1. Following a general ceiling determined by the Finance Committee, each subject-matter committee should be responsible for one portion of the budget. Each chair would introduce a budget bill for that portion, and treat that bill like any other, with hearings, votes, and so on.

2. Upon arrival in the Finance Committee, these individual budget bills would be assembled and printed together to represent the first "programmatic" budget proposal, based on the best thinking of each subject matter committee at that time. This would ensure that the priorities of each committee, and of the public who participated in their hearings, would be on the table in the final budget conference committee.

3. All budget worksheets would be open for public review, and would be posted on the official legislative website.

4. All bills sent to the Finance Committee would receive a public hearing in that committee.

- The session would adjourn no later than June 1, and no extensions would be permitted. The public regards extensions as a failure of the system.

- Each committee would be required to hold an electronic hearing for those in remote areas at least one time per month for each of the neighbor island counties.

- At least one conference room in the House and another in the Senate would be equipped to provide interactive distance testimony with the neighbor islands.

- Each committee would be required to hold at least one fourhour public hearing per month at a convenient time and location (with free parking) outside of the Capitol in the community to allow working citizens to testify on any measure before that committee.

- The Legislature would arrange for free parking and a shuttle service if necessary for anyone who is attending legislative meetings.

- All conference committee rooms would be equipped with the technology to project the measures and language under discussion onto a large enough screen to allow citizens to follow the proceedings easily.

- These large-screen projections would also be fed to a public viewing room, where individual monitors could display any conference committee that is in progress or replay a videotape of any conference committee that had already met.

- All committee meetings, briefings, and hearings would be recorded on videotape and would become part of the official archival records. This is in addition to the written folders that are normally prepared for such purposes.
- Public bids would be accepted from private firms to prepare the official written and multimedia records of the legislative session.
- In addition to the individual office staff, each standing committee would employ two permanent, twelve-month researtchers, one of whom would serve as the permanent clerk of the committee.
- All voting by legislators in committees or on the floor would be recorded electronically and posted on the Legislature's official website within twelve hours.
- Each house would arrange for periodic community floor sessions during which all non-substantive presentations and certificates would be scheduled.
- All House and Senate floor proceedings would be recorded by video and audio technology for use by the media and the public.
- nonpartisan commission would be established to produce a written summary of each legislative day in tabloid form for distribution to the public within twenty-four hours (much like major conferences do for participants).

Such changes would transform the Legislature into a system in which there is time to do homework and include the public; a system that is more program-driven and less budget-driven; a system that nurtures a respect for standing subject-matter committees, and, by extension, for all their members and the public who testify before them; and a system that uses modern technology to facilitate public input and discussion.

DIRECT DEMOCRACY

Even with the aforementioned internal reforms, there will still be an ongoing need to revitalize public participation and faith in the overall system. No matter how well the representative forms operate, more direct democracy will be appropriate, in part because technology now permits more. A modified form of direct initiative that fosters greater public awareness and enforces a certain degree of honesty in the media is outlined below:

- Any bill, excluding those dealing with financing, taxation, the state's bill of rights, or collective bargaining measures in any of their official drafts, would be placed on the next general election ballot if a petition to that effect were signed by 15% of the registered voters in the state in the last election.
- Any public initiative law may be placed on the ballot in the next general election in accordance with the following process:

  1. The full text must be made available in printed form and on an official web site no later than July 1 of the year in which it is to be considered.
  2. A signed petition of no fewer than 20% of the number who voted in the last election shall be submitted no later than August 1 of the year in which it is to be considered.
  3. An official committee of those submitting the petition shall be established to receive contributions for the purpose of informing the public about the measure.
  4. A nonpartisan commission shall be established to monitor the content in materials and advertisements funded by the petitioning committee.
  5. No fewer than four town meetings shall be arranged per county to review and discuss the initiatives proposed each year.

- The Legislature would pass by resolution in each regular session a list of no fewer than five issues to be included in an official telephone survey to be conducted in the following manner:

  1. The issues of interest would be presented in the form of yes-or-no questions, plainly stated, and clearly explained.
  2. A joint House and Senate public input committee would be established for the purpose of wording and

framing the survey questions, and preparing a written background statement.

3. The questions would be published in a newspaper of general circulation no later than one month before the telephone survey is to be conducted. It would also be published a second time one week before the survey is to be conducted.

4. Following the survey, the results would be made available to the public on the official government website, and in written form.

- The Legislature may also, through passage of a resolution of referendum by both houses, place on the ballot of any election one or more nonbinding referendum questions designed to sample public opinion on issues of statewide importance.

Any system of direct democracy needs to avoid the temptation to use that system to punish the government or the political community as a whole. It should also encourage public scrutiny of proposals, insist on a fair and honest debate and dialogue, and nurture a regular and satisfying public dialogue on issues of importance without overwhelming the citizenry with lengthy and obscure amendments at each election. A final objective would be to minimize the influence of agenda-laden money from well-funded advocates who seek to manipulate the public's consciousness about such proposals.

The above section on direct democracy is based on the following assumptions:

- More idealism is possible, but it must be rewarded and nurtured.
- More thoughtfulness is possible, but it must be encouraged.
- More participation is possible, but it must be facilitated.
- More accountability is possible, but it must be fostered.

There is an old saying that a brilliant idea is a job half done. This prescription for reforms represents only one person's dream, based on a fair amount of firsthand experience. Our government has flaws and limitations. Only a community with a sense of its own goals and direction can change the way it operates. What is sad is the number of people who have given up trying, who have concluded that our system cannot be fixed. It is one thing to be skeptical, another to succumb to cynicism.

My own hope is that by exploring the nuts and bolts of institutional and legislative reform, we can persuade more and more of our citizens to join the dialogue. Like it or not, there will always be a government. We may as well make it work for us. We may as well learn to dance as one again.

13 | THE DECLINE OF COMMUNITY AND SOCIAL CAPITAL: THE CASE OF FLUORIDATION

···

I do not support fluoridation. In fact I hate water that has fluoride in it. Coffee is awful made with water that has been fluoridated.

— Unsolicited e-mail, January 2001

I pondered this opinion, recognizing the author as someone who had spent considerable energy in the community working for minority rights. Not a word about dental health of poor kids. Not a word about social justice, or access to health care. It was, in my view, one of the most selfish of statements. Unfortunately, it was not unusual. In the 2001 legislative session, even committed environmentalists who normally based their arguments on sound science urged rejection of fluoridation in part based on a mainland friend's assertion that it made the water taste funny. That any chemist could tell them fluoridated water has no detectable taste or odor mattered little. They were not interested in even asking. They knew.

THE AGE OF SKEPTICISM

Members of the baby boomer generation have a part of their brain that responds to the bumper sticker: Question Authority. We questioned racial discrimination, the Vietnam War, and the right of corporations to pollute our air and water. Our hopefulness and belief in society was chipped away with the assassinations of President Kennedy, Bobby Kennedy, Martin Luther King Jr., and many others. Even our conservatives lost face and faith with Richard Nixon. As a generation we have been disillusioned again and again, and too many political and sports heroes left the scene in disgrace. At the same time, we cultivated a subculture of independence and personal gratification. In our youth, we experimented with drugs; in our maturity, with alternative medicine, herbal teas, holistic and naturopathic approaches. We ran marathons and recycled our wastes. In other words, we were not going to take the word of the authorities without question. The "experts" had misled us too often.

In 2000, Robert Putnam published Bowling Alone: The Collapse and Revival of American Community. He used the phrase "social capital" to refer to connections among individuals. These include "social networks and the norms of reciprocity and trustworthiness." There is, by many accounts, a kind of civic malaise at the beginning of our new century. Putnam cites 1999 surveys where two-thirds of Americans said that civic life was weakening and that social and moral values were higher in the past. Americans longed for a greater sense of community, social bonds, and engagement. He has statistics to back him up.

In the last twenty years of the twentieth century, the number of Americans who attended even one public meeting, including those at schools, declined by 40%. The number who had worked for a political party declined by 42%; the number who had served on a committee for a local organization declined by 39%; the number who had attended a political speech: declined by 34%; the number who had signed a petition declined by 22%. Twelve participatory activities were selected, and the number who participated in even one of these declined by 25%. Interestingly enough, the declines were greatest among the better educated. Among college graduates, attendance at public meetings dropped from 34 to 18% (Putnam, pp. 45-46).

It wasn't only political activities that saw a drop-in involvement. PTA membership per 100 families with kids in school peaked in 1960 at around 47, but was at 17 by the year 2000 (Putnam, p. 57). There was a similar trend in church attendance, peaking around 1960 at just under 50%, and dropping to just over 35% in 2000 (p. 71). Union membership was highest in the late 1950s at about 33%, and is now down to below 15% (p. 81). Even membership in professional associations, such as the American Medical Association, the American Bar Association, or the American Nurses Association, follows this trend (p. 84). We don't even entertain at home, go to the movies, pay cards with friends, or sit down to eat with our families as often as we did in the past. Perhaps the most social of all informal sports, bowling has declined so precipitously as to threaten the livelihood of bowling lane proprietors. In Honolulu, we have seen some of our most cherished alleys razed and replaced with convenience stores. About the only activities that have increase is attendance at major spectator sports, particularly football, basketball, baseball, and auto races.

Calling this the "mystery of disengagement," Putnam offers some of the most common reasons for our antisocial behavior of the last thirty years:

- Busyness and time pressure
- Economic hard times
- The movement of women into the labor force and the pressures on two-career families
- Moving residences
- Suburban sprawl
- Television
- Globalization and the replacement of small stores with chain stores
- Decline in marriage fidelity and family ties
- The growth of welfare
- Civil rights
- Vietnam, Watergate, and other disappointments

We as Americans suffer from a proliferation of screens: TVs, computers, and so on. Rather than interact face-to-face, we prefer to connect to the Internet. One of the most disturbing of trends is the difference of civic engagement among different age groups. Looking at the 18-29, 30-44, 45-59, and over-60 age brackets, Putnam found declines in forms of civic engagement from the early 1970s to the late 1990s (Table 1). This civic disengagement and decline in social capital must relate to attitudes toward community in general, and in an unwillingness to frame issues as social problems rather than personal crises.

FLUORIDATION AND THE DISTRUST OF AUTHORITY

In 1987, as I assumed the chair of the House Committee on Health, I felt it was high time Hawaii reached out for the state-of-the-art in dental health: fluoridated water. I had grown up on it, and knew it not only passed the taste test, but it kept my mouth cavity-free for the first thirteen years of my life. Friends and relatives did not suffer from mysterious epidemics of genetic deformities, liver damage, cancer, or dementia. It was taken for granted as a sensible public health measure. I was totally unprepared for the firestorm that would be unleashed from a passionate segment of the community in Hawaii. I have never seen an issue that was so lopsided with science on one side and emotion on the other.

Table I. Change In civic engagement by age (early 1970s to late 1990s)

Activiy	18-29	30-44	45-59	60+
Read newspaper daily	-57%	-52%	-22%	-10%
Attend church weekly	-30%	-25%	-22%	-3%
Signed a petition	-46%	-27%	-8%	-0%
Union member	-64%	-41%	-32%	-42%
Attended public meeting	-57%	-50%	-34%	-21%
Wrote Congressman	-47%	-34%	-27%	-15%
Officer or committee member of local organization	-53%	-53%	-41%	-24%
Wrote letter to newspaper	-49%	-18%	-9%	-4%
Worked for political party	-64%	-54%	-49%	-36%
Ran for or held public office	-43%	-49%	-8%	-22%
Took part in any of 12 civic activities	-44%	-31%	-22%	-11%

Source: Putnam 2000, p. 252.

Fluoridation lost that year, and seemed to remain dormant until in 2000 the Department of Health decided it was time to try once again. The proposal again failed. It was decided in the fall of 2000 to mount a more effective effort, and I was asked by the Department of Health to provide some assistance.

This is not so much the story of how policy makers react as how the community has lost its trust in authority and, perhaps more importantly, its willingness to think critically about complex issues. It is also part of the continuing saga of how personal choice has replaced notions of community responsibility.

It is important to first recognize that the mainstream healthcare system, mostly financed through insurance, has not yet embraced oral health as an integral part of overall health. Most health insurance plans do not include dental health in the benefit package. If you want dental coverage, you purchase it separately, usually from a different company. In Hawaii, nearly 90% of the population enjoying some health insurance, but over a quarter of our citizens have no dental insurance. The poor have difficulty accessing dental care, particularly in rural communities. The reimbursement rate for Medicaid dental services is so low that many dentists must opt out of providing services.

In the fall of 2000, the state's Department of Human Services, which pays the bills, estimated it needed an additional $37 million just to create an economic incentive for dentists to take Medicaid patients. To complicate matters more, traditional medical education often omits crucial oral heald1 issues. Some physicians were advising new parents to give their infants a bottle with juice to keep them from crying. They had never heard of baby-bottle tooth decay.

A few disturbing statistics tell us we have a problem here in the "Health State." Baby-bottle tooth decay is defined as having three or more cavities in primary teeth, often caused by an infant who spends too much time sucking on the nipple of a bottle of sugar water or juice. On the U.S. mainland, approximately 5% of babies have this condition. In Hawaii, the rate is 13.6%. Over 16% of children on Molokai have baby-bottle tooth problems, and on Lanai, the rate is over 23%. Among children aged 5-9 years, the average number of filled or decayed primary teeth for children on the mainland is 1.8, while in our state is it 3.9. Various ethnic groups fare differently in their dental health profiles. For children with so-called "unmet" dental needs, nearly 40% of Native Hawaiians, 62% of other Pacific Islanders, and 46% of Filipinos in Hawaii are underserved.

Obviously, we have a problem. Yet the healthcare establishment has been only mildly interested. They rely on the Department of Health, the Dental Association, and the primary care clinics to carry the ball on such policy issues. HMSA, our largest health insurance company, has been aggressive in its support of fluoridation. Kaiser Permanente, normally ahead of the curve in prevention, not only would not lend its name to the effort, it would not allow its physicians to voluntarily provide information on fluoridation to patients. In general, it is left to the usual advocates for the poor to push a community perspective on health. In tough economic times, and certainly throughout the 1990s, Hawaii did not respond to the dental health needs of minorities or the poor.

With the shortage of money on its mind, the state's administration observed that on average it would cost about $1 per year per person to fluoridate the water, which would reduce dental disease by 25-40%. Put another way, to fluoridate the water for one person's lifetime costs approximately the same as filling one decayed tooth! Hawaii could spend a million dollars a year on preventive fluoridation, or it could spend tens of millions each year for additional dental health benefits for the poor. Children could enjoy the same levels of dental health and bright smiles as their mainland counterparts, or they could continue to chew through life with a mouthful of metal. From a public health and prudent financing point of view, fluoridation would be, as they say, a slam-dunk.

Not so fast. These basic statistics are not only not well known among Hawaii's general population, they are also unknown or unappreciated by politicians and policy makers. But if prudent investments in dental healtl1 were the only criteria, Hawaii would probably be fluoridating its water today. There are deeper and more troubling myths, attitudes, and beliefs that stand in its way.

THE ARGUMENTS

The pro-fluoridation people say tl1at it works and it is safe. Over 360 million people in over sixty countries have fluoridated water. In the United States, it is over 145 million. Many communities have been studied for decades in search of reliable evidence of the negative health effects of fluoridated water. To date, the National Science Foundation, the American Medical Association, the U.S. Centers for Disease Control, the World Health Organization, the American Cancer Society, the American Dental Association, and many other professional scientific organizations have concluded that it is both safe and effective.

These conclusions are based on credible science, which the U.S. Supreme Court summarized as meeting four criteria:

1. whether the expert's theory or technique can (or has been) tested, using the scientific method;
2. whether it has been subject to peer review and publication;
3. whether a study has a known or potential error rate and the existence and maintenance of standard in controlling its operation; and
4. whether it has attracted widespread acceptance within a relevant scientific community.

Claims that water fluoridation causes cancer, genetic damage, Down's syndrome, AIDS, kidney disease, allergic reactions, and many other ailments have been repeatedly studied using large population samples, and the scientific community has concluded there is no credible evidence for such wild claims. Pro-fluoridation advocates and scientists commonly refer to such claims as "junk science" and their advocates as "quacks" with questionable credentials, methodology, and conclusions. Small rates of dental fluorosis are acceptable trade-offs to prevent high rates of permanently damaged teeth with fillings everywhere. Fluoride is a naturally occurring substance which, in the proper amounts, can significantly reduce tooth decay and can have a lifetime benefit for children who ingest appropriate amounts of fluoride up to the age of sixteen.

The anti-fluoridation people say that it doesn't work and it isn't safe. There is a vast international and national conspiracy to cover up evidence that fluoridation of water does not reduce tooth decay and that the ingestion of any amounts of this poison over time will significantly increase one's risk of cancer, genetic damage, cardiovascular disease, kidney disease, neurological disease, AIDS, Down's syndrome, and so on. In addition, there are people who are proven to be allergic to fluoride. Fluorosis is worse than having cavities! The scientific community must be part of this conspiracy because they are constantly questioning the credentials, methodology, conclusions, and tactics of a handful of brave researchers who are allowed to publish only in a small number of non-peer-reviewed journals, many published in foreign countries. Because large doses of fluoride are toxic, it therefore follows that even small amounts are harmful. There is enough fluoride in a tube of toothpaste to kill a child! Fluoride consumption can be compared to the smoking of cigarettes. Studies show that fluoride doesn't work to reduce tooth decay. People should avoid fluoride treatments at the dentist's office, fluoride toothpastes, fluoride tablets, and the preparation of many foods with fluoridated water. Fluoride spills occur and are frequently not reported. Some are so serious as to be life-threatening to entire populations. Fluoride has been implicated in the recent high school shootings.

How can there be such completely opposite views when looking at the same information?

How can the collective experience of millions be so irrelevant to so many?

TOP TEN FACTS ABOUT FLUORIDATION

1. All the top scientific and public health organizations support it. Many of the "antis" are fruitcakes.

2. In 1993, the results of 113 studies in 23 countries were compiled and analyzed Review proved water fluoridation effective for tooth decay prevention: 40- 49% reductions for baby teeth, 50-59% for adult teeth.

3. Dosage counts. Salt, vitamins A and D, chlorine, and many other substances are safe in appropriate amounts, but could be harmful if consumed in high amounts.

4. Fluoride is a naturally occurring substance, usually in tiny concentrations. Low concentrations are healthy, not toxic. Where water already has high amounts of fluoride, there is no need to fluoridate.

5. Fluoride not only is not linked to bone fractures, some studies indicate it should be used to strengthen bones.

6. Over 50 epidemiological studies throughout the world indicate no links to cancer. In 1990 a 36-year study involving 2.3 million cancer deaths found no links. A recent British study reviewing 50 years of research found it was safe.

7. Studies show no links of fluoridated water to other diseases. Credible scientists regularly examine new claims and find them unreliable. With 145 million people over 50 years, there would be many links found. They are not.

8. The technical process of fluoridation is well known, is cost-effective (about the cost of filling one cavity per person per lifetime), does not damage other equipment over time, and uses reliable technologies that prevent the injection of inappropriate amounts at any one time. Agricultural areas with fluoride show no damage to crops.

9. Public health measures like fluoridation provide general benefits for whole populations in which individual behavior, access to affordable health care, and education place various groups at a disadvantage. There is a social equity issue here, especially for the poor. It is the role of scientific organizations to read and interpret the data for those who cannot.

10. Since 1998 more than a dozen U.S. municipalities have initiated fluoridation for over 6.3 million people, and national polls indicate a consistent level of support at 70%.

WHAT THE ANTIS SAY

1. There is a vast international and national conspiracy. They think we are fruitcakes.

2. Can cite several studies with different methodology that "prove" fluoridation does not work. Even one study, with proper interpretation, is enough to justify banning fluoridation.

3. If any concentration of fluoride is bad, all levels are bad. Fluoride is just like cigarette smoking, bad over time. If you hate cigarettes, you should hate fluoride.

4. Fluoride is a poison and is toxic, period. There is enough fluoride in a tube of toothpaste to kill a child. There is fluoride to the right of us, fluoride to the left of us. Boy, are we in trouble.

5. Fluoride causes hip fractures. Look at all those hip fractures among the elderly. Look what fluoride has done!

6. Liar, liar, pants on fire. It causes cancer. We can show that people who live in fluoridated cities often have lots of cancer. We can quote doctors! Don't believe those epidemiologists. What about those high school shootings?

7. Not only does it cause cancer, it also causes AIDS, DNA damage, Down's syndrome, Alzheimer's disease, kidney damage, etc. There is an obligation to exhaustively study every possible concern. We cannot trust science. They are duped. Only we can interpret.

8. There is documentation that occasionally workers have not followed safety precautions and have become ill. This proves fluoridation is a bad idea. If it makes workers ill, it can make everyone ill. What about the cost of replacing other equipment damaged by fluoride in the water?It will ruin crops.

9. It is a matter of choice. It is wrong to chlorinate water, regulate secondhand smoke, immunize, pasteurize, or otherwise force anyone to "benefit" from government schemes. Public health is a left-wing conspiracy. Parents and children should read the scientific literature and interpret it for themselves. This is Big Brother. This is socialism.

10. Occasionally our tactics can convince politicians or the public to oppose it. This proves we are right. We are the only responsible voices in this debate.

THE LOGIC OF FLUORIDATION

When all is said and done, after insults and exaggerations have been hurled from one side of the room at the other, there is a certain logic to the argument that should be helpful to policy makers. The following frequently asked questions and their answers were circulated during the 2001 debate, to no avail.

WHAT IS THE PROBLEM?

Hawaii's culture and climate encourage greater consumption of soft drinks and juices that contribute to tooth decay, yet nearly 300,000 people in Hawaii have no dental insurance. Hawaii's children have one of the worst rates of dental caries in the nation. Certain groups, such as Native Hawaiians and Filipinos, have even greater dental health problems. Nationally, about 5% of babies suffer from baby-bottle tooth decay. Hawaii's average is 16%, and some areas of the state are over 30% (six times the national average). The average number of decayed or filled primary teeth in children from 5 to 9 years old is 1.9 nationally, but for Hawaiians this is 3.7; for Filipinos, 5.6; and for Southeast Asians, 4.3.

WHAT ARE SOME OF THE SOLUTIONS?

Preventive dental care, topical fluoride treatments, the use of fluoridated toothpaste, and the purchase of fluoride pills are strategies that can be partly effective. All of these require personal compliance and can be costly. However, none can replace the effectiveness of fluoridation for the prevention of tooth decay over an entire population, for an entire lifetime, from infancy to our golden years. The disabled, the homeless, and other special populations without access to alternatives also benefit from fluoridation. The small amounts added to drinking water are on the U.S. government's recommended daily requirement list for vitamins, minerals, and so on.

WHAT DOES FLUORIDATION COST?

Fluoridation is estimated to cost about $1 per person per year. That would mean that a lifetime of fluoridation would cost the same as filling one decayed tooth. Put another way, for every dollar spent of fluoridation, $80 is saved in dental expenses. There are reduced dental insurance premiums, and fewer tax dollars spent on the dental care of the poor.

WHAT ARE SOME MYTHS ABOUT FLUORIDATION?

Some say it makes water taste funny, but this is not true. Some say it ruins agricultural crops, but many successful agricultural areas irrigate with fluoridated water. Some say it causes cancer, but scientists say this too is not true. After years and years of study by reputable scientists, there are no serious health effects found to be caused by fluoridated water. Many critics have a deep distrust of traditional science, and believe in conspiracy theories.

HOW CAN WE JUDGE WHAT IS GOOD SCIENCE AND WHAT IS JUNK SCIENCE?

This last issue, of how the average citizen who is not an expert might judge good information from poor or exaggerated information is at the core of the problem. If we no longer trust any authority, and we are no longer engaged in social and civic affairs that place us in a community context for problem solving, then we are left to our own personal analytical quirks to sort out fact from fiction.

I do not mean to imply that the general public is made up of defective thinkers, and that public officials are smarter. I do mean to suggest that the decline in social or community consciousness affects all segments of society. I spoke length with one of the neighbor island mayors and was told in no uncertain terms that by saying there were facts about this issue was an arrogant put down of his people, who have their own facts. The view was that it was just another example of the patronizing attitude of Oahu bureaucrats. Sometimes, the level of paranoia that creeps into arguments is astounding:

> It is important to know that fluoride is a toxic waste product of the fertilizer industry. If they didn't sell it to us to dilute in our water and poison us, they would have to

pay to dispose of it safely! The fluoride industry is multi-billion-dollar industry. Follow the money.

If scientific data is always suspect or open to question by the next website devoted to saving humanity from yet another sinister plot, this has enormous implications for public policy, and the very role of a legislative body.

> Whether the subject is Spaceport, U.S. Navy low frequency active sonar, irradiators, tree plantations spraying organic farms out of business, or fluoridation, we find that common sense and reasons are usually left far behind when someone has a private agenda foisted upon the public.

We must ask ourselves, quite seriously, are we as a society losing our ability to think clearly and critically about complex problems? Is our common basis of knowledge so fragmented among pet cable channel that we no longer share a common body of accepted knowledge about the world? Have there been so many betrayals, so many government cover-ups, that many of us have become fearful of just about anything, even tried and true public health measures?

If the answers to these questions are possibly yes, then democracy is in big trouble. The decline in social capital is one of the primary reasons a more deliberative and thoughtful context for decision making is needed. It is why we cannot afford to continue this rejection of democratic life, alienated from the very processes and connectedness that can protect our interests and our rights.

The case of fluoridation may be one that is debatable among the well intentioned. But I would argue that the tone and tactics of those who reject this common public health measure have crossed over into a twilight zone of nonsocial, everything-is-a-personal-issue existence.

The legislative institutions of this county may be out of step with the felt needs and desires of a Third Wave information age population, but they are adaptable if we want them to be. Do we really want to nurture and expand our sense of community? Do we really want to tear ourselves away from the TV and the computer screen to engage once again in what we once called society?

There are serious members of Hawaii's community who are pondering this loss of social capital. Leaders in Hawaii's Aloha United Way, the Hawaii Community Foundation, and civic-minded corporate organizations are beginning to wrestle with a society that seems to want to self-destruct. At the same time, almost as if it were an unconscious impulse, both nonprofits and government organizations, particularly at the University of Hawaii, are groping for ways to resuscitate policy analysis.

Many sense a disturbing drift away from a common language, a common civic bond, and a common way of thinking about problems that extend beyond our personal ability to cope. The current alienation from government must be reversed if we are going to re-engage in a collective dialogue.

In our own way, we are all pondering the alienation referred to at the beginning of this book, the dancers out of step. This is not just a government reform problem. It is an issue that goes to the very heart of our collective life.

I am an optimist. I believe that we can reinvent not only our government, but also our society. It will not look or feel the same as the community of our grandparents, but it will be able to satisfy our most basic need to belong to something larger than ourselves.

POSTSCRIPT: A POLITICAL FAREWELL

There is no poignant statement to be made on my personal exit from the Legislature, other than this book, which hopes to convey the richness of the experience and the potential to make a difference. One of my former colleagues, David Hagino, whom I have followed many a time into political battle, did issue his own postscript to a successful electoral career. While many of David's thoughts are only his, others, and the overall sense of his statement, is a fitting way to conclude this book.

> Passing the Torch
> Statement by Rep. David Hagino on Leaving Public Office
> July 28, 1994

This is a good time to leave public office. That was m thought during last Sunday's dedication of Korean and Vietnam Memorials. The completion of that public work of are represented six years of effort by my brother Senator Gerald Hagino and many others, including myself, dating back to 1988 when his bill was enacted into law. But it was a much longer time coming.

It was back in 1971 when I learned that a childhood friend of mine had died in Vietnam. He was not the first friend to die. He would not be the last. But I remembered him vividly. Back then I said that someday I would honor his memory, as well as the memories of the many other members of our generation that died in that war. It has been done

There is a purpose to this story and it fits in with my farewell to public office. I come from the traditions of the 60's movements - civil rights, peace, environment, and women's rights. I have my roots in the plantation era and I worked in the pine fields during high school at a time when picking pine or working in the cannery was a mandatory rite of passage in Hawaii. Those movements and those roots have instilled certain values in me. As I leave office after 16 years of public service I can say that I have kept the faith. The issues that I have raised, the legislation advocated, the principles enunciated, reflect those beliefs forged over several decades. I have kept the faith just as I have kept a promise for a friend that was made over twenty years ago.

It was in 1970 when I first ran for office and lost. I knew that someday I would run again and that I would be successful. I laid down three rules for myself about holding public office:

1. Know when to leave office. Too many of my colleagues cling to public office. Some because they have nothing better to do. Others, because they are hoping for that prized appointment to a well-paying position.
2. Leave gracefully. Too many of us hold on until we are defeated for re-election. Some us lose and then continue to run again. I say leave gracefully and don't look back.
3. When you leave, help the next generation of leaders get elected to office or, if already in office, help them to attain leadership positions. One of the reasons to leave at this time is because this is an important year. I would rather spend my time helping others get into public office and into leadership than to elect myself again.

My view of holding public office differs sharply from that held by most of my colleagues. I do not believe that some divine right of kingship is conferred upon us. Holding elected office is both a privilege and an honor. Many of used to complain about the sacrifices that we have to make to hold office. This was prominently stated in the debate over the legislative pay raise. The current Speaker even said that we were not paid enough. It is true that we sacrifice much by serving in public office. But again, let me say as I said in that debate: We know what we were getting ourselves into when we sought office. If the sacrifice is too much, then we can simply get out. The voters are not demanding that we continue to stay in office.

Because I consider it a privilege to hold office I can say that I am not going to seek a reward such as an appointment from the next administration, nor will I apply for a judgeship, nor will I apply for a trusteeship with the Bishop Estate. In fact, as some may already know, I am not even on the State retirement system. When I leave office in November, I take no pension or the free medical plan with me. I came to do public service. I leave having accomplished that.

But that's not enough. My concept of leadership differs with that held by many. I believe that the best leaders lead by example. Two of the people that I admire today are Ah Quon McElrath and Edward Nakamura. Both are in their 70s. Both continue to work for the poor and the working class. What is amazing is that neither have ever held or even sought elected office. Both continue to function as leaders and sources of inspiration.

Over the past two years, we have had many stories about corruption in government. I will not dwell on that subject, but I do want to close by saying that public service is still a noble profession. The best of our citizens from all walks of life should consider public service and elected office for a portion of their lives. Democracy works best when all of us take the time to participate. This participation cannot be limited solely to voting because it will not guarantee good leaders and decision-makers. I had hoped to leave public office quietly once I made my decision, but I have chosen to make this public statement in the hope that it will encourage others to run for public office, especially young people.

— David Hagino

www.ingramcontent.com/pod-product-compliance
Lightning Source LLC
Chambersburg PA
CBHW020533030426
42337CB00013B/841